Alexis Wright, *Carpentaria*: The Law of the Land

Alexis Wright, *Carpentaria*: The Law of the Land

Susan Barrett
Estelle Castro-Koshy
Laura Singeot

CNED
Belin
ÉDUCATION

www.cned.fr
www.collection-major.com

ISBN : 979-10-358-1649-0
ISSN : 1242-4935
Dépôt legal – 1re édition : 2021, octobre

170 bis, boulevard du Montparnasse 75680 Paris cedex 14

CONTENTS

PART ONE
CULTURAL THEMES

Part two
Writing and literary techniques

Part three
Going further/perspectives

To my daughters, Mélisande and Kerry
and in memory of my brother Donald (1968-2021).
Susan

Aux nouvelles rencontres
et à toutes celles qui m'ont accompagnée jusque là.
Laura

À Kael, Aidan et Arun
À ma grand-mère Yvette, ma famille et mes amis.
Estelle

I am greatly honoured to have my work *Carpentaria* included in the national curriculum of the French agrégation. I am excited by the prospect that the book will be read and discussed by distinguished scholars in France. It is the first book ever to be chosen for the agrégation that was written by a First Nation Sovereign author of this Continent, and the first Australian book in fifty years, since *Voss* (1957), by Patrick White.

I am delighted that my work will reach a broader audience and will encourage readers to explore the literatures of the world more broadly.

I hope you go well with your exams. The best way to read *Carpentaria* is just to enjoy it, which was the way that I wrote it.

Alexis Wright, June 2021

Notes sur les abréviations utilisées

Pour faciliter la lisibilité du propos, les titres des essais d'Alexis Wright seront abrégés comme suit :

"A Dream of Belonging for Indigenous Australians, the Fabled Outback is Home"	"Dream"
"The Inward Migration in Apocalyptic Times"	"Migration"
"In Times Like These, What Would Oodgeroo Do?"	"Oodgeroo"
"A Self-governing Literature"	"Self-governing"
"A Journey in Writing Place"	"Journey"
"The Ancient Library and a Self-Governing Literature"	"Ancient Library"
"We All Smell the Smoke, We All Feel the Heat: This Environmental Catastrophe is Global"	"Smell the Smoke"
"Telling the Untold Stories: Alexis Wright on Censorship"	"Untold"
"The Power and Purpose of Literature: Boisbouvier Oration 2018"	"Power"
"What Happens When You Tell Somebody Else's Story?"	"What Happens"
"Deep Weather"	"Weather"
"On Writing *Carpentaria*"	"Writing"
"The Politics of Writing"	"Politics"
"Broken Sense of Place"	"Broken"
"Breaking Taboos"	"Breaking"

INTRODUCTION

1

GENERAL INTRODUCTION

Susan Barrett

Carpentaria (2006) is the second novel by the Waanyi Aboriginal Australian author Alexis Wright. Its title refers to the region in which it is set in the north of Australia, not just the land but also the sea – the full geographical name for the area is the Gulf of Carpentaria. This is a remote region on the Australian mainland, rarely visited by tourists and unfamiliar to most white Australians, and yet the novel is anything but regional since it addresses serious issues about Aboriginal rights which are to be found throughout Australia. Lynda Ng goes even further, suggesting that the themes the novel covers make it a transnational work of literature which can resonate with readers all over the world.[1]

Initial reception of the book after its publication in Australia was overwhelmingly positive with many reviewers praising it fulsomely; Carole Ferrier, for example, called it "the best Australian novel for years" (2006), while Adam Shoemaker described it as "the greatest, most inventive and most mesmerising Indigenous epic ever produced in Australia" (2008, 55). Inevitably there have been a few critics over the years who have claimed to find it puzzling[2] but its extraordinary literary qualities were rapidly recognised both within Australia – where it went on to win five literary prizes and it has become one of the most widely studied works in Australian universities – and abroad.[3]

In all countries, works of literature have always been a way of challenging the status quo. The people who read novels and poems, or

1. Lynda Ng says in the introduction to her book, *Indigenous Transnationalism: Alexis Wright's* Carpentaria (2018), the only full-length study of *Carpentaria* until 2021 when the novel was on the French Agrégation syllabus, "one of the key aims of this volume is to show the ways in which *Carpentaria* bypasses the standard national Australian framework, to reposition Aboriginal experiences and identity within global coordinates" (Kindle).

2. See for example William Syson (2006), and Chester Eagle (2010).

3. For further details about the prizes the novel won and its publishing history see the biography on Alexis Wright in the next chapter.

go to the theatre to watch plays, are not necessarily the same as those who read history books or who follow current affairs. In current and former colonies this need for a literature of protest is perhaps even more acute, and it is widely acknowledged that Indigenous literature can play an important role in "challenging, disrupting and, indeed, transforming claims to historical, juridical and literary 'truths'" (Birrell, 2016, 197).

Carpentaria thus offers its readers an insight into what life is like for Aboriginal Australians in rural north Australia, alongside a damning criticism of the colonisation and continual occupation of the area by white people, which started in the nineteenth century. However, as Alexis Wright herself has said, *Carpentaria* was never intended to be a historical novel:

> I did not want to write a historical novel even if Australia appears to be the land of disappearing memory. [...] I have had to deal with history all of my life and I have seen so much happen in the contemporary Indigenous world because of history, that all I wanted was to extract my total being from the colonising spider's trap door. (Writing, Kindle) [1]

For Wright, like so many other Indigenous and First Nation writers, alongside the desire to challenge the ideas of the majority, goes the need to create a subversive literary form in which to do so. Drawing on the work of Gilles Deleuze, Kathleen Birrell argues that rather than copying the "indigeneity created by controlling discourses," works of Indigenous literature have become "an opening into the space of alterity, of creation, of *becoming* (2016, 199) which "provoke people to *think* rather than to merely recognise, represent or consume" (italics in original, 2016, 201). *Carpentaria* is, thus, an invitation to reflect, and to examine our own often unconscious, pre-conceived ideas.

As its title indicates, *Carpentaria* is a novel anchored in place. Non-Aboriginal readers should be aware, however, that a sense of place means something very specific to Aboriginal people. This is how Alexis Wright describes it:

> I understand the reality of place in my Aboriginal background where we say we belong to a place through our story laws since time began. This meaning of place

1. For ease of reading, Wright's essays will be referenced in the text by a key word from their title. A list of the key words, and the essay to which they refer, can be found page 13. "Writing" refers to her essay "On Writing *Carpentaria*" that was initially published in *Heat*, 2007, n° 13, p. 79-95 and subsequently reprinted in Lynda Ng (ed.), *Indigenous Transnationalism: Alexis Wright's* Carpentaria, Artarmon, Giramondo, 2018. "Kindle" refers to the Kindle edition of Ng's book, in which there are no page numbers.

> is of complete submersion in a sphere of relatedness to the total environment, and to every single thing contained in the natural world with the same closeness as being related to a mother, father, brother, sister, grandmother, grandfather, etc. The traditional landscape is then the house, home of the spirits, land, family, and relatedness to all of its stories, ancient beliefs, sacred stories and laws and culture. Land is a holy place. (Broken, Kindle)

Just like the word "place," the word "country" also means something specific to Aboriginal people. It is a Kriol term used by Aboriginal people all over Australia to designate "their traditional land estates inherited from their forebears as a matter of custom and according to traditional land tenure laws of each people or society" (Langton, 2018, 72). For Arnaud Barras the experience of reading *Carpentaria* is:

> [...] like hearing the voice of Country mapping its own creation. This literary mode blurs—when it does not erase altogether—the ontological boundaries between story, body and ecology, and it celebrates the entanglement of Law, Country and Dreaming[1] in storytelling. (2021, 171-172)[2]

It is impossible for a book of this length to analyse fully all the elements of such a long and complex novel as *Carpentaria*. Therefore *Carpentaria: The Law of the Land* provides those with little or no prior knowledge of Australia and Australian literature with the keys necessary to understand the novel, and also includes footnotes throughout the text with suggestions for further reading on the points raised, as well as an extensive bibliography at the end, organised thematically with the most important works clearly indicated.

This book is written in both English and French to enable those students working towards the French Agrégation exam to feel comfortable discussing the novel in both languages. For their benefit, the introductory section is followed by a chapter summary in English, and a list of characters, with the pages on which they appear, in French. A glossary at the end of the book provides an explanation of which terms are recommended to use in both English and French when discussing matters concerning Aboriginal Australians, as well as a list of Australian-English words with which non-Australian readers may be unfamiliar.

---

1. For an explanation of the meaning of "Law" and "Dreaming" see Part one, 1. "The Indigenous World"
2. An earlier version of this essay is available at: https://arnaudbarras.ch/documents/barras_mapping%20carpentaria_unpublished.pdf

The aim of this introductory section is to introduce the reader of *Carpentaria: The Law of the Land* to Alexis Wright and her world. A detailed biography of Alexis Wright is followed by a chapter giving an overview of Aboriginal Australian literary history, and its role in Aboriginal self-determination and self-definition by the writer and researcher Eugenia Flynn. This section concludes with a short chapter by the anthropologist David Trigger who discusses the meaning of country for the Waanyi people. *Carpentaria: The Law of the Land* is then divided into three parts. The first part, "Cultural Themes" weaves together literary analyses of the novel, and close textual readings, with essential knowledge about Aboriginal culture, Australian history and the geographical region of the Gulf of Carpentaria. Contemporary issues such as mining, ecology and pollution are also addressed. The important topic of land rights and Native Title is covered in a chapter by the anthropologist Jessica De Largy Healy. In this first part the continual references to the novel, and the numerous quotations, allow the reader to see how contextual knowledge is never just background knowledge but can be used to form a personal interpretation of the novel.

The second part, "Writing and Literary Techniques" focuses more specifically on literary and stylistic analyses of *Carpentaria,* drawing on the theoretical ideas of both literary theorists such as Mikhail Bakhtin, Gérard Genette and Julia Kristeva and contemporary critics. After an introduction in French analysing Wright's own thoughts about writing literature, the second part continues in English with sections on genre, literary influences, intertextuality and subgenres. This part concludes with an analysis of point of view and other narrative techniques in French. Short definitions of key literary terms are included throughout, either in the text or in the footnotes, and indications for additional reading are provided.

The third part is an invitation to "go further" with chapters providing tools for a more in-depth understanding of the novel and its context. The first chapter, by the historian and writer Victoria Grieve-Williams, discusses Aboriginal spirituality. The second, by the linguist Mary Laughren, is an introduction to the Waanyi language and includes a section with an English translation of most of the Waanyi words used in *Carpentaria.* The third and final chapter, by the scholar of First Nations literatures Mylène Charon, offers a comparative reading in French of *Carpentaria* and Wright's first novel, *Plains of Promise* (1997).

2

BIOGRAPHY OF ALEXIS WRIGHT

Susan Barrett & Estelle Castro-Koshy

Alexis Wright is from the Waanyi[1] people whose traditional country is in the highlands of the southern Gulf of Carpentaria in northern Australia. She was born in Cloncurry (Queensland) in 1950, the daughter of a Waanyi mother and a white cattleman.

In her 2021 essay about the meaning of the Australian Outback, Wright wrote that she understands her father, Jack Wright, was of English, French and Portuguese heritage. His father's family initially arrived in New South Wales from Sussex and Middlesex in the UK in the 1800s. She said,

> Beginning with their haulage business, a part of the family became established in rural Queensland. My father's father, John Wright, was instrumental in setting up Duchess, a thriving mining town in the early 1900s. My father was born on his father's Fishers Creek pastoral property near Cloncurry, where he grew up in the drought-stricken cattle industry. As an adult he was left the lease of the Oorindimindi cattle station (41,000 hectares near McKinlay on Kalkadungu land) by a man he worked for called Alex Murray. My father's world evaporated from our lives soon after he died when I was five. It was left to my imagination to visualise his life, and I saw him as being a man of great inner strength, grown through his love of isolation on his cattle property that I never saw nor knew. (Dream)

In an earlier essay, she also wrote,

> [...] it is quite possible that his cattle station was under water in this flood, part of the inland sea. Perhaps this land is now starting to bound with new life – all the grasses and pretty flowers bringing butterflies and birds on the breeze, something that he would never have seen in the droughts of the 1950s. (Smell the Smoke)

Wright was brought up by her mother and grandmother in Cloncurry where they lived after they were forced to move from their traditional

1. The word is also sometimes spelt Waanji in English.

homeland. Her mother's family had been displaced from their traditional homelands as a result of the colonisation of northern Australia. Wright describes the killing era as a time when her Waanyi ancestors were constantly moving over Aboriginal sovereign lands in the border region of North West Queensland to the east, and to the west, in what has become the Northern Territory. Her great-grandmother Opal was found by a pastoralist up a tree when she was a child, presumably after the massacre of the rest of her family (Vernay, 2004, 119).

Wright also has Chinese ancestry through her Cantonese great-grandfather, Chui Saam Bo who, in the late 1800s, emigrated from the Pearl River Delta region of China to North Australia's Gulf of Carpentaria where he married her great-grandmother Opal.

Her grandmother always wanted to return to her Waanyi homeland, but was not able to do so until she was in her eighties (Vernay, 2004, 120).

Wright has said of the time she spent as a child with her grandmother:

> I adored my grandmother [...]. Even today many years later I think she was one of the most fascinating people I ever met. She would take me on long walks in our landscape of dry and windswept yellowing grasslands, through dry sandy riverbeds with a few remaining water holes, and through the winding sandy beds of red gullies, and over the hillsides of goat tracks in the dirt where people walked. In her garden were mango trees, and seedlings germinating in rusty tins collected from the rubbish tip, and vegetables that surrounded her corrugated tin house with a dirt floor and lit at night by a carbine lamp. There were her dogs, chooks and ducks, and the bush turkey down the backyard. (Power of Story, 32)

The "wonderfully strange stories" her grandmother told her as a child have had a huge influence on her throughout her life (Writing, Kindle).

Wright received an education to junior level, the highest level offered at her local school in rural Far North West Queensland. She later studied Social Studies, Media, and Creative Writing at universities in Adelaide, Melbourne, and Sydney. She holds an Honorary Doctorate in Communication from RMIT (Royal Melbourne Institute of Technology), and an Honorary Doctorate in Letters from Western Sydney University. She was a Chief Investigator for several research projects funded by the ARC (Australian Research Council), and is an adjunct Professor in The Writing & Society Research Centre at the

University of Western Sydney. She has held the Boisbouvier Chair in Australian Literature at the University of Melbourne since 2017.

As well as her work as a writer, Wright is an activist for Aboriginal rights and environmental concerns. In her essay "Politics of Writing" Wright says that she "was dragged into working" for Aboriginal political movements in North West Queensland when she was in her twenties (10). Since then she has worked for government departments and Aboriginal agencies in four different States and Territories. She has been involved in numerous campaigns which have included work on land rights and acquisition of land to return to traditional land ownership, Native Title, mining negotiations, protests and agreements, campaigns for Aboriginal rights including Aboriginal self-government and sovereignty, alcoholism and fund-raising.

In 1984-1985, she was involved in the McLelland Royal Commission on the Maralinga Nuclear Tests conducted by Britain between 1956 and 1963 at Maralinga in South Australia. In 1993, she was the coordinator of the Northern Territory Aboriginal Constitutional Convention and wrote "Aboriginal Self Government" for *Land Rights News*, which has become one of the seminal texts on Indigenous land rights. Her non-fictional book *Grog War* (1997) drew attention to the fight by the traditional Aboriginal Elders and community of Tennant Creek in the Northern Territory to limit the sale of alcohol on their land.

She has been the community writer-in-residence for the Central Land Council. Her non-fictional edited collection *Take Power, Like This Old Man Here: An Anthology of Writings Celebrating Twenty Years of Land Rights in Central Australia* (1998) is an oral history of the Central Land Council. Hundreds of people were approached to contribute to the book, which tells the stories associated with the struggle for land rights in Central Australia.

In more recent times, she has written widely on the important planetary concerns of global warming, the environment, oral storytelling practices, and censorship, with an urgent call for writers to create the literature that will be necessary for these times. She writes in her 2021 essay "The Inward Migration in Apocalyptic Times" which appeared in *Emergence Magazine*:

> We will need the bravest of writers, those who will search ceaselessly through the backwaters of their minds, hearts, and souls to find ways to powerfully articulate the new stories, the new sagas, the new imagination, and the new epics of the world, inspired by their doubt, fear, love longing, and wondering.

> They will need to see beauty despite the destruction, experience deep sorrow, and find that incorruptible truth amid the growing dust storms. These visionaries must be capable of seeing that all time is intertwined, important, and unresolved, just as Aboriginal people see time immemorial in our culture.

Her first literary success came in 1994 when one of her short stories won the Northern Territory Literary Award; another story was highly recommended for the Award in 1996. Her first novel, *Plains of Promise*, was published in 1997 and remains in print thanks to several new editions of the book. It is the story of three generations of Aboriginal women, and draws attention to many of the problems faced by Aboriginal people during the twentieth century, including the practice of removing Aboriginal children from their parents. [1]

Carpentaria (2006) is Wright's second novel. After initially being rejected by every major publisher in Australia, it was finally accepted by the small independent publisher Giramondo. The following year it won the most prestigious Australian literary prize, the Miles Franklin Literary Award, and four other major literary prizes. It was subsequently published in the United States, the United Kingdom and India, and translated into different languages including French, Italian, and Chinese.

The French publisher, Actes Sud, has long taken an interest in Alexis Wright. The translation of *Plains of Promise* (*Les Plaines de l'espoir*) was published in 1999 and received favourable reviews leading the editor, Marc de Gouvenain, to commission an essay about Aboriginal beliefs, *Croire en l'incroyable* (2000), which has only ever been published in French. Actes Sud also published an anthology of her short stories under the title *Le Pacte du serpent arc-en-ciel*, something which has never been done by an English language publisher.

Wright has also had links with China for many years. *Carpentaria, The Swan Book*, *Tracker*, and *Odyssey of the Horizon*, a novella commissioned by the Australia Council for the Tracey Moffatt exhibition at the Venice Biennale in 2017, have all been translated and published in China. The Chinese edition of the *Odyssey of the Horizon* is in Chinese, English and Japanese. Wright has been a guest writer at several literary events and universities in China where her work is studied and aroused the interest of a group of young scholars in translating and introducing Australian Indigenous literature, culture

1. This historical injustice has become known as the "Stolen Generations" and was brought to public attention by the publication of the *Bringing Them Home Report* in 1997.

and history. As a result, two *International Symposia on Australian Indigenous and Chinese Mongolian Culture* were held in Inner Mongolia in 2015 and 2017.[1] When Wright visited Inner Mongolia in 2018, she was awarded the title of Visiting Professor by the Inner Mongolia Normal University.

Wright's third novel *The Swan Book* (2013) won the Australian Literary Society Gold Medal, and was also short-listed for several literary awards. Her biographical work *Tracker* (2017), a tribute to the Eastern Arrernte (Northern Territory) Aboriginal economic visionary and political leader Tracker Tilmouth, won the important Stella Prize, an annual Australian literary award for writing by women.

Wright is a regular participant in domestic and international writers' festivals, writers' workshops, conferences, and readings. Her new novel *Praiseworthy* will be published by Giramondo Publishing in 2022.

1. We thank Professor Li Yao, the translator of Wright into Chinese, for providing this information.

3

ABORIGINAL LITERARY HISTORY THROUGH SELF-DETERMINATION AND SELF-DEFINITION

Eugenia Flynn

The history of Aboriginal literature in English has been strongly contested (van Toorn, 754; Heiss, 2003, 25) and speaks to aspirations of Aboriginal self-determination in all facets of life, inclusive of cultural production and storytelling. The establishment of the first British colony on the continent now known as the country Australia in 1788 signalled the onset of English language dominance (Heiss & Minter, 1), the suppression of Aboriginal cultural practices (Wilson & Wilkie), and a loss of autonomy (Maddison) for Aboriginal Peoples. Throughout this complex history, Aboriginal storytelling has endured, with Aboriginal writers asserting their sovereign power through the act of writing and making clear interventions designed to challenge the status quo. This includes the Aboriginal poetry movement of the 1960s and 1970s, life writing and Aboriginal women's narratives across the 1980s and 1990s, and the proliferation of fiction across a variety of genres and forms from the 2000s onward, inclusive of emergent works of world literature such as Waanyi author Alexis Wright's award-winning 2006 novel *Carpentaria*. As a result of this enduring storytelling practice, within what is a complex context of power and domination, Aboriginal writers today continue to place primacy and importance on self-determination and self-definition in and through the production of literature.

I | CONTESTING ABORIGINAL LITERARY HISTORY

The history of Aboriginal literary culture has been contested by non-Indigenous literary scholars, anthropologists, and linguists. Non-Indigenous interest in Aboriginal literature began in earnest in the late 1980s with the publication of Adam Shoemaker's literary history *Black Words, White Page: Aboriginal Literature 1929 to 1988*. However, prior studies of Aboriginal storytelling traditions rarely considered Aboriginal writing as a literary force. Instead, research related to Australian Aboriginal peoples and literature was primarily concerned with anthropological studies of Aboriginal song and story, or with:

> [...] the efforts of white Australian writers to come to grips with the Aborigine. Clearly, in all cases, their interest in the Aborigine is touched by an interest in themselves, in Australia itself as a land and as a social-political structure. (Healy, 1978, 2-3)

Originally written in 1978, J. J. Healy's book *Literature and the Aborigine in Australia* presents a survey of literary works written about Aboriginal people, perspectives, and stories, contributing to the obfuscation of Aboriginal literary history. Updated to a second edition published in 1989, Healy acknowledges that he made a conscious choice in 1978 not to consider Aboriginal literature (Healy, 1989, XIX), opting instead to make mention of a small selection of Aboriginal writers and referring to emerging contexts that would see Aboriginal literature taken more seriously in the future.

However, by 1989 Shoemaker and others had already started foregrounding Aboriginal literature as a literary force that would then begin to be 'taken more seriously' by non-Indigenous literary critics, writers and scholars. Much of this early work of tracing the history of Aboriginal literary culture focuses on the publication of two seminal texts, Ngarrindjeri writer David Unaipon's 1929 text *Native Legends* and the 1964 book of poetry *We Are Going* by Quandamooka poet Oodgeroo Noonuccal. However, by 1996 literary scholar Penny van Toorn began to question this history by arguing that Aboriginal writing pre-dates Unaipon's 1929 text *Native Legends* and continues between 1929 and the publication of Noonuccal's *We Are Going*, over 30 years later in 1964. In this way, van Toorn opposes the conception that Aboriginal writing is a recent phenomenon and positions contemporary Aboriginal literature as part of a long continuum of literature and text (van Toorn, 754), contesting the previously established literary history.

The history of Aboriginal literature is further contested through the revisioning of what constitutes and defines Aboriginal literature, directly challenging the notion that Aboriginal literature can only be located within "the rubric of Literature-with-a-capital-L, looking primarily at the genres of poetry, drama and fiction and, to a much lesser degree, biography and autobiography" (van Toorn, 758). Here, van Toorn is joined by non-Indigenous anthropologists and linguists such as Jennifer Biddle and Stephen Muecke who argue that Aboriginal literature, writing, text and publishing is comprised of a broad range of material that ranges from letters, newsletters, pamphlets, petitions and speeches to dots and circles in the sand and visual art (van Toorn, 754; Muecke *et al.*; Biddle, 28). However, in seeking to expand definitions of Aboriginal literature van Toorn is careful not to reinscribe Eurocentric hierarchical distinctions related to Aboriginal text and literature:

> When texts from the oral tradition count as literary writing but early Aboriginal-authored printed documents do not, the history of Aboriginal textual practice becomes absurd. As well as reinvoking colonial anthropological distinctions between oral and literate cultures, these apparently inclusive anthologies reinforce the line between literature with a capital 'L' and the many so-called sub-literary modes. (van Toorn, 757)

In revisioning the very definition and conceptualisation of Aboriginal literature, to include more expansive understandings of Aboriginal writing and reading, van Toorn, Biddle and Muecke challenge traditional literary norms. The term 'literature' is defined within traditional literary studies as a category of text, as historical and cultural phenomena, and as:

> [...] the entirety of written expression, with the restriction that not every written document can be categorised as literature in the more exact sense of the word. The definitions, therefore, usually include additional adjectives such as "aesthetic" or "artistic" in order to distinguish literary works from texts for everyday use such as telephone books, newspapers, legal documents, and scholarly writings. (Klarer, 1)

By including speeches, dots and circles in sand (Aboriginal sand paintings), and visual art as part of a more expansive definition of Aboriginal literature, published texts written in English can then be viewed as one mode within a range of Aboriginal storytelling traditions, inclusive of Aboriginal oral narratives and oratory. Oral storytelling traditions are repositioned as part of the Aboriginal literary continuum, not as part of the 'pre-literary history' to contemporary Aboriginal literature. This is confirmed by Wiradjuri writer and academic Anita Heiss who contends:

> The oral tradition is still very evident in Aboriginal writing today [...]. There is a great difference between what is spoken and what is written in the Anglo world, but in Aboriginal society, spoken and written traditions are more closely aligned. (Heiss, 2003, 28-29)

In summary, non-Indigenous scholars such as van Toorn, Biddle and Muecke have all played important roles in the historiography of Aboriginal literature by challenging traditional notions of literature, arguing for more expansive ways of defining Aboriginal literature, and therefore contesting the history of Aboriginal literary culture previously established by scholars such as Shoemaker. This contestation aligns with Aboriginal conceptions of Aboriginal literature and involves increased inclusion of Aboriginal modes of storytelling, writing and reading, leading to new understandings of the origins of Aboriginal literary culture that move beyond the publications of *Native Legends* in 1929 and *We Are Going* in 1964.

II | ABORIGINAL WRITERS SELF-DETERMINING AND SELF-DEFINING ABORIGINAL LITERATURE

Aboriginal writers and scholars involved in tracing the history and development of Aboriginal literature seek to define Aboriginal writing for themselves – an exercise arguably more important than non-Indigenous theorising on the definitions of Aboriginal literature and historiography of Aboriginal literary culture. As early as the 1980s, Aboriginal and Torres Strait Islander scholars such as Cliff Watego have documented and interrogated the origins of contemporary Aboriginal literature, a history that is inclusive of early playwrights and poets such as Jack Davis, Oodgeroo Noonuccal (then known as Kath Walker), Kevin Gilbert and Gerry Bostock (Watego, 11-24). Extending this early work, scholars such as Heiss have documented the history of Aboriginal literary publishing and interrogated issues of authenticity in Aboriginal literature, non-Indigenous writing on Aboriginal people and story, and Aboriginal identity (Heiss, 2003, 2-24).

Importantly, Heiss provides extensive documentation of contemporaneous Aboriginal discourse on what constitutes literature within an Aboriginal context, the possibilities of an 'Aboriginal style' of writing, and genres of choice for Aboriginal writers (Heiss, 2003, 25-46). In this way, Heiss weaves together various opinions by Aboriginal writers, enabling Aboriginal writers themselves to self-define Aboriginal literature, contending that "[a]t the outset it could be argued that any definition of Aboriginal writing should be coming from Aboriginal writers themselves" (Heiss, 2003, 26).

The notion that Aboriginal people should themselves define what is Aboriginal literature, its origins and history, and the various contours of its style, form and content reflects the aspirations of Aboriginal self-determination. As expressed by Aboriginal people, Aboriginal self-determination involves several rights that speak directly to Aboriginal literature. Speaking at the 4th Vincent Lingiari Memorial Lecture, Yawuru leader Patrick Dodson outlined such rights to be included in any potential treaty between Aboriginal Peoples and the Australian nation-state:

> [...] The right to maintain and develop our distinct characteristics and identities, whilst taking part in the life of the country as a whole.
> [...] The right to self-determination. A right to negotiate our political status and to pursue economic, social and cultural development.
> [...] The right to our own law, customs and traditions, and equality before the national law.
> [...] The right to our unique cultural traditions and customs. The right to own and control our cultural and intellectual property.
> [...] The right to our spiritual and religious traditions.
> [...] The right to our languages, histories, stories, oral traditions and names for people and places [...]. (Dodson, 29-30)

Eualeyai/Kamillaroi writer and academic Larissa Behrendt further summarises the concept of rights and self-determination:

> The rights enmeshed in the concept of "self-determination" includes, I would argue, everything from the right not to be discriminated against, the rights to enjoy language, culture and heritage, our rights to land, seas, waters and natural resources, the right to be educated and to work, the right to be economically self sufficient, the right to be involved in decision-making processes that impact upon our lives, and the right to govern and manage our own affairs and our own communities. (Behrendt, 2002, 45)

The impact of colonisation has left Aboriginal people with little political or social autonomy (Maddison, 24-43). Extending this to cultural autonomy, not only has the historiography of Aboriginal literary culture been dominated by non-Indigenous scholars as gatekeepers of the origin, definitions and contours of Aboriginal literature, so too has the act of literary practice been historically dominated by non-Indigenous writers. Although credited as one of the first texts published by an Aboriginal writer in English, the manuscript for Unaipon's *Native Legends* (variously titled *Legendary Tales of the Australian Aborigines* or *Myths & Legends of the Australian Aboriginals*) was appropriated and published under the name of W. Ramsay Smith, a non-Indigenous anthropologist and Chief Medical Officer for South Australia, and only subject to literary repatriation in 2001 (Leane, 2015, 29). Contemporary literary hoaxes such as those run by non-Indigenous writers Leon Carmen and Marlo Morgan indicate ongoing desire by non-Indigenous people to assume positions of authority over the literary representation of Aboriginal people, culture and histories – posing as a member of the Stolen Generations by the name of Wanda Koolmatrie, Leon Carmen published the text My Own Sweet Time in 1994, later revealed to be entirely fictional (Morrissey, 299-307); Marlo Morgan published the book *Mutant Message Down Under* in 1994 as an autobiographical account of her New Age experience with a 'lost tribe' of Aboriginal people in the desert, later revealed to be untrue (Behrendt, 1998, 256-279).

Further, as indicated by Healy in 1978, numerous texts have been written by non-Indigenous Australians interested in 'coming to grips' with 'the Aborigine'. Often this has led to harmful representations of Aboriginal people in Australian literature. One such text is the 1972 novel *The Chant of Jimmie Blacksmith* by Thomas Keneally which depicts Aboriginal men as emasculated and presents the reader with "images of [Aboriginal women] with a loose, available sexuality and the overwhelming impression that Aboriginal women are easy sexual sport" (Behrendt, 2000, 360). As Wright argues:

> When it comes to how our stories are being told, supposedly on our behalf, or for our interest or supposed good, it has never been a level playing field. We do not get much of a chance to say what is right or wrong about the stories told on our behalf—which stories are told or how they are told. It just happens, and we try to deal with the fallout. (What happens)

Throughout this history, Aboriginal writers have continued to advocate for their autonomy, self-determination and rights while asserting their sovereign power through the act of writing. Aboriginal sovereignty is defined by Aboriginal people as more than western legality. Here, Yamatji scholar Crystal McKinnon argues that Aboriginal literature, text and writing are an extension of Aboriginal peoples' embodiment of sovereignty:

> Aboriginal and Torres Strait Islander people embody sovereignty [...] the things those bodies produce are sovereign texts. These texts tell stories, and if we know

> the right ways to read and see them, it deepens our understandings of sovereignty. These texts tell the stories of Aboriginal people and communities which have been passed down for generations and form a part of the fabric of the expressions of sovereignty, constituting sovereignty itself. (McKinnon, 201)

Positioned in this way, Aboriginal literature becomes a practice in self-determination and self-definition for the Aboriginal writers who produce literary work within such a complex context of power and domination. This is affirmed by Wright, who, in reflecting on her literary practice, contends:

> But what becomes clearer to me the more I write, is that I have been trying to create a self-governing literary landscape through what I have learnt from our ancient library, and our knowledge of always governing ourselves. (Ancient Library)

Here, Aboriginal storytelling is a continuum where modern Aboriginal literature written and published in English is self-determined and self-defined, part of an embodied Aboriginal sovereignty tied to place.

III | ABORIGINAL LITERATURE ON ABORIGINAL TERMS

As previously discussed, the commonly accepted history of Aboriginal literature acknowledges Unaipon's *Native Legends* as the earliest Aboriginal work published in English, and Noonuccal's *We Are Going* as the first published book of modern Aboriginal literature. Challenging this accepted literary history, Watego positions *Native Legends* as political in nature and thus part of the same Australian Indigenous contemporary literary culture as *We Are Going*, arguing:

> The protest or consciousness-raising element within Aboriginal literature therefore begins, not in the mid-1960s as popularly interpreted, but with the writings of Unaipon forty years previously. (Watego, 17)

First posited in 1988, Watego's repositioning of Unaipon's work within a modern Aboriginal literary culture that centres around a 'protest or consciousness-raising element' resonates with other Aboriginal writers and scholars through to today (Heiss, 2006; Grieve-Williams; Wright, "Oodgeroo"). Published in 1964, *We Are Going* was Noonuccal's first book of poetry and the first by an Aboriginal woman (Heiss & Minter). The beginning of modern Australian Indigenous literature is often thought to have begun with the publication of *We Are Going* (Grossman, 2005, 12; van Toorn, 754) and Noonuccal is identified as "paving the way and opening the doors to publishers, and alerting the wider community as to the strength and value of Aboriginal literature" (Heiss, 2003, 2).

We Are Going is known for its significant contribution to the establishment of modern Aboriginal literature, due to its form as a book of poetry and the political nature of its content: "*We Are Going* marks the arrival of Aboriginal poetry as one of the most important genres in contemporary Aboriginal political and creative literature" (Heiss & Minter, 4). From *We Are Going* onward, across the 1960s and 1970s, poetry became an important literary form for Aboriginal writers, particularly as a political tool during the Australian Black Power Movement of the same period and stretching into the 1980s (Foley). Noongar writer Jack Davis published his book of poetry *The First Born and Other Poems* in 1970, Murri poet Lionel Fogarty released his first collection of poetry *Kargun* in 1980, and Wiradjuri author Kevin Gilbert edited the poetry anthology *Inside Black Australia*, released in 1988. Notably, both Davis and Gilbert also published groundbreaking plays – *The Cherry Pickers* (1968) by Gilbert and *No Sugar* (1985) by Davis – with playwrighting a common form of choice for Aboriginal writers from the 1980s onward.

By the mid-to late 1980s, not only were poetry and plays genres of choice for Aboriginal writers, but autobiographical narratives and testimonial fiction were becoming important modes of self-determined Aboriginal literature (Heiss & Minter, 6-7). Across the 1980s and into the 1990s, Aboriginal women were of particular prominence in this genre, which came to be known as 'life writing' (Brewster, 1995; Grossman, 2013; Moreton-Robinson, 2000, 1-4). In 1986 Palyku writer Sally Morgan published *My Place* to considerable commercial success, in 1987 Glenyse Ward (Noongar) released *Wandering Girl*, Bundjalung writer Ruby Langford Ginibi released *Don't Take Your Love to Town* in 1988, and in 1996 author Doris Pilkington Garimara (Mardu) published *Follow the Rabbit-Proof Fence*. Through writing their story, and the stories of their families, Aboriginal writers of autobiography, biography and testimonial fiction were able to share the truth of Australia's forced removal of Aboriginal children from their families (the Stolen Generations), their lives as domestics and labourers, and the experiences and perspectives shared by many Aboriginal people living with the legacies of colonisation.

By the late 1990s and into the 2000s, Aboriginal communities were renewing their interest in Aboriginal culture, inclusive of an increased uptake in writing and the form of the novel, and in addition to the production of significant works across other creative forms such as theatre, dance, music, visual art, film and photography (Heiss & Minter, 7). In 1997 *Plains of Promise* became Alexis Wright's first novel and Bundjalung Yugambeh writer Melissa Lucashenko published her first novel *Steam Pigs* in the same year. In 1999, Noongar writer Kim Scott published his second book *Benang*, co-winning the prestigious Miles Franklin Literary Award the year after its release. By 2007 Aboriginal literature had its second Miles Franklin Literary Award, its first full winner (Heiss & Minter, 185), in the form of Alexis Wright's *Carpentaria* (2006).

Across this same period and into contemporary times, Aboriginal writers have taken up a variety of genres and forms, inclusive of academic and other non-fiction, short fiction and children's books (Heiss, 2003, 37-41). Young adult books have also been part of this history with Birri-Gubba and Kunggandji writer Boori Monty Prior publishing *Maybe Tomorrow* in 1998, Jared Thomas (Nukunu) releasing his first young adult novel *Sweet Guy* in 2005, and *Grace Beside Me* (2012) by Wiradjuri and Torres Strait Islander author Sue McPherson was made into a television series in 2018. With young adult fiction has come a natural intersection with the genres of speculative fiction and the emerging transnational literary movement of Indigenous Futurisms. In 2012, Palyku author Ambelin Kwaymullina published the first of many young adult speculative fiction works – *The Interrogation of Ashala Wolf* – and in 2014 Mununjali writer Ellen van Neerven published *Heat and Light*, a collection of short stories that includes works of speculative fiction and engages with the experiences and perspectives of young Aboriginal people.

As a work of short fiction, *Heat and Light* sits alongside other important Aboriginal literary works that make use of the short story form. In 2006, Koori writer Tony Birch published his first book, a collection of short stories titled *Shadowboxing*. Although Birch has since become a prolific novelist and essayist, his latest work *Dark as Last Night* (2021) also utilises the short story form. Contemporary Aboriginal literature also includes other genre and form such as crime, romance, satire, social commentary, polemic and other non-fiction. Nicole Watson's first book *The Boundary* (2011) is a fast-paced crime novel, and in 2007 Anita Heiss released the first of a series of Aboriginal chick lit novels (*Not Meeting Mr Right*) going on to publish three more chick lit books in subsequent years (including *Paris Dreaming*). Across the late 1990s and early 2000s, Anita Heiss published social commentary and satire in *Token Koori* (1998) and *Sacred Cows* (2000). More recently, Victor Steffensen (Tagalaka) released *Fire Country* (2020), which is part autobiography, part polemic and engages with issues of Indigenous cultural knowledge and land management practices. Further, Wiradjuri journalist and writer Stan Grant has published several books of social commentary that provide insight into Aboriginal perspectives on Australian society: *Talking to My Country* (2016), *Australia Day* (2019), *On Identity* (2019), and *With the Falling of the Dusk* (2021).

IV | CONCLUSION

Aboriginal literature has changed and developed across its history, moving from its origins in oral storytelling to published works in English with a specific concentration in poetry, playwrighting and life writing. As modern Aboriginal literature has further developed into other forms and genre – fiction, short fiction, young adult, speculative fiction and Indigenous Futurisms, crime, chick lit, satire, social commentary, polemic and Indigenous cultural knowledges and practice – self-determination and self-definition remain critical. Contesting the prior history of non-Indigenous writing about (or indeed fraudulently as) Aboriginal people, Aboriginal writers have asserted their sovereignty and challenged traditional literary norms. Today, Aboriginal literature continues to push boundaries while simultaneously remaining firmly grounded in its roots. For example, fiction novels like *The Yield* (2019) by Wiradjuri writer Tara June Winch and poetry books like *Kindred* (2019) by Gunai writer Kirli Saunders use traditional literary forms to engage with Aboriginal languages. Likewise, works like Wright's *Carpentaria* present Aboriginal oral storytelling modes and Indigenous knowledges within the form of the traditional literary novel.

As Aboriginal literature becomes increasingly part of world and transnational literatures (Brewster, 2010, 89; Ng, 2018; Sharrad, 2020), self-determination and self-definition also increase in importance:

> So, the argument is essentially the same as what other people in the world generally want for themselves, and that is, to be able to tell their own story, to

> be heard and understood. Our story is whether Aboriginal people have the right to tell or govern their own story and on what terms, or have we relinquished the right to tell the truths about our story. (Self-governing, 95)

With Wright one of Aboriginal literature's most profound writers with global and transnational reach, her words on the importance of a self-governing literature indicate the ongoing challenge that Aboriginal writers pose to traditional literary norms.

4

WAANYI COUNTRY, NORTH AUSTRALIA

David S. Trigger

The language name "Waanyi" is the identity term used to distinguish the group of contemporary Aboriginal people who assert traditional connections with, and rights and interests in, an area that straddles the Queensland/Northern Territory border in the Gulf Country of north Australia. The dimensions and boundaries of Waanyi country are broadly supported among territorially adjacent Indigenous groups in the region. The overlaps with the cultural system of the Garawa language group to the north and west of Waanyi country are substantial.

The spatial extent of "Waanyi country" is understood in terms of the actions of particular ancestral spiritual beings, occupation and use of the land by earlier generations of Waanyi people, and associated bodies of traditional knowledge about species and geographic features of the landscape. Waanyi connections to the land derive from cultural knowledge about both the spiritual and material properties of plants, animals and topography. This knowledge has been diminishing among younger generations of Waanyi people but there continues to be energetic embracing of inherited connections to land, waters and adapted cultural beliefs and practices.

The Waanyi conception of "country" is understood especially in terms of the actions of ancestral "Dreaming" beings who arise in, travel through, and inhabit the land. Narratives concerning these beings may be said to constitute the intellectual basis for traditional connections to Waanyi country. Beliefs about Dreamings in the land also inform those traditional Waanyi customs and practices that have continued in the face of changes arising from the relationship over more than 150 years with the wider Australian settler-colonial society. Each major Dreaming has a place in what is termed in English the "skin" system. The "skin" (or *nginyin*) of a spiritual entity, and also of the country it inhabits and the Waanyi people connected to it, is an internal spiritual essence. In the traditional system of land tenure and social organisation an individual's skin is the same as his or her father. The skin system is complex and traditionally entailed preferred marriage rules regulating the skins inherited by children from their parents. Nowadays people do not generally marry correctly according to the skin system but the "skin" significance of country and Dreamings remain part of the knowledge older people wish to transmit to the younger generations.

To the extent that its dimensions prior to European intrusion can be reconstructed, "Waanyi country" included a large area south and southeast of the China Wall, a major escarpment running east-west on the north side of the Nicholson River, and forming part of the northern boundary of Waanyi land claims over the past few decades. In my research since the late 1970s, now deceased senior Waanyi people spoke of an important site defining the western boundary of Waanyi country, where *Bujarda* (Python, "Piebald" Snake) Dreaming began speaking Waanyi language on its travels to the south and east through Waanyi country. In the Northern Territory, Waanyi country extends south to the vicinity of the Carrara Range and Carrara Creek, this area said by now deceased Waanyi elders Roy Seccin and Jack Hogan to be where *Gundugundu* ("Short Devil Men")[1] begin their travels along Carrara Creek and spread northwards. In the course of these movements, *Gundugundu* are said to encounter *Bujarda* (Python) and *Jumburuna* (Yellow Goanna) Dreamings. Further west, the place Jamunygula (known as Tobacco Hole in English) was described as a "corner post" marking the boundary of Waanyi and Wagaya country. Gudawudangiri, or Border Waterhole, located near the Queensland/Northern Territory border, demarcates the location where a travelling band of mythic "girls" from the west known in the Waramungu language as *Mungamunga* ("desert girls") and in Waanyi as *Marrarrabana* ("water girls") began speaking the Waanyi language. From here, they travelled on through Waanyi country further east into Queensland.

Waanyi country extended as far eastwards as the vicinity of the foot of the hills marking the eastern extremity of the Barkly Tableland. In the area of Lawn Hill Station in Queensland, these hills include the Constance Range and the Edith Range, and they run roughly in a

1. See Mary Laughren's list of Waanyi words p. 213.

north-south direction along a route to the west of Lawn Hill Creek. Contemporary Waanyi people assert traditional connections with an area further to the east than these ranges. Senior Waanyi men and women have explained that Waanyi people "took over" an expanse of plains country running eastwards from Lawn Hill Creek to the Gregory River, this area having initially been country of the Nguburindi people. Senior Waanyi people also acknowledge their historical succession to part of Injilarija country centred on the upper reaches of Lawn Hill Creek and the middle reaches of the Gregory River.

Both Injilarija and Nguburindi language groups had their numbers fatally depleted in the wake of early European settlement. Thus, Waanyi people succeeded to traditional ownership of land once part of Injilarija and Nguburindi territories, in accordance with traditional law and custom and with the circumstances of Waanyi historical movements eastwards from late in the nineteenth century. While senior Waanyi people are often careful to acknowledge these historical processes of "take over", they also confirm Waanyi rights and interests as far east as the Gregory River and south to a boundary running along Lawn Hill Creek and then extending to the Gregory River in the vicinity of Riversleigh homestead. As it is put by one of the most conservative senior Waanyi men, Roy Seccin, the Waanyi people now hold traditional law and custom over a large domain: "they got a big land that Waanyi".

The majority of contemporary Waanyi people have lived most of their lives in close proximity to some part of their traditional country. A large number now live at Doomadgee, with others resident at Mornington Island, Burketown, Robinson River, Borroloola, and Mt Isa. Since the early 1980s, a small number of families have lived periodically on outstations within the area of the Nicholson River Land Trust in the Northern Territory, country that was claimed successfully in the 1980s by Waanyi and Garawa traditional owners under the *Aboriginal Land Rights (N.T.) Act*.

The literature available regarding Waanyi people and culture in the Gulf Country addresses criteria for membership of the group, the nature of Waanyi law and custom concerning traditional land tenure, the details of identifiable "countries" and associated families within the overall area of Waanyi traditional territory, contemporary acknowledgement of changing and adapted aspects of traditional law and custom, and the nature of traditional rights and interests asserted by Waanyi people through legal options available to them. There are also accounts of historical relationships among Waanyi people as they have been impacted and engaged with aspects of the wider Australian society and economy.

5

GETTING STARTED

I | CHAPTER SUMMARY, SUSAN BARRETT

Carpentaria is divided into fourteen chapters of unequal length, which are subdivided into unnumbered sections visually separated by a typographic space. The first letter of each chapter is in a much larger font, and the first two chapters are preceded by a short passage in capital letters that acts as a kind of epigraph. These typographic features have been interpreted in various ways; Chester Eagle sees the large first letter as a way of "giv[ing] the coming pages a push start" (362), while Geoff Rodoreda suggests that the short capitalised text is a way of setting the stage and preparing the reader to listen (161).

Rather than having a linear plot with chapters that are linked chronologically, *Carpentaria* advances through a series of stories about the different characters and significant events. This episodic structure is characteristic of oral traditions in which themes tend to be more important than plot and the episodes are very often interchangeable (Loomes, 132). It is also reminiscent of how memory works, with one thought leading to another with the links between them clear only to the person whose thoughts they are.

The stories in the novel are framed by changes in the land – the novel begins with a description of how the ancestral serpent created the rivers, and it ends with the destruction of the town of Desperance by a cyclone. The character of Norm is another structural feature as he is the first and the last character to appear. Arnaud Barras (2021) argues that further cohesion is given by the three journeys undertaken in the novel: the first is by Norm to return Elias's body to the sea, the second by Mozzie who is constantly journeying across the land, and the third by Will who goes in search of Hope and Bala.

The plot of the novel is not easy to summarise, indeed Jeanine Leane cautions against trying to do so arguing that:

> To offer a plot summary would be reductionist, as the narrative is a complex layering of stories. It collapses time and space to honour Aboriginal past, present, memory, future and the sense of collectively experienced time like the serpent described in the opening passages, 'collapsing tunnels' that represent confined spaces to form 'deep sunken valleys' that are expansive and vast like the Aboriginal stories in the narrative. (2015, 152)

The chapter summary which follows should be read keeping the points made above in mind.

Chapter 1: From Time Immemorial (1)

The first chapter focuses on the land. After an epigraph drawing attention to the existence of an Aboriginal story about the history of Australia and the current state of affairs, which is different to the white nation's story, the novel opens with a description of how the ancestral serpent formed the country before withdrawing underground, where it continues to live. The character of Normal Phantom is introduced. There is a description of how the white inhabitants' ceremony to rename the river is ruined by a dust storm and the chapter ends with an invocation to listen to the real story of the place.

Chapter 2: Angel Day (12)

Chapter two is centred on Norm's wife Angel Day. It describes how she built her house and how Norm went away to sea for five years, perhaps in protest for where she had chosen to build it or perhaps simply because he did not want to help her. Most of the chapter concerns Angel's trip to the rubbish dump, where she finds an old clock and a statue of the Virgin Mary, and which culminates in a fight with the other Aboriginal women. Her son Will lights a fire to stop the fighting. The council later try unsuccessfully to investigate the origin of the fire. During the night the Aboriginal families who are not part of the Phantom clan move to the other side of the dump giving rise to two Aboriginal communities, the Eastsiders and the Westsiders. The white inhabitants of Uptown consider Norm to be the leader of the Aboriginal people and a delegation sets off to see him. Instead of talking to Norm, they end up in a confrontation with Angel Day.

Chapter 3: Elias Smith comes ... and goes (42)

There is a cyclone at sea and all the clocks stop working. The town's inhabitants go down to the water's edge and see a man with long white hair and a beard walking out of the sea. Several embedded stories follow. The first focusses on Joseph Midnight, who claims to belong to a tribe that does not exist. He is in league with the mining company and is thought to be responsible for the wild pigs overrunning the Aboriginal camps. The narrator then moves on to the Aboriginal inhabitants' attempts to get their children to find out the white secrets which they believe are hidden in their schoolbooks. The embedded stories conclude with the State Governor's attempt to change the town's name to Masterton which is fiercely resisted by the Desperanians. The narrator then returns to talking about the man from the sea. Truthful, the local policeman, who has so little to do that he grows plants in the prison cell and roses in the prison garden, takes charge. Captain Nicoli Finn, an old man keeping watch of the coastline, decides to call the man Elias Smith. It is decided that Elias should guard the town but there are a series of mysterious fires which are blamed on him and he is asked to leave.

Chapter 4: Number One house (89)

Elias leaves the town in his boat. Norm reflects on the time he used to spend at sea with Elias. Norm's sea skills are well known but the arrival of the mine has changed things in Desperance. The new mine technology is blamed for stealing people's words and sending them elsewhere. Norm's youngest child Kevin takes a job in the mine and is brain-damaged in an accident on the first day. Kevin tries to attack Norm with a knife. Later a group of young white men try to run Kevin over but his sisters defend him and get into a fight using iron bars and a rifle. His sisters then put Kevin to bed brutally.

Chapter 5: Mozzie Fishman (114)

The story shifts from Norm and the inhabitants of Desperance to Mozzie Fishman and his zealots who drive around the country in a thirty-three-car procession. Mozzie is afraid of the sea but he can detect water inland. He returns to Desperance every year at the start of the wet season. Will Phantom is travelling in Mozzie's car. The convoy arrive at a lagoon where they intend to spend the night but they find Elias's dead body sitting in a boat in the middle of the lagoon. The other men leave immediately but Will stays behind. Mozzie realises that Norm is waiting for Will to come home and remembers how Will left his family and moved Eastside when he married Hope. He thinks back to when Norm was arrested for murdering one of the Eastsiders, and how the white judge eventually dismissed the case.

Chapter 6: Knowing Fish (152)

Will is sitting by the side of the lagoon. He went into hiding after being accused of sabotaging the development of the mining industry. He thinks about the journey Elias would have had to make to bring the boat inland to the lagoon. He realises that Elias cannot have made the trip by himself, that he was murdered, and his body has been tied into the boat. A helicopter appears overhead and Will tries to attract its attention before discovering that the passenger in the helicopter has a rifle and is trying to shoot him. Will hides in the water of the lagoon and is saved by the arrival of a storm. When the helicopter leaves, Will takes Elias's body out of the lagoon, hides the boat and carries the body away with him. Two mine vehicles arrive with six men inside them, including two of Will's brothers, but they fail to see him. Will takes shelter in a cave with Aboriginal paintings in it. The Irish priest, Father Danny, turns up and the helicopter lands to question him about where he is going. The men in the helicopter slash all Father Danny's tyres before leaving. Will comes out of hiding and Father Danny drives him, and Elias's body, to Desperance. Will takes Elias's body to his father's fish-preserving workshop. He remembers his childhood and his father being arrested after finding a dead body in the dump. Will leaves Elias's body in the workshop for Norm to find and rows out to sea in search of Hope and Bala.

Chapter 7: Something about the Phantom Family (196)

Norm believes that some sort of supernatural power helps him to restore the fish and he believes his workshop stores other people's memories. Norm thinks about Angel. He finds Elias's body and screams. His three daughters come to see what is happening. They set fire to tyres with the intention of burning Elias's body but Norm stops them. Truthful arrives to find out why there is a fire, and ends up sleeping with Girlie.

Chapter 8: Norm's responsibility (219)

Norm decides to take Elias's body to the gropers' place to lay him to rest. He holds a conversation with Elias's body as he rows out to sea.

They talk about Angel, and they watch a manta ray. Norm remembers a groper caught by white fishermen dying on the beach. Gropers come to meet the boat. He puts Elias's body into the water and the fish take him away. Norm is alone in his boat. He has a series of troubling dreams, is unable to catch any fish and is attacked by people from the spirit world. He lands on a beach covered in dead fish. During the night he is visited by the devil woman Gardajala who tries to seduce him.

Chapter 9: Bala, the child of hope (264)

Norm is lost in his own world talking to the spirits when he realises that a small boy is trying to move his boat. At first he thinks it is Will but the boy comes back with some cooked fish for him to eat. The boy tells Norm that his name is Bala and that it is his father who is called Will. Norm once again thinks of Angel and blames her for the way their children have turned out. Bala tells Norm that they have to hide. Norm thinks he has ended up on the island as punishment for what Will has done and is unwilling to listen to Bala. A storm arrives and Norm runs away from the flood water accompanied by spirit people who put him in his boat and launch him on the river flowing towards the sea. He rescues Bala who is clinging to a tree. Bala tells him that the bad men took his mother Hope and that he saw her falling out of the sky. Norm concludes that it is Elias who helped him find his grandson.

Chapter 10: The giant in the cloak (295)

The narrative returns to Desperance with a description of the arrival of the wet season – a time of year when strange things happen in the town. Three young Aboriginal boys are arrested for Gordie's murder, which happened on the night Norm left with Elias's body. The Mayor Bruiser beats the boys up, initially aided by Truthful, but eventually Truthful has second thoughts and stops Bruiser by threatening him with a gun. Kevin is picked up on his way back from the bar by a group of young, white-hooded white men. They beat him up and torture him, dragging him along behind their car. Girlie finds him seriously injured and he is taken to hospital. No one is arrested for the attack and Girlie points out the contrast between how quickly people were arrested for Gordie's murder and how little is being done to find Kevin's attackers. Truthful has a disturbing dream of his rose garden filled with grey-skinned Aboriginal people and goes back to the cell to discover that the three boys have hanged themselves. He unties them and tends to their dead bodies tenderly, bringing them food several times a day. Bruiser eventually realises what has happened. He wants to cover up the boys' suicide by blaming it on Truthful having gone mad. None of the town people oppose his decision.

Chapter 11: The mine (350)

The narrative shifts again to Fishman who left Desperance on the same day as Norm. Two years previously, Fishman had helped Will escape from Desperance after he had damaged the pipeline which the mine had built to carry the ore from the mine to the coast. The mine gave Joseph Midnight a new house but Midnight sent Hope and Bala away in Elias's boat because he feared for their safety and knew that Will would go looking for them. When Will turns up, he gives him his boat and sings him directions to find Hope and Bala. Will realises that Elias's body was a trap set up by the mine to catch him. Will is at sea following Midnight's directions and comes to an island made of rubbish that has been taken over by pelicans. There is a storm and afterwards Will explores the neighbouring islands. He hears an Italian tenor voice singing and wakes up tied up in a helicopter with Hope. Hope is pushed out of the helicopter and Will watches her fall. Will is taken to the mine where he is spotted by two of Fishman's men. Fishman sends a rescue party who start a fire. Will wants to kill the guards and is reluctant to leave. The two guards are killed as they chase after Will. A massive explosion destroys the mine.

Chapter 12: About sending letters (402)

Mozzie fears that Angel's life is in danger and he tells his men to take her to a town in the South. Will tells Mozzie that he wants to put the two mine workers' bodies in Elias's boat but Mozzie tells him he needs to bury them. Mozzie believes that everything started to go wrong when Elias left the town and the mine arrived. He believes that Bruiser killed Gordie because he knew too much. He tells Will that Truthful hanged himself. Two of Mozzie's men bring Elias's boat back; they put the men's bodies in it and anchor it in the middle of the lagoon. They take the bodies of the Aboriginal boys, who died in prison, to a cave with an underground sea inside it. They place the bodies in paperbark canoes and push the canoes off to take the boys to their final resting place. As they head back towards the entrance to the cave, they can hear helicopters outside looking for them. Will says he is leaving. Meanwhile the police arrest the boys who were driving Angel to safety. She decides to hitchhike back to town but is picked up by a truck and disappears.

Chapter 13: The wash (440)

Will looks down on Desperance and thinks about the fruit bats. The town is flooding as a result of the storm. He takes refuge in the pub where he finds Lloydie Smith talking to his mermaid. Will takes refuge in the upper room. While he waits for the waters to rise, he remembers things from his childhood. He also remembers the people who are important to him: Joseph, Norm, Fishman, Hope, Bala, Elias. Will is swept away by the flood water and is washed ashore on a floating island of rubbish. Initially the island is fertile with crops growing, but it gradually starts to fall apart, destroyed by white ants and invaded by seagulls.

Chapter 14: Coming back (484)

Norm has been at sea for forty days and nights with Hope and Bala. He realises that Hope is afraid of both the sea and the night sky, and he decides that he needs to take care of Bala. Norm lands the boat where Desperance should be, but there is nothing left. The town has been washed away by the floods. He walks towards where the town once was with Bala on his shoulders, planning where he will rebuild his home. Hope returns to the boat to go and look for Will, helped on her way by the gropers.

II | TABLEAU DES PERSONNAGES, LAURA SINGEOT

> *« All the main characters of this book are like islands of self-sufficiency that act alone. » (Writing, Kindle)*

Les personnages principaux apparaissent trop souvent pour que ce tableau soit exhaustif mais certains épisodes importants les concernant y sont toutefois mentionnés. De même, on aurait pu ajouter comme personnages « the town/the townsfolk of Desperance » (p. 30, 31) ou encore les clans aborigènes (« Eastside » ou « Westside ») et les anciens (« elders »), mais les instances en sont trop nombreuses.

Les personnages sont classés par ordre de première apparition.

Personnages	Pages et chapitres	Descriptions succinctes
Ch1 From time immemorial		
Serpent ancestral	Ch1, p. 1-2	Création des fleuves.
	Ch2, p. 13 et ch5, p. 134	Esprit du serpent sur lequel a été construit la maison d'Angel Day et de Norm.
	Ch3, p. 59	Réapparaît un siècle plus tard pour ramener le fleuve jusqu'au port de Desperance.
	Ch13, p. 448, 453, 457 et ch14, p. 490	Autres mentions lors du cyclone ou du voyage de Norm, Hope et Bala.
Abdul et Abdullah	Ch1, p. 4-6	Les frères afghans et leurs chameaux.
Normal Phantom	Ch1, p. 4, 6-8	Première description qui insiste sur son lien avec l'eau, les étoiles.
	Ch4, p. 97-99	Raconte l'histoire violente du massacre des parents de son père et de leur tribu.
	Ch5, p. 148-150	Accusé des crimes « perpétrés par Abilene ».
	Ch7, p. 196-201	Description de son atelier et de son art de la taxidermie.
	Ch7, p. 204-205	Découvre le corps d'Elias.
	Ch8, p. 225-suivantes	Voyage en mer pour célébrer la cérémonie funéraire d'Elias (237-242).
	Ch14, p. 484-498	Voyage de retour avec Hope et Bala, puis seul avec Bala, il arrive là où se trouvait Desperance avant le cyclone (499).

Personnages	Pages et chapitres	Descriptions succinctes
Uncle Micky	Ch1, p. 10	A récupéré toutes les preuves qu'il pouvait concernant les massacres d'Aborigènes dans la région, archives qui sombrent dans l'oubli.
Ch2 Angel Day		
Angel Day	Ch2, p. 13-15	Construit sa maison avec des détritus récupérés dans la décharge à l'orée de la ville. Querelles de ménage avec Norm.
	Ch2, p. 18-24	Recherche des trésors sur la décharge et initie la guerre des clans.
	Ch2, p. 38	Discours face à la délégation municipale après la guerre des clans.
	Ch5, p. 132-133	Relation avec Mozzie.
	Ch12, p. 429-436	Envoyée dans une autre ville par Mozzie, se retrouve à faire le voyage seule après que ses chauffeurs ont été arrêtés par des policiers.
	Ch12, p. 437-439	«Lettre» reçue par un homme du convoi de Mozzie, qui raconte la vie d'Angel Day après son départ de Desperance.
Femme aborigène	Ch2, p. 24-25	Ressemble aux falaises blanches de Douvres et initie la bataille des clans en répondant à Angel Day.
Will Phantom	Ch2, p. 27	Jeune, il met le feu à la décharge pour arrêter la guerre des clans.
	Ch4, p. 100	Troisième fils de Norm, son favori, jusqu'à ce qu'il le renie.

Personnages	Pages et chapitres	Descriptions succinctes
	Ch5, p. 144-145 et ch6, p. 156-169	Va récupérer le corps d'Elias sur le lagon, enquête sur la scène du crime, jusqu'à ce qu'il se fasse tirer dessus par les hommes de la mine (165-167), puis il s'enfuit dans le bush.
	Ch6, p. 154-155	Description par Joseph Midnight.
	Ch6, p. 185-195	Will dépose le corps d'Elias dans l'atelier de Norm. C'est l'occasion pour lui de repenser à sa famille et son enfance.
	Ch10, p. 312	Ses frasques et actes de sabotage de la mine sont énumérés brièvement.
	Ch11, p. 351-356	Récit de ses premiers démêlés avec la mine et tentative infructueuse de la police pour l'arrêter.
	Ch11, p. 366-375	Voyage d'île en île jusqu'à ce qu'il soit arrêté par les hommes de la mine. Après avoir assisté à la « mort » de Hope, il s'échappe de la mine et y met le feu avec l'aide des hommes de Mozzie (386-390).
	Ch13, p. 440-445	Retourne à pied jusqu'à Desperance.
	Ch13, p. 453-473	Trouve refuge au pub lors du cyclone. Se rappelle ses souvenirs d'enfance, de pêche avec son père, Elias et Mozzie.
	Ch13, p. 475-483	Arrive sur son île de déchets, heureux, jusqu'à ce qu'il devienne mélancolique et ait peur que l'île ne se désintègre (480).

Personnages	Pages et chapitres	Descriptions succinctes
Stan Bruiser	Ch2, p. 32-34	Maire de la ville, brutal, raciste.
	Ch2, p. 39-40	Violeur de femmes aborigènes.
	Ch10, p. 310, 312-315	Discours à propos du meurtre de Gordie, décide d'arrêter les 3 jeunes renifleurs d'essence.
	Ch10, p. 345	Essaye de ramener Truthful à la raison, sans succès. A une vision des 3 garçons et parle avec une voix d'enfant lorsqu'il raconte la scène aux habitants (347), puis décide d'agir sans se soucier des lois sur les armes à feu (348).
	Ch12, p. 412	Mozzie pense qu'il a tué Gordie car ce dernier avait découvert des choses sur lui.
	Ch13, p. 449	Quitte Desperance avant le cyclone dans la voiture de police, comme un « 'stand-in' policeman » (451).
Cilla Mooch	Ch2, p. 36	Aborigène qui « tente de rentrer dans un moule blanc », membre du conseil municipal, tente de négocier avec Norm après la guerre des clans.
	Ch13, p. 451	Conduit l'un des camions lors de l'évacuation de Desperance, défiant envers la politique d'évacuation et remise en question du rôle de Bruiser.

Personnages	Pages et chapitres	Descriptions succinctes
Ch3 Elias Smith comes… and goes		
Elias Smith	Ch3, p. 48	Description physique, comparé plusieurs fois au père Noël (46, 66) et lien avec le « Dreamtime » (49-53).
	Ch3, p. 74-78	Sa vie à Desperance.
	Ch3, p. 81	Désigné gardien de Desperance, il est ensuite accusé d'avoir fait exploser la mairie (83), ce qui mène à son exil (86).
	Ch4, p. 89-93	Son départ de Desperance.
	Ch5, p. 140-142	Son corps est découvert par les hommes de Fishman et Will sur le lagon.
	Ch8, p. 225-suiv.	Cérémonie funéraire en mer orchestrée par Norm.
Joseph Midnight	Ch3, p. 50-52	Nom donné à son groupe, querelle de territoire.
	Ch11, p. 357-366	Raconte à Will ce qui s'est passé avec Hope et Bala, l'aide à préparer son voyage.
	Ch13, p. 452	Voit pour la dernière fois Will, depuis l'arrière du camion qui l'évacue de Desperance.
Nicoli Finn	Ch3, p. 62-66	Description précise, découvre Elias sur la plage.
	Ch3, p. 73-74	Interrogatoire d'Elias, lui donne son nom, prédit le temps (77).
	Ch8, p. 224	Mort et veille funéraire.
Truthful E'Strange	Ch3, p. 68-70	Policier de Desperance, description générale.

Personnages	Pages et chapitres	Descriptions succinctes
	Ch7, p. 214-218	S'invite et s'impose chez les Phantom après que les filles ont essayé de faire disparaître les preuves du meurtre d'Elias. Confrontation avec Girlie, avant de l'accompagner dans sa chambre.
	Ch8, p. 223	Norm imagine sa mort en mer.
	Ch10, p. 333-334, 337-339	Les frères et sœurs Phantom l'accusent de ne pas vouloir retrouver les agresseurs de Kevin ; rumeurs sur sa sexualité.
	Ch10, p. 339-341	Perd la raison, notamment après la découverte des corps des garçons dans la cellule (343-346).
	Ch12, p. 414	Suicide par pendaison.
Lonely, aka A.D. Smith	Ch3, p. 79-81	Inventeur du filet de protection invisible entourant Desperance. Marié à une Aborigène, Glenny.
Sallyanne Smith	Ch3, p. 81	Rédactrice municipale, elle suggère de donner à Elias le poste de gardien de la ville. Elle conserve la saga des Smith, « the Book of books » (82).
Captain Matthew Desperance Flinders	Ch3, p. 59	Évocation seulement : fondateur de la ville.
Beatrice Smith	Ch3, p. 65-66	Joue du Handel sur son orgue à pédalier. Autre mention sans son nom (97).

Personnages	Pages et chapitres	Descriptions succinctes
Mrs C. (Carmen) Caucus	Ch3, p. 86	Propriétaire de : « It's Flaming Hot Fish fish and chip shop ».
	Ch10, p. 345	Initie la manifestation devant la prison, à cause de l'odeur des cadavres des garçons.
	Ch13, p. 447	Pyrotechnicienne lorsqu'il s'agit de se débarrasser des chauves-souris.
Libby Valance	Ch3, p. 66, 68	Secrétaire de mairie, conduit l'interrogatoire d'Elias, marié à Maria-Sofia (68).
	Ch10, p. 308-309	Sonne la cloche pour le meurtre de Gordie, puis questionne les méthodes de Bruiser quant à « l'enquête » (313-314).
	Ch10, p. 348-349	Méprise les méthodes de Bruiser, concernant le traitement des jeunes garçons en prison et les armes à feu, le hait mais ne peut pas le tuer.
Jay Smith	Ch3, p. 70	Ancien sergent de la police.
Danny Real	Ch3, p. 87	Nouveau maître d'école, aime les oiseaux et écrit dans le journal de l'école qui remplace les archives municipales détruites par le feu.
	Ch13, p. 449	Quitte Desperance avant le cyclone dans la voiture de Bruiser.

Personnages	Pages et chapitres	Descriptions succinctes
Ch4 Number One House		
Sea Lady	Ch4, p. 94	Première description.
	Ch8, p. 250-254	Hante Norm et le rend fou, scène de combat et de joute verbale. Description physique (262).
	Ch9, p. 264	Confrontation avec Gardajala.
Pirate, le cacatoès blanc	Ch4, p. 99-101	Écoute les histoires de Norm, prophète de la famille Phantom, diseur de bonne aventure de la communauté.
	Ch7, p. 201	Interdit de séjour dans l'atelier de Norm, pour éviter qu'il se mette à imiter les grillons.
	Ch7, p. 213	Béni par le Pape.
	Ch9, p. 268, 275	Rejoint Norm sur l'île de Bala.
Dallas	Ch4, p. 100	Le chien blanc de Norm.
Kevin	Ch4, p. 101	Septième enfant de Norm, très intelligent mais un accident dans la mine où il travaillait le laisse handicapé et dépendant. Ne se sentait pas à sa place à l'école malgré ses excellentes notes. Très maladroit.
	Ch4, p. 104-108	Conséquences de l'accident à la mine, querelles avec son père (t-shirt nazi), harcelé par les brutes de Desperance.
	Ch4, p. 113 et ch7, p. 209-211	Contrôlé et attaché sur le lit par ses sœurs lorsqu'il fait une crise.
	Ch10, p. 326-331	Soirée au pub, est kidnappé dans la Holden, battu et laissé pour mort. Envoyé à l'hôpital par la voie des airs.

Personnages	Pages et chapitres	Descriptions succinctes
Inso et Donny	Ch4, p. 104	Les deux premiers fils de Norm, boxent et travaillent pour la mine.
	Ch6, p. 169-174	Font partie du groupe qui essaye de retrouver le corps d'Elias après l'attaque de Will sur le lagon.
	Ch10, p. 332-333	Rendent visite à Kevin à l'hôpital.
Abilene	Ch4, p. 108-109	Monstre porcin qui hante les bords du fleuve et dont on dit qu'elle mange les pêcheurs, entraînée par Norm. Elle aurait notamment mangé « l'Oncle ».
Girlie, Janice et Patsy	Ch4, p. 110	Les trois filles de Norm, respectivement la maigre, celle qui est tout le temps enceinte et celle qui est une femme battue. Elles font déguerpir les brutes qui poursuivaient Kevin (112).
	Ch7, p. 206-211	Essaient de faire disparaître les preuves du meurtre d'Elias en y mettant le feu.
Noelie	Ch4, p. 111	Cousin et ex de Girlie, avec qui il a eu des enfants, harcèle Kevin.
Ch5 Mozzie Fishman		
Mozzie Fishman	Ch5, p. 114-119	Description du convoi, attribution du nom et enfance.
	Ch5, p. 121-123	Mozzie et ses visions.
	Ch5, p. 132-133	Son succès auprès des femmes.
	Ch11, p. 392	Discours après l'explosion de la mine : « talking globally, acting locally ».

Personnages	Pages et chapitres	Descriptions succinctes
« The snake lizard »	Ch5, p. 120	Le convoi de Fishman suit le chemin de l'ancêtre.
Father Danny	Ch5, p. 134	Tente d'exorciser la maison des Phantom avec les crucifix qu'il apporte.
	Ch6, p. 175-185	Description, puis confrontation avec les hommes de la mine qui tentent de lui barrer la route (177-182). Ramène Will avec le corps d'Elias à Desperance (182-185).
« Guru man »	Ch5, p. 134	Tente d'exorciser la maison des Phantom avec du pain et en jouant des percussions. Sans succès.
Cyclone Midnight	Ch5, p. 146-147	Père de Joseph Midnight, a initié la guerre des clans. Créateur d'Abilene.
Le juge	Ch5, p. 149-150	Juge Norm pour les meurtres dont on l'accuse, ornithologue râté, met fin aux poursuites et s'enfuit en van vers Surfers Paradise. N'est plus jamais revu.
Ch6 Knowing fish		
Aucun nouveau personnage		
Ch7 Something about the Phantom family		
Aucun nouveau personnage		

Personnages	Pages et chapitres	Descriptions succinctes
Ch8 Norm's responsibility		
Gordie	Ch8, p. 224-225	Nouveau gardien de la ville, après Nicoli. Trois jeunes garçons sont accusés de son meurtre (Ch10, p. 300, 302-305).
Devil woman, Gardajala	Ch8, p. 262-263	La plage est son royaume et elle est associée à une image de luxure.
	Ch9, p. 264, 267-268, 289	Affronte la « sea lady », puis revient hanter Norm régulièrement.
Ch9 Bala, the child of hope		
Esprits Gundugundu et Kadajala (« white-man devil »)	Ch9, p. 264-265	Règnent sur la mer : les Gundugundu, qui vivent dans les cyclones, sont plus dangereux que Kadajala.
Bala	Ch9, p. 266-271	Rencontre Norm, pêche et chasse pour lui.
	Ch9, p. 285-286	Se noie presque à cause d'une inondation alors qu'il chasse le canard pour Norm. Est sauvé par ce dernier (292).
Yinbirras	Ch9, p. 286-287	Êtres féériques liés au peuple Yannguny, tentent d'échapper à l'inondation.
The « bush people » (290) ou « ghostly tribe » (294) dont la vieille femme au visage de poisson	Ch9, p. 287-292, 294	Des feuilles d'eucalyptus poussent de leurs doigts; courent aux côtés du bateau de Norm pour échapper à l'inondation.

Personnages	Pages et chapitres	Descriptions succinctes
Ch10 The Giant in the cloak		
Tristrum Fishman, Junior Fishman Luke et Aaron Ho Kum	Ch10, p. 297-300, 316-318	Arrestation pour le meurtre de Gordie, description de leur famille.
	Ch10, p. 318-322	Sont presque battus à mort par Bruiser, puis se pendent dans leur cellule (343).
	Ch12, p. 417-423	Leur cérémonie funéraire est célébrée par Mozzie Fishman.
Aaron Ho Kum's uncle	Ch10, p. 317-318	Éleveur de chèvres dont le travail est reconnu par Uptown, s'occupe d'Aaron.
Lloydie Smith	Ch10, p. 317	Père d'Aaron, l'un des trois garçons arrêtés pour le meurtre de Gordie, ne l'a jamais reconnu car sa mère est aborigène.
	Ch10, p. 327-328	Est hypnotisé par son amour pour la «sirène», tête de proue, qui lui sert de comptoir, jusqu'à mourir avec elle lors du cyclone final (454-456, 471).
Ch11 The mine		
Hope	Ch11, p. 374	Les hommes de la mine se débarrassent d'elle en la jetant de l'hélicoptère.
	Ch14, p. 486-498	Lors du voyage de retour avec Norm et Bala, elle a peur de la mer, des étoiles. Après les avoir retrouvés sur la plage (488), le début du voyage est chaotique car elle se dispute avec Norm, puis elle part seule pour retrouver Will (497-498).

Personnages	Pages et chapitres	Descriptions succinctes
Cookie and Chuck	Ch11, p. 377-380	Hommes qui surveillent Will à la mine, meurent lors de l'incendie (389, 390). Après une dispute avec Mozzie sur le sujet, Will décide de laisser leurs corps dans le bateau d'Elias, à la merci des animaux sauvages au milieu du lagon où le corps d'Elias avait été abandonné (416-417).
Ch12 About sending letters		
Graham Spilling	Ch12, p. 427	Patron de la mine, donne des ordres pour retrouver les fauteurs de trouble.
Deux jeunes hommes de Mozzie	Ch12, p. 433-434	Chauffeurs d'Angel Day lorsqu'elle quitte Desperance, histoires de jeunesse teintées de violence au contact des policiers blancs, raison pour laquelle ils ont rejoint le convoi.
Ch13 The wash		
Old Queen of the Pricklebush world	Ch13, p. 459-461	Vieille et maigre, elle a été éduquée dans une mission. Will voit son esprit dans l'une des chambres de l'hôtel de Lloydie lors du cyclone.
Ch14 Coming back		
Aucun nouveau personnage		

PART ONE

CULTURAL THEMES

1

THE INDIGENOUS WORLD

Susan Barrett

I | "SINCE TIME IMMEMORIAL"

> *"The Indigenous world is both ancient and modern, both colonial experience and contemporary reality, and the problem right now for us, is how to carry all times when approaching the future" (Wright, Writing, Kindle)*

a. The Dreaming and Dreaming Tracks

If you talk to an Aboriginal person, they will tell you that they have lived in Australia "since time immemorial" (1). The term "Dreaming" [1] has often been used in English to translate the Aboriginal words which describe the period of time when the ancestral beings created the geographical features, the different species and the Laws of existence by which life is sustained (Rose, 2000, 44). In Aboriginal cosmology the rivers and the valleys were created as the ancestral beings travelled across the land and the animals we see around us today acquired their physical characteristics during the Dreaming. According to Deborah Bird Rose, most life-forms initially had a basic human shape which the

1. "Dreaming" was also translated into English as "Dreamtime." There is considerable debate over which is the best translation for the different words. The presence of the word "time" in "Dreamtime" suggests that it refers to an era that is over. This is in contradiction with the Aboriginal belief that it is a part of contemporary life. "Dreaming" is a present participle which conveys the idea of something which is ongoing, yet even the word "dream" is problematic in English as it can suggest something transitive and imaginary with little real importance. Aboriginal people increasingly use the terms "Law" or "Ancestral Law" instead.

ancestral beings could change at will, but eventually they lost their ability to change and assumed their current form:

> [...] they became immobile and at the same time they lost their range of options. The power of each was focused in a particular direction [...]. Compared to the species alive now, Dreamings had a vast range of options. They changed in size, becoming small or huge in different places. They changed shape; the Nanganari women, for example, changed into possums and then changed back to humans again [...] they imprinted their tracks in the landscape in the forms of hills, valleys, rivers. They carried seeds and tubers establishing plant communities that persist. (Rose, 2000, 46)

The stories of the Dreaming found in different parts of Australia share some common features but there are regional variations that account for the local geographical features and the specific flora and fauna which are found in the different parts of Australia. The Rainbow Snake or Rainbow Serpent is found in Dreaming stories all over Australia. It is also represented visually in paintings on rocks and in caves. In some Dreaming stories the Serpent's main role is as the "'first mother' of all subsequent beings" (Taçon *et al.*, 102), while in others it is responsible primarily for creating the features of the landscape. The first story told in *Carpentaria* is the story of how the Rainbow Serpent shaped the landscape of the Gulf of Carpentaria:

> The ancestral serpent, a creature larger than storm clouds, came down from the stars, laden with its creative enormity [...] to crawl on its heavy belly, all around the wet clay soils in the Gulf of Carpentaria [...] leaving in its wake the thunder of tunnels collapsing to form deep sunken valleys. The sea water following in the serpent's wake [...] filled the swirling tracks to form the mighty bending rivers spread across the vast plains of the Gulf country. (1-2)

Its position at the opening of the novel is a reflection of the importance of the Rainbow Serpent Dreaming for Waanyi and other Aboriginal people. One particularity of the Dreamings in northern Australia, where there is a wet season and a dry season, is that the Serpent is "associated with seasonal fertility through the creation of rain" (Taçon *et al.*,102), while during the dry season it inhabits deep waterholes. This belief is incorporated in the story about the Serpent told at the beginning of *Carpentaria*:

> When it finished creating the many rivers in its wake, it created one last river, no larger or smaller than the others [...]. This is where the giant serpent continues to live deep down under the ground in a vast network of limestone aquifers. (2)

The ancestral beings are not only literally visible in rock and cave paintings,[1] they are also spiritually present in the landscape itself. Marcia Langton suggests that one way for non-Aboriginal people to begin to understand the idea of the continued presence of spiritual beings all around us is to think of them as stars:

> We know that stars are what can still be seen now of some cataclysmic event in the universe many thousands of light years ago. That is, the light of the explosion emanating through time and visible to our eyes in the present. Likewise, Aboriginal people perceive the spiritual presence of Elders in the landscape as what has emanated through time since the ancestor died. (2018, 11)

This is a very helpful analogy for non-Aboriginal readers, but it is important to read the whole of Langton's section on "Cultures and Languages" in her book *Welcome to Country* as she describes how the "Old People" are much more than just inanimate objects. Aboriginal people are aware of the landscape as a living force. As the narrator in the novel says, "Claypans breathed like skin and you could feel it, right inside the marrow of your bones" (*Carpentaria*, 357). People's lives are intimately entwined with the land on which they live forming a reciprocal relationship:

> The person takes care of the country and the country takes care of the person. [...] Damage to people is damage to country. [...] Damage to country, and to Dreamings in particular, causes death or injury to people. (Rose, 2000, 107-108)

The land therefore has an agency, and this is what explains how a rock is able to save Will when he is trying to escape from the Gurfurritt mine whilst being pursued by two security men: "the rock was ready, waiting for this moment. [...] The murderer struck dead, died instantly [...] And there was the stone, still there, unmoved" (389-390). Similar agency can be seen when the land protects Will and the other men from the explosion by "throw[ing them] down for shelter behind the boulders, in the fold of the ancestral spirit who governed the land" (390-1).

The close relationship that Aboriginal people have with the natural world is emphasised throughout the novel. Normal Phantom's

1. The Rainbow Serpent can be found in several rock paintings in the Gulf of Carpentaria. The most significant Waanyi Rainbow Serpent painting, a huge red and yellow snake, 5.8 metres long by 2.3 metres high, can be seen at Lilydale Spring. According to two Waanyi elders, the old people "put it there so everyone would know about it, so its story would be told and not forgotten" (Taçon, 166). Reproductions of the painting can be easily found on line.

ancestors are "the river people" and Norm is "like ebbing water [...]. He knew fish and was on friendly terms with gropers" (6); he tells the other Pricklebush inhabitants "we are the flesh and blood of the sea and we are what the sea brings the land" (32). Will Phantom is able to escape from the mine officials, not just because he hides in the bushes, but because he quite literally "is mud" (174); later in the novel Joseph Midnight only knows that Will is not "the trunk of a dead tree" because "he had looked at this country hundreds of times, and he knows for darn sure that there was no dead tree of any description along this stretch of road" (452).

In order to maintain the equilibrium of the natural world, Aboriginal people in some parts of Australia follow traditional practices carrying out rites and rituals to "mark the sacred in everyday life" (Langton, 2018, 11). One of these rituals is to travel along the paths taken by the ancestral beings which are known as "dreaming tracks" or "songlines". These tracks criss-cross the whole continent and are of different lengths – some are quite short, while others go through the country of many different tribal groups. All along the tracks are places that have meaning and purpose for Aboriginal People (Wright, 2000, 11-12, English adaptation mine).

In *Carpentaria*, it is Mozzie Fishman who takes on the role of travelling along the tracks and performing the rituals: "Their convoy continued an ancient religious crusade along the spiritual travelling road of the great ancestor whose journey continues to span the entire continent and is older than time itself" (114). Fishman and his men provide a clear illustration of the way Aboriginal culture is both unchanging and capable of adapting to new circumstances. He and his followers no longer travel the country on foot; instead they drive in "battered vehicles" (119). However, they do so in a way that is reminiscent of the ancestral Serpent Dreaming story; they travel in a formation that resembles "a long black snake" (350) and they move "in reptile silence" (119). Knowledge of the tracks is not limited to Fishman; it is kept alive in people's memories, something that requires a constant effort to maintain: "They always watched the goings-on of Uptown with restrained interest, and shortly afterwards, began their memory revisions. This was a daily task" (50). Knowledge is handed down orally from one generation to the next. Despite the antagonism between Norm and Joseph Midnight, Midnight shares his knowledge of sea tracks with Will to help him go in search of Hope:

> The old man gave him the directions to the safe place in his far-off country – a blow-by-blow description sung in song, unravelling a map to a Dreaming place he had never seen [...] He went on and on, fully believing he was singing in the right sequence hundreds of places in a journey to a place at least a thousand kilometres away. (360)

b. Archaeology

Archaeological research suggests that the first inhabitants came by sea to the northern shores of Australia. From there they moved south along the coastlines and also inland across the semi-arid and arid central zones following the availability of water (Langton, 2018, 9). These first inhabitants arrived at least fifty thousand years ago, possibly as long ago as 120,000 years – it has proved impossible to determine whether charcoal found at Lake George near Canberra is evidence of human habitation or simply the remains of fires caused by lightning. Radio-carbon dating has, however, revealed human remains that are about 30,000 years old at Lake Mungo in New South Wales, 45,000 years old at Keilor near Melbourne (Broome,13-14), and 65,000 years old in Arnhem Land in the Northern Territory (Langton, 2018, 2). Contrary to popular European belief, which saw Australia as an isolated place, cut off from the rest of the world until the English arrived in 1788, Aboriginal people have always traded with the inhabitants of the South East Asian islands that lie to the north of the continent.

Before the arrival of Europeans, it is estimated that there were between 250 and 400 different Indigenous languages and 500 different tribal groups. Although there were similarities between them, cultural practices varied across the country since they took into account the widely different geographical features and climatic conditions that exist in Australia. The terms "Aborigine" and "Aboriginal people" were initially used by the British settlers in order to homogenise what were, in reality, heterogeneous nations.[1]

1. For a full discussion about the different terms used now, and in the past, to refer to the first inhabitants of Australia see Glossary "Terminologie."

II | "THE LAW OF THE DREAMTIME" (*CARPENTARIA*, 239)

> *"I am country. Listen to me!*
> *I am your government – I am the land.*
> *This country speaks proper way.*
> *Law right up top.*
> *It has to be above other laws." (Wright qtd in Birrell, 2016, 15)*

The Dreaming does not only provide an explanation of how the universe and everything within it came into being, it also provides a set of rules for living which Aboriginal people call "the Law." Anne Brewster gives a succinct definition of the Law as something that "describes indigenous social and cosmological relationships to land and sea, to ancestors, and those that pertain to the domain of social intercourse" (2010, 88). The Law is mentioned in the first pages of the novel, immediately after the story of the Rainbow Serpent when the narrator says, "The inside knowledge about this river and coastal region is Aboriginal Law handed down through the ages since time began" (3).

The Law stands above all other laws and, unlike European law, is not enforced by a judiciary system but by the land, waters and sky (Birrell, 2016, 213-214). It is extremely powerful and the cyclone, and subsequent flooding, at the end of the novel that destroy the white town of Desperance can be read as an example of how the Law "becomes an annihilating force, which destroys non-indigenous law" (Birrell, 2016, 214), perhaps as a reaction to the damage that white people have done to the land.

The novel ends with a reaffirmation of the strength of the Law and the power of the ancestral Serpent. Norm and his grandson Bala walk towards where Desperance used to be. As they walk, Norm is

> [...] sizing up the flattened landscape, already planning the home he would rebuild on the same piece of land where his old house had been, among the spirits [...] where the snake slept underneath. (499)

The narrator comments: "there was so much song wafting off the watery land, singing the country afresh as they walked hand in hand" (499), suggesting that Norm and his grandson will be able to found something which is at the same time new, and a return to the ancient Law of the land.

Comparisons are made in the novel between Aboriginal Law and white knowledge. The narrator says, for example, that "Men such as Norm Phantom kept a *library* chock-a-block full of stories of the old country stored in their heads" (italics mine, 235), Fishman describes himself as "the living bible of all times" (410), his and his men's "crossing of the continent to bring the ceremony north-east to the Gulf, to finish it up, was a rigorous Law, laid down piece by piece in a *book of another kind* covering thousands of kilometres" (italics mine, 119). If this perhaps makes it easier for non-Aboriginal readers to grasp the importance and seriousness of the Law, the narrator makes it clear from the very first pages of the novel, that knowledge of the Law comes from knowledge of place:

> Can someone who did not grow up in a place that is sometimes under water, sometimes bone-dry, know when the trade winds blowing off the southern and northern hemispheres will merge in summer? [...] It takes a particular kind of knowledge to go with the river, whatever its mood. It is about there being no difference between you and the movement of water as it seasonally shifts its tracks according to its own mood. (3)

Passages like the one above have led Alison Ravenscroft to warn against the temptation for non-Aboriginal people to believe that they can ever have a full understanding of what the Law actually is:

> Indigenous Law cannot be 'seen' from a Waanyi point of view if one is not Waanyi, [...]. Indigenous Law remains as a fragment, distorted by the light cast by the scene we can see; in our scene it cannot appear. It makes no sense in a white Western epistemology, and at best its traces are translated into English, into modern Western discursive frames such as 'ecology' or 'natural history' or 'science'. That is, it is translated into our own nexus of intelligibility—a process through which Indigenous Law as an object of knowledge is made into a different object. (2010, 214)

She argues that we, as white readers, cannot know what the cyclone means in terms of the Rainbow Serpent Dreaming, and that consequently we should be wary of seeking to impose our own interpretation. Nor should we attempt to read *Carpentaria* ethnographically as a source of information about the Waanyi people and their beliefs. Rather we should embrace the novel as a text with its "own quite specific qualities of unknowability, and undecidability" (2010, 214). Our reading of *Carpentaria* should thus be undertaken not with the aim of arriving at a full understanding of the Law, but as a movement *towards* understanding of another culture (2010, 215).

III | ORALITY AND STORYTELLING IN CARPENTARIA

> *"I wanted to return something of what I have learnt and to continue the story of this country of my forefathers" (Wright, Writing, Kindle)*

As we have seen, Aboriginal Law cannot be separated from storytelling. As Kathleen Birrell reminds us, the Law is "articulated not in a court of law, but in storytelling, its juridical force made manifest not in judicial decision but in the ancestral governance of country" (Birrell, 2016, 213). Marcia Langton describes storytelling for Aboriginal people as "the original classroom where history, morality and knowledge about people, places and the world are relayed to each new generation" (2018, 24). Storytelling is thus an integral part of Aboriginal culture and carries a more profound meaning for Aboriginal people than it does for Europeans.

In her interview with Jean-François Vernay, Wright spoke, however, about the importance not only of continuing to transmit knowledge through storytelling but also of the importance of making this knowledge available in books: "We're an oral tradition, but I think that it is important to have our memories of who we are and all sorts of people we are in the form of books for future generations" (2004, 121). The existence of the stories in books is important not only for future generations of Aboriginal Australians but also for non-Aboriginal people. As the Noongar Aboriginal writer, Kim Scott, said in *Kayang and Me* (2005), a book about how he came to write a novel based on his ancestors' stories, "The way to keep country and culture alive - and not like a museum - is to have its people welcoming and introducing others into its stories" (257).[1]

How *Carpentaria* is written is therefore not just a question of literary style, it is also about respecting the Law. In her essay "On Writing *Carpentaria*", Wright goes as far as to say that it is "as if the land was telling a story about itself as much as the narrator is telling stories to the land" and for her the question of how to tell the story was just as

1. Kim Scott is a member of the Noongar people in Western Australia. He is the author of five novels: *True Country* (1993); *Benang: From the Heart* (1999); *Lost (*2006); *That Deadman Dance* (2010); *Taboo* (2017). He was the first Indigenous Australian writer to win the Miles Franklin Award which he was awarded for *Benang* in 2000 conjointly with the white novelist Thea Astley.

important as the story itself: "[there were] two principal questions: firstly how to understand the idea of Indigenous people living with the stories of all the times of this country and secondly how to write from this perspective" (Writing, Kindle). Her inspiration for the narrative voice finally came after hearing two old men talking on a footbridge over the Todd River (Writing, Kindle). When she realised that she wanted to write the novel as if it were someone telling one long story, she was aware that this was not without risk:

> I [...] knew that I would pay a price for my decision to write a novel as though some old Aboriginal person was telling the story. I think what I feared most was that this kind of voice and style of telling would be flatly rejected in Australia. Every day I was writing the novel, I would begin the day by arguing with myself about how a manuscript written in this voice was taking a big risk." (Writing, Kindle)

She felt that it was a risk worth taking, however, and that while it might alienate some white readers, it might also be a narrative voice to which Aboriginal readers could relate (Writing, Kindle).

Just as the white reader is always outside the Law, Geoff Rodoreda suggests that as white readers we are similarly outsiders to the story in the novel. We are eavesdropping on the narrator of the novel in much the same way as Wright eavesdropped on the old men's conversation, "listening in" on a story being told by Aboriginal people to Aboriginal people (9). It is therefore important to remember as we are reading that "these tellers and listeners have their own discourse, their own jargon, their own shared ways of understanding the world" (10). We need to accept that we may not always be able to fully understand things that are beyond our experience and outside our own culture.

The first chapter can be read as a prologue to the rest of the novel, and the way it is framed makes it very clear that storytelling is going to be a central feature of *Carpentaria*. The chapter starts with a sort of epigraph in capital letters: "A NATION CHANTS, *BUT WE KNOW YOUR STORY ALREADY*" (1). The opposition of "we" and "your" makes the existence of two separate groups very clear and draws attention to the fact that white people are generally not good at listening. The chapter ends with an invitation to the white reader to come and listen to a different story:

> If you are someone who visits old cemeteries, wait awhile if you visit the water people. The old Gulf country men and women who took our besieged

> memories to the grave might just climb out of the mud and tell you the real story of what happened here. (11)

The capital letters at the beginning of the chapter can be seen as a visual equivalent of the storyteller raising their voice to attract the audience's attention. The epigraph concludes with a dramatic statement designed to shock the audience into listening: "ARMAGEDDON BEGINS HERE" (1). The opening story of the Dreaming of the ancestral serpent that formed the landscape of the Gulf of Carpentaria by "crawl[ing] on its heavy belly, all around the wet clay soils" (1) is very much an oral story; the narrator addresses the reader directly as "you", "if you had been watching with the eyes of a bird hovering in the sky far above the ground" (1),"you need the patience of one who can spend hours doing nothing. If you wait under the rivergum [...] you will see" (2). Rhetorical questions are used to encourage the listener to reflect on what they are hearing:

> Can someone who did not grow up in a place that is sometimes under water, sometimes bone-dry know when the trade winds blowing off the southern and northern hemisphere will merge in summer? Know the climatic change better than they know themselves? (3)

Imperatives are used to invite the reader to imagine the scene for themselves: "Picture the creative serpent, scoring deep into – scouring down through – the slippery underground of the mudflats" (1), "Imagine the serpent's breathing rhythms as the tide flows inland" (2). The accumulation of sibilants: "scoring [...] scouring [...] slippery" (1), "ripples that shimmer silver, similar to the scales of a small, nocturnal serpent [...] slippery translucent body" (2-3), echo the hissing of a snake and lend themselves to an oral performance. Sentences are compound rather than complex with their length and rhythm reflecting the serpent's journey; the description of how the serpent formed the many rivers found in the Gulf country is relatively long and the repetition of prepositions provide a regular rhythm, reminiscent of a chant: "The serpent travelled *over* the marine plains, *over* the salt flats, *through* the salt dunes *past* the mangrove forests" (italics mine, 2). Its return to the sea, on the other hand, is a single simple sentence: "Then it went back to the sea" (2).

In the last paragraph of this first section (1-4), the Aboriginal storyteller is replaced by what at first appears for Western readers to be a more familiar third person narrator: "In one moment, during a Wet season early in the last century, the town lost its harbour waters when the river simply decided to change course, to bypass it by several kilometres" (3). The aside "Just like that" (3) is, however, characteristic of an oral rather than a written story. The same is true of the sentence without a verb a few lines further on: "A dreadful vision, a long yellow streak marching behind an arrowhead, pointing straight for the little town of Desperance" (3-4). As the paragraph progresses, it becomes apparent that far from being a neutral omniscient narrator, as the opening sentence of this sub-section suggested, it is in fact the voice of a particular type of rural white Australian. The narrator uses the racist term of "Yellow Peril" (3), accumulates clichés: "a dreadful vision" (3), "duty was everybody's business" (4), "decent society" (4); and uses a possessive adjective to talk of "the state of *their* blacks" (italics mine, 4).

In fact this narrator had already made a brief incursion a few paragraphs earlier with the shockingly racist comment about how "those up-to-no-good Mission-bred kids accidentally hanged Cry-baby Sally" (2). Both the long compound adjective, and the colloquial expression "Cry-baby," are characteristic of spoken rather than written language. The way the two different voices of Aboriginal and white Australians are entwined in the first pages of the novel seems designed to draw the reader's attention to the complicated relationships between the population groups that live in and around Desperance, and to the different stories that they tell themselves.

Several critics have commented on the characteristics of oral language that occur throughout the novel.[1] These include the frequent use of "you" mentioned above, alliteration, consonance, onomatopoeia, phonetic spellings of words such as the name of the "Gurfurritt" (Go-For-It) mine, grammatically irregular forms: "more louder," and the use of fillers characteristic of oral language: "Oh!" (54), "In any case" (53), "Well! (52).

For Louise Loomes the frequent use of parataxis and apposition are both ways of resisting "the typical hierarchical structures of the European novel, in particular the necessity for linearity and progress, or plotting" (131). She suggests that parataxis, with its accumulation of clauses using coordination rather than subordination supports the idea of "things being in an equal relationship," and "prevents the description from progressing" because there is no temporal movement

1. See in particular: Arnaud Barras (2021), Louise Loomes (2014), Geoff Rodoreda (2016).

(131). She gives as an example to illustrate her point the description of the young petrol-sniffers who are arrested for Gordie's murder:

> Everyone had seen these boys walking about town, speeded up upon petrol fumes and looking like zombies, walking straight past people as though they did not exist, sometimes with their little girls in tow, initiated by older boys on petrol as well. (*Carpentaria*, 313)

Similarly she suggests that apposition (the grammatical construction where two elements are placed side by side, with one identifying the other) is used as a way of accumulating information with description dominating action. It thus becomes a technique that "serves to disrupt linearity by holding the moment still" (Loomes, 131-2). For her, this can be seen in the following passage:

> So the 'edge' people, all of the blackfella mob living with quiet breathing in higgily-piggerly, rubbish-dump trash shacks, all popped any old where in the prickly bushes, all along a cobweb of dirt tracks running crooked, left, right and centre outside of town [...]. (*Carpentaria*, 53)

2

THE WHITE WORLD

Susan Barrett

I | THE ARRIVAL OF THE WHITE MAN

"A history only as old as the cemetery down the road" (Carpentaria, 59)

While Aboriginal people have lived in Australia for tens of thousands of years, the first Europeans to land on the coast did so less than 400 years ago. In 1623, an expedition, sent in search of new sources of raw materials by the Dutch East India company towards what is today Papua New Guinea, landed on the Gulf coast to take on board fresh water. The leader of the expedition, Jan Carstenszoon, named the gulf "Carpentaria" in honour of Pieter de Carpentier, the Governor General of the Dutch East Indies at the time.

British colonisation started in 1788 when the First Fleet of convicts and their guards landed in what is today Sydney in New South Wales. Although the British were aware of the existence of the north of Australia – Cook had sailed around the east and north coasts of Australia in 1770 – the North was initially thought to be of little interest as a place for European settlement. In 1802 the English navigator and cartographer Matthew Flinders (1774-1814) was sent on an expedition to examine and chart the Torres Strait and the coasts of the Gulf of Carpentaria. Flinders arrived in the Gulf on 3, November 1802 and spent two and a half months mapping the area.[1] The town of Desperance takes its name from Matthew Flinders' fictitious middle name: "Desperance named after the founder, Captain Matthew Desperance" (59).

1. https://www.burke.qld.gov.au/our-region/history/a-brief-history-of-the-gulf-of-carpentaria

Almost a further thirty years passed until Captain John Lort Stokes explored the area in more detail in 1841. He landed at the mouth of a river which he called the Albert River, after Queen Victoria's husband, and travelled fifty miles up the river in search of fresh water. It was the end of the wet season and he was impressed by the endless grassy plains, which he named "The Plains of Promise", the title Alexis Wright used for her first novel.

By the mid-nineteenth century Europeans were starting to explore inland Australia by travelling overland rather than round the coast. Ludwig Leichardt was the first explorer to arrive in the Gulf country in 1848; he was followed by Augustus Gregory in 1855-56, then Burke and Wills in 1861, who died on their way back to Victoria. In the early 1860s, the first white pastoralists arrived who took over huge tracts of land to farm cattle.[1] By 1864 it had become apparent that a port was necessary, both to export the cattle and to import the goods the white inhabitants needed. As a result, the town of Burketown was officially established on the banks of the Albert River in 1865. Unlike the fictional Desperance, the river that flows through Burketown has never disappeared, but the town was devastated by a cyclone in March 1887 which flooded the town, killing 7 of the town's 138 white inhabitants.[2]

The area was of course already inhabited by several Aboriginal groups, including the Waanyi people to whom Alexis Wright belongs. Violence between the white settlers and the Aboriginal inhabitants was almost inevitable since the whites had stolen the Aboriginal land and resources. The worst recorded atrocity was the massacre of twenty-eight Aboriginal people by the police in Burketown in 1868, which was carried out in retaliation for the spearing of several horses outside the town.[3] There is a brief reference to the settlers' violence in *Carpentaria* with the character of Uncle Micky who uses a metal detector to collect spent bullet cartridges:

---

1. "Cattle station" is the term used in Australia to refer to large farms whose main activity is raising cattle. Because of the sparse vegetation in central Australia the stations can exceed 10,000km². The Aboriginal population were displaced from their land by the arrival of the pastoralists.
2. https://www.burke.qld.gov.au/our-region/history/a-brief-history-of-the-gulf-of-carpentaria
Mention is made of the important stock losses, and the destruction of Aboriginal humpies (shelters), but loss of Aboriginal lives was not recorded. This is typical of newspaper reports of the time.
3. https://c21ch.newcastle.edu.au/colonialmassacres/detail.php?r=751

> [...] all of those forty-fours, thirty thirtys, three-o-threes, twelve-gauges – all kinds of cartridges used in the massacre of the local tribes. He had maps, names of witnesses, details, the lot. A walking encyclopedia. Now his voice lives on in the great archive of cassettes which he left for the war trials he predicted would happen one day. But no tourists go to Micky's museum. (10)

Later on in the novel, Norm tells the story of the massacre of his father's parents and tribe, "an ode to his parents' memory" (99), and there is a reference to "the boulders with a peephole view where cartridges were as many as stones on the ground from the massacre of the local tribes-people" (99).

The 1860s saw the arrival not only of white people but also of camels. As early as 1835, white Australians began to advocate for the importation of camels, which they saw as a

> [...] robust, reliable and inexpensive form of transport for exploration and exploitation of the roadless arid interior, due to the combination of their biophysical characteristics and those of the continent's inland landscapes. (Gibbs, *et al.*, 9)

Camels were imported on a large scale from 1862 onwards. It was estimated that by the time of the last shipment in 1907, some 6,000 camels had been brought into Australia. Until the development of the combustion engine, they were used both by station owners to travel around their extensive properties, and to transport goods across central Australia. With the arrival of the motor car they were no longer needed so in the 1920s and 1930s the camels were released into the wild where they have proliferated. Killing the camels, "the screaming, uncooperative animals [who] didn't comprehend English, or barbarian either" (5) is the first entry in the records of the Municipal Council of Desperance. The laconic description of "Camels Removed" (6) conceals the true barbarity of what the townsfolk did; the camels were "hounded for several hours by their pursuers on foot and horseback, and stoned and whipped, the camels were eventually moved out over the claypans and shot" (6). This is just one of many examples in the novel where the words used by the white inhabitants to talk about their actions underplay the violence of what they have done.

The camels came with their handlers who were from both Afghanistan and Pakistan but became collectively known in Australia as "Afghans," regardless of their country of origin. The white Australians needed the handlers' skill with the animals but were openly racist towards them. The "Afghans" lived on the outskirts of towns and although most spoke English, they were never fully integrated. The description in *Carpentaria* of "Abdul and Abdullah" (4) as "shifty dogs, dodgy dogs, murdering dogs and unreliable [...] dark-skinned foreigners" (5) is characteristic of many rural white Australians' attitude towards the people they had brought into the country to work for them, ignoring the fact that they themselves were also foreigners in the Gulf country.

As Gibbs *et al.* point out, the ambivalence white Australians showed towards the Afghans was part of the wider anti-Asian prejudice which underpinned the White Australia Policy of the late 19th and early 20th centuries (13). The White Australia Policy is the term given to the government policies, starting with the Immigration Restriction Act in 1901, which aimed to stop people of non-European ethnic origin, in particular Asians and Pacific Islanders, from immigrating to Australia. The north of Australia was thought to be particularly threatened by the mass arrival of Chinese and other East Asian people, a fear which became known as "The Yellow Peril" (*Carpentaria*, 3).

The initial reaction of Uptown to the arrival of Elias Smith[1] is one of panic over the fear that his arrival is the start of "boatloads of illegal people" (71) and the inhabitants attribute to him all the fears normally associated with the "Yellow Peril": "What if the man is dangerous, contagious, riddled with all kinds of incurable diseases, a violent maverick, or a murderer or a foreigner trying to gain illegal entry?" (71). Anne Brewster suggests that for the reader he can be seen as "metonymic of successive generations of European occupation" and an ironic vision of myths of discovery and exploration (2010, 94). He is initially absorbed into white society but eventually his differences are "foregrounded in order to expel him from whiteness" (Brewster, 2010, 96). The Desperanians decide he is a "new Australian" (*Carpentaria*, 160), a term used in the 1960s for non-Anglo-Celtic (mainly Greek and Italian) immigrants who came to Australia after the Second World War, perhaps because of his "Slavic eyes" (61). Their racist tendencies surface once again – they call him "a low-down dog, a complete useless loafer" (160), accuse him of "burning up the Queen's picture" (159),

---

1. Elias's name may refer either to the prophet Elijah (from which the name Elias is derived) or to Saint Elias of Enna. Elijah performed many miracles and is said to have entered heaven alive in a chariot of fire. It is possible to see Elias's body being taken away by the gropers as an inverted version of this story. Saint Elias of Enna travelled over three continents after the Arabs invaded his home town in Sicily, which has a more obvious parallel with Elias's wanderings. Smith is the most common English surname and is the most common surname in Desperance.

which for them is an act of "treachery" (160), and he is forced to return to the sea from which he came. For Arnaud Barras, the way the Uptown inhabitants react towards Elias is symbolic of their inability to "self-criticise and to rethink the history of [their own] invasion" (2015, 59).

In many ways Elias is symbolic of the condition of white Australians – he turns up one day with no memory of where he came from and no identity, just like the inhabitants of Desperance: "Uptown whitefella mob was full of people claiming they had no origins. [...] They said they were not strangers because they had originated from nowhere" (55). For Brewster, the "bewilderment" (48), and "total confusion" (68) that Elias experiences when he lands on the unknown shore "represents the vulnerability of contemporary white belonging" in Australia (Brewster, 2010, 95).

It is not just white identity that is shown to be fragile in the novel but also white history. Almost all the white inhabitants share the surname Smith and the town's scribe, Sallyanne Smith, owns the "complete collection of the Smith family's sagas" (81). The narrator disparagingly calls this collection the "Book of Books" (81) but it is, to all intents and purposes, the history of the town. These precious documents are kept in a padlocked shed where, unbeknown to the inhabitants, the many volumes are "wasting away in dozens of cardboard boxes [...] chewed by defecating vermin" (81-2). They are eventually destroyed in a fire when the shed is set alight in an arson attack. Aboriginal knowledge is stored more securely; as the narrator wryly comments: "Pretty good job vermin couldn't shit on what the Pricklebush had locked up inside their heads" (82).

II | WHITE ISOLATION

One of the main differences between the white world and the Aboriginal world is the relationship to place. The Aboriginal population of Desperance have an intimate knowledge of the natural world in which they live, which is illustrated by the description of Norm whose "ancestors were the river people, who were living with the river from before time began" (6). The white population, on the other hand, have no affinity with either the land or its creatures. Proximity to the sea, for example, is slowly turning Nicoli Finn crazy:

> Poor Finn. Crocodiles, sharks, gropers, stingrays, box jelly-fish, stonefish, hundreds and hundreds of the invaders of childhood dreams swam around his

> mind. He heard his head pulsating with voices reminiscing over every single tragedy in Uptown fishing or beach picnic history. [...] Living next to the sea was like having tragedy for a neighbour. (65)

Lacking any true understanding of the natural world, the white inhabitants interact with the landscape in accordance with a form of knowledge which is false. This is epitomised by the location of the town, which is supposedly a port but which is no longer on the water's edge: "In one moment, during a Wet season early in the last century, the town lost its harbour waters when the river simply decided to change course, to bypass it by several kilometres. Just like that" (3). Unlike the Pricklebush mob, whose knowledge is stored in their memories, "no living soul remembered what the port had looked like" (7) before because no one had thought to take a photo of it. The implication of this is that white knowledge will eventually disappear.

The town's name "Desperance" is an invented word, but even for English speakers it is easy to see that etymologically it refers to a lack of hope.[1] The fact that the inhabitants chose this as the name of their new settlement is symptomatic of what little expectation they had about its future, and is an ironic comment on the prospects of colonisation. At one point, one of the State Governors tries to change the name to Masterton, a name more fitting with colonial expectations of white dominance, but the local inhabitants are "enraged" (58) and remove all the new signs, determined that "no one would mistake Desperance for the name of some past his use-by-date Southern politician who wanted to plant his ego in the minds of the future generations" (58).

The refusal to accept a new name has the effect of cutting the town and its inhabitants off completely from the rest of Australia since "with all the official road maps to Masterton regarded locally as some place different, strangers only had a snowflake's chance in hell of finding their way around" (58). Not that this isolation particularly bothers the Desperanians since "Uptown never liked to talk much to strangers" (58-9). This is probably just as well because it is a place of no interest to anyone else: "they were changing guards at Buckingham Palace but nobody in the world cared what happened to Desperance" (71).

---

1. It is interesting to reflect on the difference in French between 'espoir' – «le fait d'espérer, d'attendre quelque chose avec confiance» et 'espérance' – «le sentiment qui fait entrevoir comme probable la réalisation de ce que l'on désire; une des trois vertus théologales» (*Petit Robert*). In the light of these definitions, Desperance is a profoundly pessimistic word.

For Europeans it is easy to underestimate the size of Australia, and the remoteness of some places from the Federal Parliament in the capital city, Canberra. Australia is an island nation covering 7,692 million km² with only 25.36 million inhabitants,[1] 64% of whom live on the east coast corridor between Brisbane and Melbourne. In the 2016 census, the whole of the Gulf of Carpentaria had a population of just 1,958[2] spread over an area of 64,169.6 km².[3] Karumba, one of the major ports in the Gulf of Carpentaria, is over 2,600 km from Canberra, a distance that is estimated to be a 28 hour drive by the quickest route. Brisbane, the home of the State Governor, is not much closer – 2,100 km and a 23 hour drive.

It is not only the town that white people would like to rename, but also the river. The river renaming ceremony ridicules the way colonisers tried to take possession of the land by naming it. Instead of being named by the explorer who "discovered" it and whose exploits are lauded in history books, the person who wanted to rename the river in Desperance has been forgotten by the white historians and is simply "someone in town whose name is not worth a mention" (8). He wanted to name the river after a person, and wants to call it "Normal's River" (9) because "everybody knew that this was Normal's river" (8). What the local Shire Council do not realise is that for Norm Phantom it is not an honour to have a river named after him because "the river only had one name from the beginning of time. It was called *Wangala*" (italics in original, 9). As an Aboriginal person, Norm does not have the presumption of the white inhabitants that he can control the landscape simply by giving it a new name. At the renaming ceremony, the white inhabitants' failure to learn to speak Waanyi means that they are blissfully unaware that Norm's "short thankyou address [... is] a fruit salad full of abuse" (9).

The distrust that the inhabitants of Uptown have for the Southern politicians occurs regularly throughout the novel. The narrator comments, for example, that on the radio, all they ever got "were the Southern politicians who talked about themselves and what they were doing but had

1. In comparison the United States covers an area of 9,834 million km² but with a population of 328.2 million.
2. Ethnically 46.1% of the Gulf inhabitants identified as Australian and 2.9% as Australian Aboriginal in the 2016 census. (Figures for Australia as a whole were 23.3% and 0.5% respectively). https://quickstats.censusdata.abs.gov.au/census_services/getproduct/census/2016/quickstat/LGA32250
3. For comparison, this is only slightly smaller than the French region Auvergne-Rhone-Alpes, which has a population of around 8 million.

nothing to do with the little people of Desperance" (78), while the politicians who fly in for the day for a ceremony organised by the mining companies are deemed to be a "bunch of fly-by-nighters" and are greeted by "a diatribe of insults" (9). This lack of understanding and feelings of distrust between rural and urban Australia makes a mockery of the unified nation mentioned in the opening sentence of the novel.

III | TIME

> *"Time is represented by the resilience of ancient beliefs overlaying the inherited colonial experience" (Wright, Writing, Kindle)*

The Aboriginal and the European conceptions of time are very different. Europeans believe in linear time, that is to say the concept that time constantly moves forwards with one event happening after another. This belief in linear time, together with the idea that there is a causal link between events, is what makes it possible to write history. Aboriginal people see time somewhat differently. Deborah Bird Rose describes it as recognising two types of time "Dreaming time" and "Ordinary time" (1992, 203). Ordinary time, which is the time of one's own life, is a time that is "sequential and bounded" (203). Social events and ceremonies provide what Rose calls "temporal co-ordinates", but space also plays a role in:

> [...] mapping the passage of time. [...] People's lives are ordered by reference to where they have been – where they have lived and worked, where they have walked, and what country they have learned. (203)

Ordinary time belongs to the present in which we live, and is characterised by change; people grow old and die, and some events never recur. Within this ordinary time, there are rhythmic patterns, such as the seasons, which recur regularly. In Dreaming time, "synchrony" is the most important feature; "Dreamings all exist, all the time" (205) and events are organised spatially rather than temporally (207).

For Angel Day a clock seems to be a symbol of white power with almost magical qualities. When she finds the still-working mantelpiece clock that used to be in the mayor's office thrown away in the rubbish dump, she "could not believe her luck" (21). Owning it, and having knowledge of white time, seems to her to be a way of helping her children to survive in the white world: "to leave without [the clock] was a betrayal of the future she was already imagining in which the Phantom children would be going to school on time" (21). And yet the novel shows time and time again that the white inhabitants' clocks are unreliable and offer false reassurance. Truthful wears a watch purely as a status symbol: "Truthful kept checking his broken gold Rolex watch, guessing the time" (69).[1] The epigraph to Chapter 2 informs the reader in a paradoxical sentence that clocks have a finite life: "The clocks tick-a-ty-tock, looked as though they might run out of time" (12), and indeed, after a particularly violent thunderstorm, they do stop working altogether:

> Time stopped tick-tocking because there was too much moisture in the air and it had interfered with the mechanical workings of dozens of watches and clocks that ended up jiggered. (43)

Without the means to measure time, life for the white inhabitants starts to fall apart:

> They were suddenly struck with a single idea, a sense of hopeless prognostication that before too long there would be another ominous piece of bad luck because all bad luck happened in threes – the storm, the clocks, so something else was sure as hell going to happen to them. (44)

They are filled with anxiety, reduced to "primordial insecurity" (45), unable to make sense of the world that has turned red.

The Aboriginal characters have their own ways of measuring time, which rely not on abstract mechanical objects but on what is happening in the natural world: "Norm Phantom's time was a spectacular clock which rang the alarm once he had caught enough: exactly ten lines bearing a large snapper each" (248). Time appears to be of less importance to them than it is to the white characters; sitting on the edge of the lagoon, Will becomes aware that "time was a fleeting whisper" (157). The narrator draws attention to the impossibility of knowing where time begins, telling the reader that "Time accumulates thought or vice versa" (157). This same idea of time stretching infinitely in both directions is found in Mozzie Fishman's statement: "I have been alive

---

1. This may be a reference to the sort of jokes Deborah Bird Rose describes which are made by the Yarralin community in the Northern Territory who see the western concept of time as a source of humour: "Various people call out for a wrist watch; they query whether it has been wound or whether the batteries are fresh. More people call out for a torch so that the watch can be seen [...] people look at the same watch and call out different times, while others offer time at random, or make up times (28 o'clock). Joking goes back and forth until a time is agreed upon" (1992, 216).

for ever" (410), and in Will's comment that Joseph Midnight's "time stretched over the millennia" (371). Midnight himself denies that there is any such thing as a contemporary world: "What contemporary world? It's the same world as I live in, and before that, and before that. No such thing as a contemporary world" (364). The novel clearly shows that what is important for the Aboriginal characters is not so much the passage of time as its cyclical repetition: "The cloud band would soon evaporate, but would return again and again [...] the big fish would return, as was the natural cycle of things" (248).

The conception of time is important not just as a theme in *Carpentaria*, but also as a way of understanding the structure of the novel. The linear vision of time has influenced the shape of traditional Western novels which have a beginning, a middle and an end, a form that is problematic for an Aboriginal Writer. As Wright says, in "On Writing *Carpentaria*" "the idea of beginning/middle/end [is] a foreign concept" for Aboriginal people. In *Carpentaria* she wanted to "portray the world of Indigenous Australia as being in constant opposition between different spaces of time" by using a temporal framework which she calls "all times" in which past, present and future exist simultaneously (Writing, Kindle). The result is a narrative that loops constantly backward and forward making it impossible to draw up a precise time line of events, or even to know exactly how the characters' different stories fit together. As Diane Molloy points out, Norm is adrift at sea with Hope and Bala for forty days and forty nights, and yet this seems to coincide with what appears to be the several years (or even decades) that Will spent drifting on the rubbish island (3).

Lynda Ng calls the temporality in the novel "collapsed time" (2013, 121).[1] For Lucy Rowland this "collapsed time" can be seen particularly clearly when Norm returns Elias's body to the sea, following the Dreamtime tracks of the gropers to the groper hole:

> [...] a circular fish city full of underground caves where the huge fish liked to live. A place where they could have returned to from the land in ancient times like the palaeontologists say, or skies if they flew like the elders say in the Law of the Dreamtime. Millions of years ago, what was it like? Remember! Were skies blue then? (239)

---

1. Lucy Rowland suggests that this may be a misquotation from an interview with Kelly O'Brien or a confusion with the expression "collapsed history", which Wright used in her essay "A Family Document" (2001, 239) to describe Indigenous story-telling (Rowland, 552).

As Rowland points out, Norm's knowledge of the place "is informed by both evolutionary narratives of time, and the Dreamtime narratives that witness the animals taking a different temporal path to their current home in the sea" (544). The use of the expression "millions of years ago," meanwhile draws attention to Norm's own links to the distant past. The novel shows that ultimately, it is not being able to keep track of the passing of time that is important but knowledge of the land:

> History could be obliterated when the Gods move the country. He saw history rolled, reshaped, undone and mauled as the great creators of the natural world engineered the bounty of everything man had ever done in this part of the world into something more of their own making. (473)

As Jeanine Leane says:

> The irony that runs through the story is that while the settlers are intent on recording their history – the 'things that are safe to tell' – they fail to realise that they are already incorporated into a bigger past that is Aboriginal land and memory and that, in this scheme of things, they are the shallowest layer. (2015, 159)

3

CONTEMPORARY ISSUES

I | « ALWAYS WAS, ALWAYS WILL BE » : DROITS À LA TERRE, TITRES FONCIERS AUTOCHTONES ET SOUVERAINETÉ EN AUSTRALIE, JESSICA DE LARGY HEALY

« Always Was, Always Will Be » est un slogan indissociable du mouvement autochtone des droits à la terre. Scandé depuis cinquante ans dans les manifestations, inscrit sur les pancartes et les bannières, déployé sur les drapeaux et les t-shirts aux couleurs aborigènes et intégré à de nombreuses œuvres d'art, celui-ci a été choisi en 2020 comme thème fédérateur de la *NAIDOC week*, une semaine de festivités organisée annuellement en Australie pour célébrer l'histoire, la culture et la résilience des Aborigènes et des Insulaires du détroit de Torres. Dans le contexte post-colonial australien, la formule originale « Always Was, Always Will Be Aboriginal Land » articule de manière implacable la longue durée de l'histoire continentale aborigène à l'affirmation continue de souveraineté par les quelques 250 nations autochtones du pays.

a. Always was...

Le roman *Carpentaria* s'ouvre sur la geste créatrice du serpent ancestral. Descendu des étoiles, il façonne l'environnement aquatique du golfe de son corps, de ses mouvements et de toute la vitalité de son être. De temps immémorial, il est toujours là, actif dans les variations des marées, le flot des rivières et les phénomènes atmosphériques. Comme d'autres êtres ancestraux, propres à d'autres régions d'Australie, il anime les écosystèmes et leurs multiples formes de vie, provoquant parfois de son courroux le déchaînement des éléments. Les savoirs associés à ses humeurs et à ses actions écologiques sont transmis de génération en génération, ils forment un corpus de la Loi (3) qui dicte les comportements sociaux, régit les activités économiques et infuse l'ensemble des pratiques spirituelles des groupes gardiens de ces lieux. Les êtres ancestraux comme le Serpent font partie d'eux : «They say its being is porous; it permeates everything. It is all around in the atmosphere and is attached to the lives of the river people like skin» (2). «Nous avons toujours été là» disent les Aborigènes partout en Australie, soulignant la relation de consubstantialité qui existe entre la terre, les ancêtres et eux.

Dans le nord tropical de l'Australie, du nord des Kimberley au sud-est de la Péninsule du Cape York, les lieux marqués par ces puissances sont toujours visités, pour la chasse, la pêche, la collecte de fruits de mer ou de matériaux utiles pour la confection de ficelles ou d'autres objets. Tout comme le faisaient leurs aïeux avant eux, les propriétaires de ces sites, les individus qui ont hérité de la charge d'en prendre soin, effectuent des rituels pour annoncer leur présence et introduire les nouveaux-venus. Plusieurs régimes fonciers coexistent en Australie aborigène, variant largement d'un groupe à l'autre, certains droits et relations d'appartenance passant par la lignée du père, d'autres par celle de la mère et d'autres encore par des esprits de conception qui impulsent la vie à la naissance. Partout sur le territoire, des campements éphémères sont établis autour d'une constellation de foyers anciens dont les couches successives de cendres témoignent du passage des générations. Les sites les plus importants sont chantés, dansés et peints, afin d'en actualiser le pouvoir et d'assurer le renouvellement des ressources naturelles. À la façon du convoi itinérant de voitures cabossées de Mozzie Fishman, cette responsabilité cérémonielle, le long des pistes chantées, peut s'assumer aujourd'hui par de nouveaux moyens.

Empruntant aux échelles temporelles géologiques enregistrées dans de nombreux mythes de création aborigène, la notion de temps profond (*deep time*) évoque les ordres de grandeurs vertigineux qui caractérisent l'ancienneté de la présence humaine sur le continent australien (Griffiths, 2018; McGrath & Jebb, 2015). L'archéologie reconnaît de plus en plus que les récits aborigènes portant sur la submersion des côtes depuis la dernière glaciation, sur le mouvement des astres ou sur l'éruption de volcans depuis longtemps éteints peuvent faire référence aux événements multimillénaires qu'elle documente avec ses propres outils. Estimée aujourd'hui à 65 000 ans par les méthodes de datation scientifique, cette profondeur historique donne la mesure du déni sur lequel s'est construite la nation australienne depuis le début de la colonisation en 1788 (McNiven & Russel, 2005). Mis en scène dès les premiers chapitres, notamment à travers la célébration ratée du centenaire de la ville pionnière de Desperance (8) dont les habitants prétendent que les frontières existaient depuis «the beginning of their time» (57), l'effet d'incommensurabilité entre ces dates se fait ressentir tout au long du livre, entre les nouveaux venus ignorants et irrespectueux du territoire, constamment soumis aux aléas climatiques et environnementaux, et les familles aborigènes qui proviennent de la terre même, qui savent reconnaître les puissances qui l'habitent, et ont appris à les comprendre et à veiller sur eux.

Loin de la fiction juridique d'une *terra nullius*, d'une île vierge et inexploitée, qui servit de prétexte à la colonisation britannique, de nombreuses études ont montré que le paysage australien était constitué d'un patchwork de domaines écologiques savamment entretenus par leurs propriétaires aborigènes, notamment grâce à l'usage de petits feux de basse intensité (Pascoe, 2014; Gammage, 2011). Adaptés à la couverture végétale, aux types de sols et aux conditions météorologiques, les feux allumés périodiquement fertilisaient les sols pauvres pour la culture d'ignames, provoquaient dans le désert la germination de graminées, et favorisaient dans le sud-est la repousse des herbacées dans d'immenses prairies où venaient paître kangourous et autres gibiers. Pour tous ces groupes, écologie, économie et religion sont intimement liées. Le clan gumatj de la Terre d'Arnhem, une région située à l'ouest du golfe de Carpentarie, chante la trajectoire du Feu ancestral, la dispersion des flammes à travers le paysage connectant plusieurs sites importants sur son propre territoire et, au-delà, sur les terres d'autres clans partageant l'ancêtre Feu. Ces itinéraires chantés durant les cérémonies révèlent toute la complexité des écosystèmes traversés par le Feu, les animaux, végétaux et autres êtres avec lesquels il interagit. De la même façon dans *Carpentaria*, le feu qui dévaste la mine Gurfurritt, à l'image du conflit acrimonieux divisant la communauté de Desperance, semble doté d'une volonté propre, «like a monster cut loose from another world», «snarl[ing] in an ugly voice... *Alright, watch while I spread right through those hangars like they were nothing, hungry! hungry! Get out of my way*» (393). Sous l'effet désastreux du changement climatique en Australie, dont les mégafeux qui ravagent régulièrement le pays, ces savoirs et pratiques écologiques autochtones ont fait l'objet d'une véritable reconnaissance institutionnelle et scientifique, ainsi que d'initiatives de réactualisations dans plusieurs États (Langton, 1998 ; Steffensen, 2020).

Depuis la sédentarisation imposée dans des missions et autres communautés permanentes de résidence, la maîtrise de ces chants qui retracent les cheminements ancestraux et des cartographies relationnelles complexes permet parfois de connaître un territoire sans jamais s'y être rendu : les chants peuvent traverser des centaines de kilomètres et passer d'un groupe à l'autre, même si leurs langues sont différentes. Ces chants consistent pour beaucoup en des énumérations de noms de lieux, liés à un ancêtre particulier. Ainsi le vieux Joseph Midnight put enseigner à un Will Phantom en fuite un chant décrivant l'itinéraire à suivre pour arriver en lieu sûr, un refuge situé à plus de 1 000 kilomètres de distance :

> The old man gave him the directions to the safe place in his far-off country – a blow-by-blow description sung in song, unravelling a map to a Dreaming place had never seen. [...] [O]ld man Midnight remembered a ceremony he had never performed in his life before, and now, to his utter astonishment, he passed it on to Will. He went on and on, fully believing he was singing in the right sequence hundreds of places in a journey to a place at least a thousand kilometres away. (360)

Ce passage renforce l'idée que, hier comme aujourd'hui, la survie dépend d'une connaissance fine du territoire. La rétention des savoirs dans la matière même du paysage assoit leur pérennité : ils peuvent ainsi être temporairement oubliés, puis remémorés, augmentés et réinvestis. Ce mouvement d'extériorisation de savoirs enfouis est à la source de nombreuses épistémologies autochtones et participe d'un processus créatif largement documenté en Australie aborigène.

b. Always will be...

Le chemin vers la reconnaissance des titres fonciers autochtones a été long et tortueux et continue de générer tensions et souffrances dans de nombreuses communautés autochtones. Lors de la prise de possession du continent australien par la Couronne d'Angleterre en 1788, contrairement à ce qui s'était passé dans d'autres colonies de peuplement britanniques, comme en Nouvelle-Zélande-Aotearoa ou au Canada, aucun traité ne fut signé avec les Aborigènes[1] : la Constitution de 1901,

1. Seul a été signé, localement, le traité de Batman à Port Phillip Bay en 1935. Ce traité a ensuite été répudié par Governor Bourke. Pour plus de détails concernant les traités et autres accords, voir https://www.atns.net.au/.

qui marque la fédération de l'Australie et la naissance de la nation moderne, ne les mentionne tout simplement pas. Cet aveuglement durable, fondé sur des doctrines racistes et impérialistes, ouvrit la voie à l'invasion, à la dépossession, aux massacres, à l'institutionnalisation et à l'exploitation des Aborigènes (Attwood, 1996; Reynolds, 1999). Le titre *Treaty* (1991) du groupe de rock aborigène Yothu Yindi, interprété en anglais et dans le dialecte de son chanteur légendaire Mandawuy Yunupingu, figure parmi les expressions autochtones contestataires les plus éloquentes qui s'élevèrent contre les célébrations officielles du bicentenaire de la colonisation en Australie.

> This land was never given up
> This land was never bought and sold
> The planting of the union jack
> Never changed our law at all
> Now two rivers run their course
> Separated for so long
> I'm dreaming of a brighter day
> When the waters will be one.
> Treaty yeah, treaty now, treaty yeah, treaty now!

Rappelant que les terres aborigènes ne furent jamais cédées, dénonçant les fausses promesses des politiciens, cette chanson devenue un véritable hymne porte depuis sa sortie la campagne politique pour la signature d'un traité entre le gouvernement et les nations autochtones du continent (De Largy Healy, 2020).

Malgré la chape coloniale écrasante, de nombreuses stratégies de résistance furent mises en œuvre partout sur le continent, et des voix aborigènes n'ont eu de cesse de clamer leur souveraineté sur les terres conquises. En 1963, les dirigeants de la douzaine de clans yolngu résidant dans la mission de Yirrkala, à l'ouest du golfe de Carpentarie, dans ce qui était alors la Réserve aborigène de la Terre d'Arnhem, envoyèrent une pétition au gouvernement fédéral à Canberra. Dans le texte apposé sur deux panneaux d'écorce, encadré par une frise de motifs peints à l'ocre, les signataires protestaient contre l'ouverture d'une mine de bauxite sur leur territoire ancestral de chasse et de pêche situé sur la péninsule de Gove. Galarrwuy Yunupingu, le fils de l'un des signataires, expliqua au sujet de ces motifs :

> [ils] représentaient le titre foncier à notre terre sous notre loi [...]. Nous peignons, comme nous l'avons toujours fait, pour démontrer notre lien continu avec notre terre et les droits et les responsabilités que nous avons envers elle. Nous peignons pour montrer au reste du monde que la terre nous appartient et

que nous appartenons à la terre. Notre peinture est un acte politique. (Yunupingu, 65-66)

Aujourd'hui, cette œuvre toujours exposée au Parlement fédéral, est considérée comme une icône de l'art politique aborigène. À travers l'usage ingénieux de leurs motifs ancestraux en tant que titres fonciers, les Yolngu permirent la remise en question de l'idée dominante selon laquelle les Aborigènes n'avaient pas de conception de la propriété foncière.

La Pétition sur écorce fut enregistrée en tant que «document traditionnel», ouvrant la voie à une progressive reconnaissance des systèmes fonciers aborigènes dans la loi du Commonwealth. En dépit des nombreux soutiens exprimés en leur faveur, les Yolngu de Yirrkala n'obtinrent cependant pas gain de cause face au consortium minier et le recours judiciaire qu'ils déposèrent à la Cour suprême du Territoire du Nord, lors d'un procès historique connu sous le nom de *Gove Land Rights Case* (1971), se solda par une défaite. Malgré ce traumatisme, et la destruction d'une vaste zone par la mine, l'activisme des Yolngu joua un rôle décisif dans la lutte pour les droits fonciers autochtones. Cette action protestataire, ainsi que d'autres comme la grève en 1966 des Gurindji, employés comme main d'œuvre sur la station de bétail de Wave Hill (Kalkaringi), pour exiger un salaire équitable et la restitution de leurs terres ancestrales, amorcèrent un processus qui aboutit à la ratification du *Aboriginal Land Rights (Northern Territory) Act* en 1976.

Cette loi déterminante ouvrit aux Aborigènes du Territoire du Nord la possibilité de revendiquer les terres sur lesquelles ils pouvaient prouver une association traditionnelle. Aujourd'hui, environ la moitié de la superficie du Territoire du Nord et 80 % du littoral appartiennent à des groupes aborigènes reconnus comme «propriétaires traditionnels». Malgré l'engagement de nombreux activistes et intellectuels autochtones dans les grandes capitales australiennes dès les années 1970, avec notamment l'érection d'une tente-ambassade aborigène en face du Parlement à Canberra pour dénoncer leur statut d'étrangers sur leur propre terre, il fallut encore attendre une vingtaine d'années avant qu'une législation fédérale ne permette la reconnaissance de droits fonciers dans les autres États.

En effet, ce n'est qu'en 1992, lorsque Eddie Koiki Mabo, un Insulaire de l'île de Mer, dans le détroit de Torres, remporta son action en justice contre l'État du Queensland devant la Haute Cour australienne, que la doctrine coloniale de la *terra nullius* fut définitivement renversée. Au terme de dix ans de procédure, le jugement historique *Mabo and Others v Queensland (N°2)* reconnaissait pour la première fois des droits fonciers traditionnels aux autochtones (Merle, 1998)[1]. L'année suivante, le *Native Title Act* (1993) était adopté, permettant, sous certaines conditions, d'étendre les revendications foncières aborigènes à l'ensemble du continent. Pour faire valoir leurs droits, les groupes concernés doivent soumettre leur demande au *National Native Title Tribunal*, un organe fédéral institué pour administrer le processus de revendication et d'octroi des titres fonciers autochtones. Cette démarche peut s'avérer particulièrement longue, compliquée et douloureuse pour les groupes provenant des régions les plus urbanisées, dont l'histoire coloniale est davantage marquée par les massacres et les déplacements forcés. En effet, c'est aux Aborigènes qu'appartient l'exercice de la preuve : ils doivent pouvoir démontrer leurs liens à la terre, la transmission d'un système culturel spécifique depuis la période pré-coloniale ainsi qu'une occupation continue de ces territoires. Dans un jugement rendu aux Yorta Yorta en 1998, la Cour de l'État du Victoria a ainsi pu recourir à la métaphore sans appel de « la marée de l'histoire emportant dans son reflux toute reconnaissance de leurs lois traditionnelles et tout réel respect de leurs coutumes traditionnelles », entérinant par ce verdict l'idée d'une culture figée dans le temps d'avant le contact, justifiant en fin de compte la poursuite de la dépossession des Aborigènes de leur terre. Si une forme de titre foncier autochtone est désormais reconnue sur un tiers du pays, des centaines de demandes sont toujours en attente de jugement.

Lorsque des groupes aborigènes sont légalement reconnus comme « propriétaires traditionnels », ils doivent être consultés pour tous les projets de développement envisagés sur leurs territoires, de l'exploration minière à la construction d'infrastructures collectives comme les routes ou les antennes relais. Les organismes chargés de les représenter, conseils fonciers ou *Native Title Representative Bodies*, sont responsables de la négociation des termes des accords et contrats passés, versements de royalties, provision d'emplois et de formations pour les membres de la communauté, fonds d'aide à la scolarité, etc. Dans les régions comme le golfe de Carpentarie riches en dépôts miniers, l'enjeu économique est considérable, surtout au regard des conditions de précarité dans lesquelles de nombreuses communautés

1. https://www.foundingdocs.gov.au/item-did-33.html

isolées subsistent. La pression générée par les mines divise souvent les communautés en factions rivales, faisant surgir des intérêts conflictuels, pour ou contre l'exploitation de leur terre. Ce contexte social tendu est mis en scène dans *Carpentaria* à travers les familles de Pricklebush, dirigée par Norm Phantom, présenté comme le «propriétaire traditionnel légitime» (50), et celle de Eastside, sous la houlette de Joseph Midnight, l'usurpateur, qui s'est inventé une tribu locale (50-1) pour s'imposer dans les négociations et en retirer tous les bénéfices. Malgré une avancée certaine pour les droits fonciers autochtones, la situation imposée par le *Native Title Act* qui oblige les groupes à se définir dans des termes qui répondent aux critères fixés par la législation australienne, reste critiquée par de nombreux acteurs politiques et militants aborigènes. Nombreux sont ceux qui plaident pour la reconnaissance de la souveraineté des nations aborigènes et insulaires du détroit de Torres.

En 2017, une importante convention pan-aborigène s'est tenue à Uluru, un site iconique du désert central australien situé sur les terres ancestrales des Anangu, afin de convenir des termes d'une proposition de referendum portant sur la reconnaissance des autochtones dans la Constitution australienne. À l'issue de la rencontre, la Déclaration du Cœur, *Statement from the Heart*, fut rendue publique, réunissant les signatures de représentants de quelques deux cents nations autochtones. Les préconisations de la Déclaration du Cœur furent officiellement présentées au Premier ministre Malcolm Turnbull sous la forme d'une peinture réalisée par un collectif de femmes anangu figurant un enchevêtrement de mythes liés au site sacré d'Uluru. Au-delà d'une reconnaissance symbolique dans le préambule de la Constitution, de laquelle les Aborigènes sont historiquement absents, la Déclaration du Cœur appelait à la double institution d'une «Voix» consacrée des Premières Nations dans le document fondateur de la démocratie australienne et d'une commission *makarrata* chargée de la négociation de traités entre le gouvernement et les différents peuples aborigènes et insulaires du détroit de Torres[1]. Au terme de cette vaste consultation nationale qu'il avait pourtant lui-même commanditée, le gouvernement australien rejeta catégoriquement cette revendication pour une «voix» permanente des autochtones au parlement fédéral. La nomination en 2019 d'un homme aborigène, Ken Wyatt, au poste de ministre fédéral des Affaires autochtones, a relancé le processus de négociation autour des questions de traités et de souveraineté dans le pays.

1. https://ulurustatement.org

II | MINING, SUSAN BARRETT

> *"Mining had changed the way people had to think about looking after themselves. If a man had to survive, he had to first think of what the mine was capable of doing to him" (Carpentaria, 370).*

The history of mining in Australia is as old as the Aboriginal people themselves who have been mining the land for pigments and stones since long before the British invasion.[1] The British began commercial mining for coal at Newcastle (almost 150 km north of Sydney) just ten years after the First Fleet arrived in New South Wales in 1788. Gold was discovered at Bathurst (200 km west of Sydney) in 1851, and shortly afterwards in the state of Victoria, leading to the first of a series of gold rushes which continued almost until the end of the century. Mining then tailed off in the first half of the twentieth century until the discovery in the 1950s of metals such as bauxite nickel, tungsten, zinc and uranium, as well as oil and natural gas. Mining currently accounts for around 10% of the Australian economy.

In 1923, lead, zinc and silver were found on the traditional lands of the Kalkadoon people around what is now known as Mount Isa in the Lower Gulf of Carpentaria. In 1924, the mining company Mount Isa Mines was formed, and commercial mining began. Mount Isa Mines has gone onto become one of the most productive single mines in the world (Neelawala *et al.*, 62).

Mining has been hugely damaging both to the Aboriginal people who lived around Mount Isa and to the land. Between 1933 and 1967, there were 28 documented removals of Aboriginal people from their traditional lands around Mount Isa.[2] Levels of environmental contaminants are high, causing often significant health problems for the local population. Lead poisoning is the major concern with lead pollution affecting soil, water sources, and also being dispersed into the atmosphere in gaseous

---

1. Rocks traditionally mined by Aboriginal people for tools include: amphibolite, andesite, basalt, blue metal, chalcedony, chert, diabase, granite, greenstone, greywacke, ironstone, limestone, mudstone, obsidian, porphyry, quartz, quartzite, sandstone, silcrete, silicified stone, siltstone and trachyte. "Mining by Aborigines – Australia's first miners." https://www.mininghistory.asn.au/mining-history/

2. For further details of population displacement see https://www.qld.gov.au/firstnations/cultural-awareness-heritage-arts/community-histories/community-histories-m/community-histories-mount-isa#:~:text=In%20the%20late%201940s%2C%20a,entire%20North%20West%20Queensland%20area

form (Neelawala *et al.*, 63-4). Zinc is another dangerous pollutant as it is toxic to aquatic life.

As David Trigger notes, white discourse around mine development is very similar to that used in an earlier period of Australian colonisation about agricultural development; both promote the idea that landscape is there for human use, but needs to be "reclaimed" by the settlers because only western use of the land is seen as valuable (1997a, 171). The mining companies were able to do this relatively easily in the late twentieth century because the media were continuing to promote the idea that there was no human presence in the areas the companies wanted to exploit. A journalist in 1972 thus described the countryside around Mount Isa as "endless scrub," thereby creating the idea of a "pristine" landscape (Trigger, 1997a, 168), and turning the area into what Philip Mead calls "a geophysical *terra nullius*" (193). In language reminiscent of nineteenth century adventure novels, where the colonial hero triumphs thanks to his greater scientific knowledge, corporate narratives around mining became stories about "success through 'vision', skills and technical achievement" (Trigger, 1997a, 165). Opening a mine was seen by both the mining companies and politicians as "a very appropriate use of the landscape in moral terms" (Trigger, 1997a, 163) because not only would the profits from mining be good for the Australian economy, but the mines themselves would provide jobs, housing, schools, sporting facilities and better roads for the local inhabitants.

Mines have not just displaced Aboriginal people, destroyed sacred sites and caused environmental damage to the land, they have also created division within the Aboriginal population with some people seeking "actively to lock into place a regime of potential benefits from mining [while] others have opposed it as inconsistent with cultural dimensions of Aboriginal relations to the land" (Trigger and Robinson, 2001, 101). In a study of the implantation of mines on Aboriginal land in Queensland and West Australia, David Trigger and Michael Robinson found that solving the differences in opinion within the Aboriginal communities required more negotiating energy than coming to an agreement with the government and the mining industry (2001, 109).

The Gurfurrit Mine in *Carpentaria* is based on the Century Zinc Mine located at Lawn Hill, 250 km northwest of Mount Isa. It is one of the largest open-pit zinc mines in the world. At the mine site itself there is a 400-man accommodation camp, offices, and an airport; a

304km underground slurry pipeline connects the mine to the port of Karumba.[1] Zinc mining began there in 1999 and, after several changes of ownership, is still in operation today. The discussions between the local Aboriginal inhabitants and CRA (Conzinc Riotinto of Australia), the mining company who originally owned the mine, were protracted, encompassing significant divisions within and between several Indigenous groups including Waanyi people who claim traditional connections with the mine site. Tensions and disagreements included conditions of the deal that was being offered and contesting views about physical and spiritual impacts on traditional country (Trigger, 1997b).

Wright has deplored the attitude of CRA:

> These [Aboriginal] communities were given little choice but to argue with each other, and forced to choose how to hold onto fragile cultural interests, from a sale that was a pittance in the scheme of things, just so that the vast interests of the company could proceed. (Writing, Kindle)

She has spoken highly of the actions of Murrandoo Yanner, a Gangalidda man from Moungibi (Burketown), who was the CEO of the Carpentaria Land Council Aboriginal Corporation at the time.[2] Yanner was particularly opposed on environmental grounds to the building of a pipeline that would take the ore to the coast. He was the inspiration for the character of Will Phantom.

For Maggie Nolan "the impacts of mining are central to any understanding of *Carpentaria* [… with] the profound and pervasive effects of mining permeat[ing] every aspect of the narrative" (n.p.). The mine is mentioned in the first chapter, and it is made very clear that its presence has not been beneficial for the town of Desperance:

> […] when the first multinational mining company came into the region. Numerous short-lived profiteering schemes were concocted for the locals, in order to serve the big company's own interests as they set about pillaging the region's treasure trove. (8)

The mine damages the land, but also exacerbates the tensions that already existed between the inhabitants of Desperance and the

1. Information taken from the New Century Resources Website. The webpage devoted to Century Mine includes a short video showing the mine and its facilities as well as an aerial view of the landscape: https://www.newcenturyresources.com/century-mine-project/
2. There are numerous videos of Yanner giving speeches available on line.

politicians "down South," the inhabitants of Uptown and the Pricklebush mob, and the Eastsiders and the Westsiders:

> Some people were talking about the jobs they would be getting. *You very, very wrong*. They were arguing against the pro-land-rights brigade. [...] Others were saying they wanted the mining company to give the country back. Others were opposed to having any mines on their sacred country. (376)

For Joseph Midnight, the mine is a way to make money by exploiting the laws on Native Title. His father, Old Cyclone, claimed that his people were the "real traditional landowners where Desperance had been built" (50), accusing Norm Phantom's group of being "*Johnny-come-latelies*" (51). Midnight's people appear to have made up a name for themselves – Wangabiya. As the narrator disparagingly says, what has brought them to Desperance seems to be more about money than about their relationship with the land:

> Lost Wangabiya started turning up in the Gulf from all over the place: Brisbane, Sydney and even one came from Los Angeles [...] It was the hint of big bickies to be had from big mining that did that. (51)

Joseph Midnight is accused of having an "extortion racket with the government" (51). Instead of using the money the government gives him to shoot the feral pigs, he allows them to breed and become even more of a nuisance. He is also responsible for the millions of cane toads in the region because his people brought the toads to Desperance in order to then be able to claim government money for catching them. The Wangabiya are, the narrator says, "unscrupulous – nasty kind of people – even without talking about the land they tried to steal (52). It is unclear, however, to what extent this might be Norm's point of view, rather than that of a neutral narrator for as David Trigger has pointed out, there were "genuine substantial differences of opinion among Aboriginal people" (1997b, 126) during the negotiations about the opening of the zinc mine at Mount Isa, which meant that:

> [...] various assertions and counter-assertions become the substance of politicking over who holds relevant knowledge, who has rights of ownership and/or use of particular lands and whose biographies are consistent with the rights to country that they are now claiming. (1997b, 122)

There were notably debates about whether right to country should be traced through the mother, father or grand-parents, with standing in the local community and age also playing a role (Trigger, 1997b, 122).

Indigenous people have been employed in mines since at least the early 1900s, and in 2007 accounted for around 3% of the total mining industry workforce in Queensland[1] (Brereton and Parmenter, 71). Although mines have undoubtedly provided a source of employment for the local Indigenous population, mining companies have been criticised for the fact that most Aboriginal people are employed in entry level jobs with few prospects for promotion or skills development. Not only are these jobs poorly paid, but there is also the risk of them disappearing completely as mining becomes increasingly mechanised (Brereton and Parmenter, 77). Even though they are Westsiders, not Eastsiders, Norm's two eldest sons Inso and Donny, like the Wangabiya, are attracted by the idea of easy money from the mine: "Everybody in the town said these two boys did nothing for anybody except for money. They worked in the mine from day one" (104).

Norm makes no attempt to profit from the mine, but nor does he attempt to oppose it, and gets angry with Will for doing so: "'It was not dangerous,' Norm thundered, pushing Will out of the yard. 'It was plain stupid because nobody can change the government'" (276). For Norm the mine is just one more thing that the white invaders have done to the land, and opposition is pointless because the government is too powerful.

Will, on the other hand, is suspicious of the motives of the mining companies right from the beginning:

> Will did not underestimate those innocent friendly meetings where the mining representatives claimed not to know what was required from Native Title claims. He believed the company knew government legislation and procedures related to Indigenous rights like the back of its hand. (376)

By the time he finds Elias's body, he has become convinced that there is something different about the way the mine wants to take their land compared to what has happened in the past:

> Life had no meaning in this new war on their country. This was a war that could not be fought on Nom Phantom's and old Joseph Midnight's terms [...] This war with the mine had no rules. Nothing was sacred. It was a war for money. (363)

The impact of the mine is so great that it is even able to interfere with the traditional Dreaming tracks. When Will finds himself on an island

1. The Aboriginal and Torres Strait Islander population in Queensland was approximately 3.3% the same year.

with a mine-worker, he realises that there is something wrong with the songlines that Midinight gave him, and which were supposed to take him to a place where he would be safe:

> So much for old man Joseph Midnight thinking the island was a safe place. Yet Will realised there was no point blaming the old man whose vision of the place was ancient. He knew his country in its stories, its histories, its sacred places [...]. His time stretched over the millennia. How would Midnight know the speed in which everything had changed at the hands of the mining company? (371)

As Nolan points out, the way mining has changed the songlines is a good example of the way mining has repercussions on all aspects of life in Desperance. Bruiser made his money thanks to a tip-off about another mine. The absence of the Aboriginal men leaves the women open to sexual abuse: "with Inso and Donny working down at the mine, Truthful felt free to come around whenever he wanted" (217). Both Mozzie Fishman and Father Danny are quite clear in their own ways about the damage the mine has caused to the community. Father Danny sums things up by saying: "This used to be a safe place before you lot started arguing and mucking around with that bloody mine" (182). Fishman provides a more thoughtful analysis:

> We never killed Truthful, and he never killed himself either, just like the boys never killed themselves. They were all killed by other hands, just like Gordie, and Elias. The mine made killers, Will, and now I've made the mine go away. May the great spirit show us some mercy one day, that is all I say. (414)

For Nolan it is the character of Kevin, however, that provides the most telling illustration of the damage Gurfurrit has caused:

> Kevin ultimately disappears from the novel, and his absence haunts its otherwise potentially hopeful resolution [...] Trapped in a body and mind not his own, Kevin exists as the novel's clearest metaphor for the destructive impacts of mining. (n.p.)

Philip Mead suggests that the destruction of the mine can be read in parallel with the story of how the bodies of the boys who committed suicide in the police cells are laid to rest in the underground sea. The two stories follow each other, and both are about the use that people make of what can be found underneath the earth's surface. Whereas the white people are interested in what is underground only for financial gain, regardless of the environmental damage and the cost to human lives, the Aboriginal people see it as a sacred place, intimately linked to the cycle of human life and death. The way in which these two stories are written reflects this difference.

The sabotaging of the mine is fast-paced. The reader discovers the danger at the same time as Will: "Mine worker! Will recognised the blue uniform. Shit! Where were the others?" (370), and shares Will's attempts to make sense of what is happening: "He tried to remember backwards. What had happened from the moment he started edging himself away from the miner's camp to now?" (373). The sudden use of the present tense plunges the reader into the heart of the action: "He feels the blow striking the back of his head" (374), while passages of direct speech add to the sense of urgency: "Will! What the fuck are you doing. Keep running" (390).

The burial of the boys, on the other hand, is slow paced and deliberate, since Fishman knows exactly where he is going and what he intends to do: "Unquestioningly, instinctively, he was following a map etched on his mind from the times of the many fathers' fathers before him" (417). The angry red of the flames has been replaced by the comforting "new, red tartan blankets" in which the boys' bodies have been wrapped. Their "going was slow" and in contrast to the noise and the chaos following the explosion of the mine "the air was so still, you could swear you heard the daydreams of lazy lizards" (418). The whole passage is characterised by long sentences, with an accumulation of clauses. The following is a particularly good example of the solemnity with which this particular story is told:

> So, it was with astonishment and awe, these men gaped at what they had been shown, and allowed themselves to be taken into the powerful spirituality, which was somehow the same, but much older than the ornate cathedrals made with stone, or the monasteries and places of worship to relics of bones and other bits and pieces of sanctified saints of old Europe and the Holy Land. (420)

These two stories about the use that is made of the elements of the natural world which can be found beneath the surface of the earth are representative of the starkly different attitudes found in traditional Aboriginal beliefs and capitalist philosophy. While Will, Mozzie and his followers see the underground sea as a part of a whole that is intimately linked to birth and death in an on-going cycle, the owners of the mine are interested only in exploiting the land for short-term financial gain, regardless of the consequences to either humans or to the environment, something which will be explored further in the chapter on pollution (Part one, III, 4). This fundamental difference is clearly summed up in Rachel Perkins' film *One Night the Moon* (2001) in the song "This Land is Mine" performed by Paul Kelly and Kelton Pell. The farmer sings: "This land is mine, all the way to the old fence line," and the Aboriginal tracker replies: "This land is me / Rock water, animal trees / They are my song / My beings here, where I belong / This land owns me / From generations past to infinity."[1]

III | COUNTRY, SEA COUNTRY, ET LE MONDE ANIMAL ET VÉGÉTAL, LAURA SINGEOT

a. « The Land has agency » : statut légal et vision autochtone de la nature et de la terre

Dans « On Writing *Carpentaria* », Alexis Wright partage sa vision du golfe de Carpentarie, telle qu'elle l'a intégrée au cœur du roman :

> I wanted to write a book that tried to examine a place of enormous energy in Australia, to understand why its energy was so concentrated in a landscape of flattened claypans. [...] Why did this country feel more vibrant to me than anywhere else in this country? Was it the claypans, seascapes, twisting ancient rivers of fresh running waters that flowed north to the sea, or the yellow tidal waters that flowed back inland? Or perhaps, in some special way, I related to the vegetation that was either spinifex-covered plains, or black soil grasslands. (Writing, Kindle)

En effet, *Carpentaria* se distingue par ses descriptions vibrantes du golfe de Carpentarie, des animaux et de la flore, qui font apprécier la connaissance intime qu'a l'auteure de sa terre ancestrale, ainsi que son travail de recherche et de précision. Si l'Australie ne compte pas moins de 8 222 îles, 887 se situent dans le Territoire du Nord, et parsèment le golfe de Carpentarie. Le récit oscille entre le continent (« mainland ») et les îles que Will et Norm explorent lors de leurs voyages nautiques. Sur le continent, les plaines de spinifex se transforment progressivement en dunes de sable ou encore en forêts de palétuviers sur le littoral; le roman se déploie entre « freshwater country » (pays d'eau salée) et « saltwater country » (pays d'eau douce).

Ni région sauvage, ni « wilderness », ces espaces sont des « paysages culturels » qui doivent être reconnus comme tels. Dans « Burning

1. The song can easily be found on line.

questions: Emerging Environmental Issues for Indigenous Peoples in Northern Australia», Marcia Langton rejette l'utilisation du terme «wilderness», qui est fortement lié à ce qu'elle nomme la «fiction légale» («legal fiction») de *terra nullius* :

> Just as *terra nullius* was a lie, so was this European fantasy of wilderness. There is no wilderness, but there are cultural landscapes, those of the environmentalists who depict a theological version of nature in posters, and those of Aboriginal people, present and past, whose relationships with the environment shaped even the reproductive mechanisms of forests. (Langton, 1998, 85)

La catégorie de «wilderness» servit au gouvernement de justification pour s'accaparer les territoires autochtones ou aujourd'hui pour les transformer en réserve naturelle, comme l'explique Langton :

> One "science fiction" concerns the widely held assumption that the Northern Aboriginal and Torres Strait Islander terrestrial, and marine domains should be categorized as "wilderness" on the basis that no economic development or introduction of technological infrastructure has occurred in these areas. [...] Until recently, most popular usage of the term "wilderness" in Australia has had the effect of denying the imprint of millennia of Aboriginal impacts on, and relationships with, species and ecologies in Australian environmental history. (Langton, 1998, 84-85)

Dans le Pacifique autochtone, le lien à l'océan ainsi qu'à la terre découle d'une relation généalogique ou de parenté, plus étendue que dans le sens européen du terme, et la traduit : les éléments naturels sont eux-mêmes considérés comme des ancêtres, doués de vie. En Nouvelle-Zélande-Aotearoa, lorsqu'un membre de la communauté māorie se présente, il est d'usage de décliner sa généalogie, «whakapapa»[1], qui englobe à la fois l'endroit où l'on est né, mais aussi les membres de sa famille. Les revendications autochtones ont entraîné récemment la reconnaissance légale en tant que personne de certains éléments naturels, comme une montagne ou une rivière, faisant la part belle à cette conception holistique du monde et de la famille étendue,

---

1. Dans «Legal and Ontological Pluralism: Recognising Rivers as More-Than-Human Entities», le terme «whakapapa» est assimilé à une «ontologie relationnelle» et se définit comme suit : «Māori identify themselves through their genealogical (whakapapa) connections and affiliated to whānau, hapū and iwi, but also to particular lands (whenua), mountains (maunga), rivers (awa) and seas (moana). These whakapapa relationships inextricably bind them (as kin) to their environment (taiao) encompassing all elements including rivers (awa) and land (whenua); as humans and more-than-humans (accordingly to Māori cosmology) alike are all descendants from Papatūānuku (Earth Mother) and Ranginui (Sky Father) [...]» (Parsons *et al.*, 238).

«whanau». Dans «We all Smell the Smoke we all Feel the Heat: This Environmental Catastrophe is Global», Alexis Wright souligne l'importance d'une telle reconnaissance légale dans le monde, et donne plusieurs exemples dont celui de la Nouvelle-Zélande-Aotearoa :

> In New Zealand, the government granted the same legal rights as a living person in 2017 to the sacred Mount Taranaki, as it also did in 2018 for the sacred Whanganui River, and as well, in the 2014 granting of legal personhood to the Te Urewera forest, and giving the local Māori tribes shared guardianship with the government. [...] All of these ideas begun with Ecuador's 2008 constitutional acknowledgment of the Rights of Nature to *exist, persist, maintain and regenerate its vital cycles. And we – the people – have the legal authority to enforce these rights on behalf of ecosystems.* (Smell the Smoke)

Pour les populations autochtones, les éléments naturels possèdent une valeur propre et ne peuvent être possédés par des êtres humains, ce qui explique la vision aborigène de se considérer comme les gardiens de leur pays («custodians»), dont ils doivent s'occuper («care for country»). Concernant le cas néo-zélandais, dans «The Whanganui River as a Legal Person», Abigail Hutchison souligne la caducité de la notion de propriété dans ce genre de cas :

> [...] the Iwi [= tribal grouping] have never considered the river as property that granted them rights such as ownership. The Iwi's relationship to the river is characterised by their belief that they are interconnected with the river – 'I am the river. The river is me' (The Office of Treaty Settlements, n° 1). One way of explaining this Maori worldview can be seen by the description of property and personhood that Radin proffers: 'Property ... refers to something in the outside world, separate from oneself ... the idea of property ... requires the notion of thing, and the notion of thing requires separation from self. This intuition makes it seem appropriate to call parts of the body property only after they have been removed from the system'. (Radin, 957 et 966, qtd in Hutchison, 181)

Dans ce cas précis, les Māoris partagent la même conception du monde que de nombreuses populations autochtones en ce qu'ils ne peuvent «posséder» un élément naturel, puisque ce n'est pas une «chose» séparée d'eux. Au contraire, il s'agit d'un élément constitutif de leur être, dont ils ne peuvent se défaire, ou qu'ils ne peuvent céder, comme ils le feraient pour un objet. Le lien possessif s'inverse même puisque le fleuve Whanganui «possède» la communauté[1], qui en retour a des obligations envers elle et doit s'en occuper (Hutchison, 181).

1. En anglais, on utilise bien le terme «to belong to a place».

Dans *Carpentaria*, «country» occupe effectivement une place particulière. Dans son interview menée par Jean-François Vernay en 2004, Alexis Wright affirme : «The land is, I suppose, one of or even the central character. Most of the images and ideas relate to the land being alive and having important meaning, which is tied to the ancient roots of our continent» (Vernay, 2004, 121). Elle ajoute que, lorsqu'elle écrit, les personnages n'arrivent qu'après la construction du lieu qu'ils habiteront dans la narration. Les nombreuses espèces animales peuplent ce «pays de l'eau», l'habitent, mais ce dernier possède également une vie propre et se retrouve agent de l'action. Cette caractérisation de la nature se détache des conceptions occidentales littéraires à la fois du lieu et du personnage : elle se différencie de la tendance romantique, où les descriptions de la nature reflètent les émotions des personnages, et de la construction du personnage post-révolution industrielle comme entité individuelle et individualiste (Watts, 15, 60). Dans *Carpentaria*, cette construction du «pays de l'eau» comme personnage envahit la narration mais prend des formes différentes.

Le roman s'ouvre sur une description de la création de la région du golfe de Carpentarie et de ses fleuves par le Serpent arc-en-ciel[1], qui vit toujours sous le sol argileux et imprègne le roman de sa présence. Cette entité créatrice introduit une conception holistique de «Country» comme personnage et lie les personnages autochtones du roman au territoire et à leurs ancêtres[2]. Le Serpent fait aussi le lien entre terre, ciel et eau car il contrôle les saisons et les éléments météorologiques qui s'abattent sur le territoire. Comme l'explique Alexis Wright dans «Deep Weather», les éclairs et les orages font partie de ses attributs : «This Rainbow Serpent is sometimes referred to as the 'Great Earth Mother', who can cause natural disasters, such as 'flash floods, torrential rain, or drought' and perhaps cyclones too [...]» (Deep Weather). Par conséquent, le Serpent arc-en-ciel incarne à lui seul cette continuité entre les éléments. Descendu des étoiles, il creuse de profonds sillons dans lesquels vient se perdre l'eau de la mer, qui

1. Pour plus de détails concernant les représentations du Serpent arc-en-ciel dans le roman et notamment des éléments tirés du travail de l'anthropologue John Bradley, lire Frances Devlin-Glass, 2008, 393-407.

2. Ici, le terme «ancêtres» ne se réduit pas à un sens purement généalogique : les éléments naturels de «Country» (arbres, rochers, cours d'eau, etc) sont également considérés comme les ancêtres des membres de la communauté qui en sont les gardiens.

brouille les frontières, et fusionne les couleurs terrestres et océaniques : «The sea water following in the serpent's wake, swarming in a frenzy of tidal waves, soon changed colour from ocean blue to the yellow of mud» (2). Cette continuité entre les différents éléments se perçoit dans le changement de couleurs mais souligne également que l'eau de mer engouffrée dans ces profonds sillons s'est finalement transformée en fleuve, la liant un peu plus aux terres du golfe : «The water filled the swirling tracks to form the mighty bending rivers spread across the vast plains of the Gulf country» (2). Ces limites poreuses témoignent encore du passage d'une eau («saltwater») à une autre («freshwater»), comme un continuum, non plus délimité, mais formant un seul et même tout. Ce fleuve-serpent («tidal river snake», 2) en vient à former la colonne vertébrale du roman, l'envahit et le modèle selon les éléments naturels qu'il engendre : «They say its being is porous; it permeates everything» (2). La respiration du serpent, qui anime tout, et se retrouve jusque dans le râle des herbes et les vents (2), imprègne le roman d'un souffle qui reparaît régulièrement à la surface comme pour donner d'autres impulsions, jusqu'au cyclone final. Les cyclones sont perçus comme autant de punitions infligées par les ancêtres, transportés par les nuages[1], envers ceux qui enfreignent la Loi : «the storm [...] searching for a Law breaker [...], that had caused the creation spirit to come after him» (462). Les esprits des ancêtres, contrôlant les éléments, mènent une guerre cyclonique sans merci :

> [Will] heard the spirit waves being rolled in by the ancestral sea water creatures of the currents, and conspiring with the spirits of the sky and winds to crash into the land as though it was exploding. The earth murmured, the underground serpent, living in the underground river that was kilometres wide, responded with hostile growls. This was the old war of the ancestors making cyclones grow to use against one another. (452-453)

Pourtant, le cyclone final devient aussi un élément créateur et régénérateur, comme le laisse pressentir Will lorsqu'il entrevoit la future destruction de l'hôtel dans lequel il a trouvé refuge :

> The bulwark of the spirits rose from the waters, and he saw nothing monstrous or hideous in this new creation taking shape, moving, rolling, changing appearance, and beauty in its strident crashing back into the water. (473)

1. «Will closed his eyes and saw the tremendous fury of the winds gathering up the seas, and clouds carrying the enormous bodies of spiritual beings belonging to other worlds. Country people, old people, said it was the sound of the great spiritual ancestors roaring out of the dusty, polluted sea all of the time nowadays. Will believed this.» (385)

Au dernier paragraphe du roman, le cyclone a laissé place à une nature comme vierge de toute présence humaine et en plein renouveau.

En outre, deux autres incarnations littérales de l'esprit du lieu[1] se distinguent dans le récit : en effet, deux femmes se disputent le contrôle de Norm au chapitre 8, «the sea lady» (250-254) et «Gardajala, the bush woman» (262-263). Leurs attributs féminins tentateurs laissent présager de la dangerosité de céder à leurs demandes, comme avec «l'ombre ténébreuse de la femme de la mer» (trad. Furlan, 261) :

> Her invisible touch she replaced with a bolt of static electricity which dipped his every movement into her stinging body. A crackling feminine wail ran around him, embracing him, coaxing compliance to her desires. There was no denying it, the voice of the wind was relaying her needs [...]. (250)

Si déjà le corps de Norm semble se confondre avec celui de la femme de la mer, ce dernier résiste pourtant à ses assauts et à ceux de son armée de veuves («he was warrior-like, in readiness to face her army of mourning ladies», 253), pour finalement succomber à Gardajala. La communion de leurs corps à l'érotisme flagrant clôt le chapitre 8 sur la capitulation de Norm face à son pouvoir d'attraction :

> The bartering for her desires to quench his, and his to quench hers, went on until he could stand it no longer. [...] Faster and faster he sang his little lines, at such an exciting pace, while pressing his hands hard onto his ears, and she in return begged faster, and he cried singing faster and thinking of her, wanting her, and she cried, until their ecstasy was consummated. Then, they both curled up in foetal positions on their earth beds, hers of grass, his of sand, and went to sleep. (263)

L'accélération du rythme du chant de Norm contamine la syntaxe, avec les nombreuses répétitions («quench», «sing», «faster», «cried») et l'accumulation des «and» avant le retour au calme final.

Hormis ces entités qui hantent le roman de leur présence, la nature se retrouve au cœur de comparaisons parsemant le texte. Ainsi, les hommes de Fishman se déplacent avec la grâce d'un mirage de grues brolgas grises en harmonie avec l'univers (442), Angel Day se pavane tel un pigeon (37) et les favoris des hommes font penser aux épines des porc-épics («sticking out like porcupine needles, were the big, mutton-chop sideburns of every man», 44). Or, loin de n'être que le

1. Ici non plus, il ne s'agit pas d'associer cette idée à la conception européenne du *genius loci* défini comme «the pervading spirit of a place» ou «a tutelary deity of a place» (*Merriam-Webster Dictionary*).

terme d'une comparaison, la nature est elle-même douée de vie. La narration est parsemée d'expressions mentionnant par exemple le fleuve qui « décide » de changer son cours (3), les mains invisibles de la mer (« as though being pushed by the invisible hands of the sea », 257) ou encore lorsqu'il s'agit de cycas, « cycad palms – *Cycas angulata*, like spirit camps, like sentries with their windswept heads staring out to sea » (367). Enfin, l'un des passages les plus splendides décrit les dépressions argileuses et occupe une place particulière au chapitre 11, séparé par des sauts de lignes :

> When the mud dried...
>
> Claypans breathed like skin, and you could feel it, right inside the marrow of your bones. The old people said it was the world stirring itself, right down to the sea. Sometimes, in Desperance, everyone heard the drying mud crack in the vast claypans. You could hear the ground groaning, splitting its epidermis into channels of deep cuts all across the ground. It looked like a fisherman's net, except it was red brown, and it trapped whatever was down below from breaking through to the surface. It made you think that whatever it was living down underneath your feet, was much bigger than you, and that gave them old clan folk real power. They said it was a good reason to keep on living right where they were. Keep it right. Everyone had to keep fighting those old spirit wars, on either side of that, *Got nothing, going nowhere neither, Uptown.* (357)

Les comparaisons avec la peau, le souffle et ses répercussions jusqu'au plus profond de soi, mais aussi ses grondements et ses entailles, donnent vie à cette terre. Le statut de personnage se lit par l'utilisation de la voix active « it made you think », où le sujet est à prendre littéralement comme « the ground »[1].

b. Sea country

Pour les populations autochtones qui y vivent, « sea country » (360)/ « le pays de la mer » (371) est, comme mentionné précédemment, un « paysage culturel ». L'expression « sea country », qui n'apparaît qu'une seule fois dans tout le roman, se distingue de « Gulf Country », souvent traduit par « la région/le pays du golfe ». « Sea country » contient la même complexité culturelle que le terme « country » pour les populations

1. Estelle Castro commente ainsi : « Les ondulations de la terre qui se manifestent dans le texte, et la description de l'épiderme blessé de la terre personnifiée qui gronde et qui craquelle à la saison sèche renforcent l'idée que la terre est bel et bien un personnage qui joue son rôle dans le roman et se fait entendre de tous les habitants de la région » (Castro, online).

autochtones d'Australie : il traduit une vision holistique de l'environnement côtier, englobant à la fois ses plages, ses eaux, son ciel, le temps qu'il y fait et les saisons qui y passent, sans oublier la faune et la flore qui s'y épanouissent, ainsi que les populations qui y vivent, avec leurs savoirs, croyances et cérémonies. Ce terme se définit également comme «an integrated cultural landscape/seascape» (National Oceans Office, 3) à la signification non pas tant géographique ou naturelle que culturelle. Ainsi, dans *Songspirals*, le collectif des femmes Gay'wu revendique cette connexion :

> Our connections are to the land and to the sea too. Sea is part of Country. We call this Sea Country. We belong to the sea and the sea belongs to us, just as with the land. We don't see any clear distinction between land and sea, rivers and mangroves, earth and sky; they are all connected through relationships. That is the basis of our authority, our land rights and sea rights. (Gay'wu Group of Women, 47)

Aussi, pour les populations autochtones côtières d'Australie, «sea» et «country» sont indissociables et ne représentent finalement qu'un seul écosystème dont ils sont les gardiens (voir Part one, 1, «The Indigenous World»).

La saison des pluies («the Wet») va de décembre à mars et les inondations à cause des cyclones et orages tropicaux sont fréquentes puisque le sol composé principalement de dépressions argileuses («clay soils» ou «claypans») est propice à l'apparition des «laisses boueuses» ou «vaseuses» (11, 71) dans le golfe («mudflats»). Entre septembre et octobre seulement, le nuage «Gloire du Matin» («Morning Glory» ou «*kangolgi*», 247) apparaît au sud du golfe : ce phénomène météorologique très localisé est devenu l'un des symboles les plus connus de cette région. Pour les Aborigènes, ce nuage prend une signification culturelle toute particulière car il les lie à leurs ancêtres et à la terre, tout en soulignant le passage d'une saison à une autre. Dans «The Inward Migration in Apocalyptic Times», Alexis Wright explique :

> My northern countryman Murrandoo Yanner said the Gangalidda believe the Morning Glory, which can be up to one thousand kilometers long and one to two kilometers wide, was created by Walalu (the Gangalidda name for the Rainbow Serpent). Murrandoo explained: "The general principle we believe is that the spirits of all our dead ancestors are watching over us and travel on that cloud to check out the lower Gulf and go across all their country." He said that the cloud is a source of energy in this cycle of renewal and regeneration [...]. (Migration)

Wright souligne en outre que les connaissances de Murrandoo Yanner s'appuient à la fois sur des savoirs traditionnels et scientifiques dans «A Journey in Writing Place» et souligne leur complémentarité :

> [The cloud] is known to create a magnetic energy that extends from the sky to the ground [...]. The cloud is of great cultural significance, and it is an energy source for his people involved in Aboriginal law and ceremony. It also signifies many things during the changing of seasons in the Gulf, such as the knowledge that there will be dew and it is time to start the coöl, slow burning of country, because new shoots will get moisture. (Journey)

Toutes les connaissances concernant Country, ses animaux, la flore mais aussi l'astronomie par exemple, transmises de génération en génération et actualisées, permettent aux populations autochtones de connaître et de prendre soin de leur environnement («to care for country»). Dans le roman, l'apparition du nuage intervient lorsque Norm se réveille après avoir fait ses adieux à Elias :

> Above the travelling birds he now saw the long morning glory cloud of the Wet season looming over his boat. Any local knew instantly what the long tubular cloud was. Stretching from the western to the eastern horizon so low in the sky, Norm thought it might touch him as it descended to the horizon of the sea. Now it occurred to him that the birds were travelling along a special route made from the evaporation left by the heat in the cooling atmosphere by the trail made by the big fish on their journeys into the sky world of summer. The cloud band would soon evaporate, but would return again and again in the morning, until the air became saturated with the humidity of the gatherings of enormous storm clouds. Then when the heavy rains finally stopped and the waters became calmer the following year, the big fish would return, as was the natural cycle of things. (247-248)

Ce nuage semble connecter tous les éléments présents dans ce tableau marin : l'ouest et l'est, le ciel et la mer, en passant par Norm, les oiseaux et les poissons qui le suivent, tel un chemin céleste qui les guide lors de leurs migrations. Enfin, il permet le retour de la faune dans un environnement régénéré par les pluies qu'il annonce, dans un cycle naturel et éternel. Dans ce passage, les migrations des oiseaux s'entremêlent aux voyages marins des poissons, dans un flottement entre ciel et mer, qui ne forment plus qu'un seul monde traversé de trajectoires et d'itinéraires saisonniers. L'air et l'eau comme composants des nuages favorisent ce passage d'un monde à l'autre, ou plutôt la création d'un monde dont les limites se révèlent poreuses ou ne servent que de seuils : «a world without end» (248), un monde sans limite.

c. Entre ciel et mer : un savoir partagé

Comme son père Norm, Will est un homme de la mer et maîtrise le savoir nécessaire pour y naviguer sans danger. Il ne fait qu'un avec «sea country» :

> Will knew how the tides worked simply by looking at the movement of a tree, or where the moon crossed the sky, the light of day, or the appearance of the sea. He carried the tide in his body. Even way out in the desert, when he was on the Fishman's convoy, a thousand miles away from the sea, he felt its rhythms. (401)

Cette connaissance du monde s'incarne littéralement chez Will et devient partie intégrante de son corps, «he carried the tide in his body». Les éléments naturels tous liés les uns aux autres sont comme autant de signes qu'il lui appartient de déchiffrer pour comprendre les mécanismes naturels qui sont à l'œuvre, comme ici les marées. Ce lien avec la mer s'avère tellement fort que l'éloignement physique ne l'amoindrit pas, au contraire : après les trois compléments de lieux qui rendent visible au sein-même de la syntaxe cette distance physique séparant Will de la mer, la proposition principale reléguée en fin de phrase («he felt its rhythms») permet de rappeler le lien avec l'élément salé, ancré par un rythme ralenti, illustré par les quatre accents successifs.

Tout comme avec «country», le savoir ancestral de «sea country» se transmet de génération en génération. C'est d'ailleurs ce savoir que Joseph Midnight partage, à sa propre surprise, avec Will avant que ce dernier n'entame son voyage afin de retrouver sa femme, Hope, et son fils, Bala. Ce savoir, Joseph n'avait pas conscience de le posséder. Pourtant, avant le départ de Will, Joseph partage sa carte mentale du pays qu'il a quitté, et en particulier les endroits où Will pourra s'arrêter sans danger :

> The old man gave him the directions to the safe place in his far-off country – a blow-by-blow description sung in song, unravelling a map to a Dreaming place he had never seen. [...] Yet, old man Midnight remembered a ceremony he had never performed in his life before, and now, to his utter astonishment, he passed it on to Will. He went on and on, fully believing he was singing in the right sequence hundreds of places in a journey to a place at least a thousand kilometres away. (360)

Cette carte mentale transmise par des chants rythmés et très détaillés («blow-by-blow») donne accès à un savoir ancestral. Les endroits dont Midnight parle lui sont inconnus, il n'y est jamais allé, pourtant il se rappelle : par la mémoire, et la transmission des chants, le territoire se livre, jusqu'à ce que Will puisse s'y retrouver, avant même qu'il ne le découvre. La mémoire est intrinsèquement liée au chant, dans une cérémonie à travers laquelle se transmettent des connaissances primordiales pour le voyage que s'apprête à entamer Will. Midnight ponctue son chant d'impératifs comme si le discours lui-même devenait performatif :

> *Sing* this time. Only that place called such and such. This way, *remember*. Don't mix it up. Then next place, *sing*, such and such. Listen to me sing it now and only when the moon is above, like there, bit lower, go on, *practice. Remember*, don't make mistakes... (360, je souligne)

« Remember », répété et entrecoupé de « sing », forme une base rythmique, presque un battement de cœur ou une respiration : l'expérience du lieu devient pratique culturelle par le chant (« practice »), les deux se rejoignant dans le terme « lower » qui peut très bien être compris comme un adverbe de lieu, ou bien un positionnement de la voix, plus bas, comme un murmure. La précision est primordiale pour la survie de Will malgré la complexité du chant dont il doit se rappeler :

> The song was so long and complicated and had to be remembered in the right sequence where the sea was alive, waves were alive, currents alive, even the clouds. 'Will, remember, you will only travel where the sea country will let you through.' (360)

Comme mentionné précédemment, le terme « sea country » n'apparaît qu'une seule fois dans le roman : ici, dans les paroles de Joseph Midnight, qui en souligne la volonté (« will let you through »), mais aussi la vie (« alive »), toujours liée au chant, comme si c'était ce chant qui rendait la mer vivante, vibrante. Puis, lorsque l'auxiliaire « be » disparaît (« currents alive »), les flots et la vie fusionnent en un courant de vie que la narration conserve tout au long du roman. Le rythme particulier de cette énumération donne vie également au texte tout en soulignant sa cohésion et en rappelant le rythme du chant, peut-être. Les quatre groupes nominaux, tous formés de quatre syllabes, s'ouvrent et se ferment sur des accentuations entrecoupées par deux syllabes non-accentuées, formant un schéma régulier fait de sommets et de creux, analogues à ceux des vagues mentionnées : « **sea** was a**live**, **wa**ves were a**live**, **cu**rrents a**live**, **e**ven the **clouds** ». Encore une fois, mer et ciel ne font qu'un, tout comme la surface des vagues et la profondeur des courants; tous vivent et procurent l'énergie avec laquelle vibre ce pays d'eau.

Cette complémentarité entre ciel et mer se retrouve également dans la connexion qui se crée entre navigation et astronomie. Après avoir dit adieu à Elias en haute mer, Norm fait appel à toutes ses connaissances maritimes, jusqu'à ce qu'il crée une carte nautique imaginaire («imaginary nautical map», 244) intégrant toutes ces connaissances et observations :

> [...] the sea kept dividing itself into greater and smaller horizontal and vertical columns, forming tributaries as thick as the matted hair of the universe, from where all manner of ocean currents were flowing, full to the brim with floodwaters. As he walked in this place, searching for an escape route, streams of water were running in every direction as though it was the history of his knowledge crisscrossing itself until it formed a watery spiderweb, a polygon structure tangled with all of the local currents he ever knew in his mind, all tracks leading home. (244)

La visualisation des courants et de la mer se retrouve au cœur de la carte mentale de Norm et repose sur des changements d'échelle constants, formant presque une super structure qui englobe tout le monde marin, en profondeur comme en surface. Cette tendance inclusive, qui opère des changements d'échelle du global («the matted hair of the universe») vers le local («local currents», «all tracks leading home»), se retrouve dans les antagonismes utilisés («greater/smaller», «horizontal/vertical»), les généralisations («all manner of ocean currents», «in every direction») ou des mouvements (ou images) de traverse qui quadrillent toute la carte ainsi créée («crisscrossing», «spiderweb», «polygon structure»).

La structure géométrique du polygone rappelle la science de la navigation avec son recours à la géométrie et au calcul pour tracer des routes nautiques globales afin de rentrer chez soi. Pourtant, il s'agit bien là du savoir de Norm, transmis de génération en génération, comme le rappelle l'expression «the history of his knowledge», qui modèle cette représentation spatiale des courants. Celle-ci s'appuie sur la compréhension des signes et la connaissance de l'eau et du ciel. Ces deux éléments sont inséparables pour Norm qui se repère sur l'eau grâce à l'océan d'étoiles dans le ciel, qu'il perçoit comme «the spirits of dead people twinkling as stars in the night ocean of the skies» (240). Itinéraires marin et céleste se rejoignent et s'entremêlent tout au long du roman, notamment lors des multiples voyages de Norm et de Will. Il s'agit de la même complémentarité pour ce qui est du lien entre navigation et astronomie. Par exemple, Norm se repère grâce à l'étoile des pêcheurs, «star of the fishermen» (227) ou encore «star of the fish»

(230), dont le nom fait référence directement à son histoire dans la «Loi du Temps du rêve» (trad. Furlan, 250-251) : «Norm knew it too as the star of navigators, or the Southern Fish. It was the groper who swam from the sea at certain times of the year to the sky and down again, falling back into the shallows of its groper's hole» (495). Puis, lorsque Norm quitte l'île et reprend le large pour rentrer avec Hope et Bala, la trajectoire est tirée de la cartographie céleste : «journeying with lee tides, on a route plotted through the Milky Way sky» (493).

Le ciel semble donc fonctionner tel un miroir, réfléchissant la surface de l'eau[1], et permettant aux mérous de faire la traversée d'un océan à l'autre, pour continuer à nager dans les courants de la voie lactée, monde des esprits :

> Norm knew if he mapped the route well, he would reach this spirit world, where the congregations of the great gropers journeying from the sky to the sea were gathered. The gropers would wait for Norm before they moved on, far away under the sea, before returning to the sea of stars, at the season's end. (226)

De par son savoir, Norm entretient une relation privilégiée avec cet animal de la Loi du Temps du rêve[2] important pour les populations aborigènes du golfe de Carpentarie, dont les plus gros spécimens peuvent atteindre 2 mètres et peser jusqu'à 400 kilos (Spicer, 150). Ces poissons sont décrits différemment selon les modes de savoirs qui sont évoqués : «The groper hole was in an abyss [...]. A place where they could have returned to from the land in ancient times like the palaeontologists say, or skies if they flew like the elders say in the Law of the Dreamtime» (239). Ces différentes visions, celles de la science occidentale ou de la science autochtone (la Loi du Temps du rêve), se côtoient au sein du texte, mais la Loi montre déjà que l'histoire du mérou insère ce dernier dans le monde céleste.

Après avoir célébré le rituel funéraire, rendant le corps d'Elias à la mer, Norm, entre veille et sommeil, est témoin de ce voyage entre les éléments, de ces poissons qui lui font comprendre qu'il a fait cette cérémonie comme il se doit :

---

1. Dans *Songlines*, Lynne Kelly explique ainsi : «The concept of Songlines in the ocean is not unique to the Pacific navigators. The ancestors of coastal Australian Aboriginal cultures created not only the landscape but also the seascape. [...] The Songlines on land and in water are mirrored in the sky» (Kelly, 139, 143). Bien que l'auteure se concentre dans ce chapitre plus précisément sur les Yolŋu et les Insulaires du détroit de Torres, ce savoir se décline dans d'autres groupes du Territoire du Nord, et notamment dans ceux des protagonistes de *Carpentaria*.
2. «Norm knew other stories about the groper coming from the Dreamtime» (238).

> As each group moved upwards, they surfaced loudly in volumes of water, raising their bodies high out of the sea, which were splashing down like waterfalls behind them. The creatures did not stop when they reached the highest level they could before falling back into the sea. Norm wiped their salty spray from his face, as he studied them swimming through the ocean of air, to ascend into the sky world of the Milky Way. They became specks in the sky until they were so far away in the distance, they became a cloudy blur in the celestial heavens of stars and spirits. (246)

Cette connexion entre océan et ciel s'appuie sur la verticalité du mouvement, de bas en haut, avec des expressions telles que «moved upwards», «raising... high out», «ascend», mais aussi grâce à des éléments qui se fondent peu à peu les uns avec les autres, et avec des changements d'échelle. L'élément liquide très présent dans la première moitié de la citation («volumes of water», «like waterfalls»), se voit associé à une corporalité accrue de ces poissons géants («bodies» and «creatures»), avant que les mérous s'éloignent de Norm. Le lecteur suit son regard, qui fonctionne ici comme un prisme et permet le passage des particules aqueuses («spray») aux particules aériennes («specks»), dans ce nouvel océan qu'est l'air, jusqu'à ce que les mérous[1] s'y confondent, «they became a cloudy blur». Toujours entre veille et sommeil, Norm les regarde ensuite s'éloigner tranquillement, après leur métamorphose céleste : « [he] caught a glimpse of the fish become stars shooting back in the skies, and finally, the night caravan moving further and further away on its journey» (246).

d. Le bestiaire du golfe de Carpentarie

Les descriptions de la faune du golfe de Carpentarie se révèlent aussi précises et documentées que celles de la flore. Le bestiaire de *Carpentaria* comprend aussi bien des mammifères terrestres que des poissons, amphibiens ou oiseaux. Cette profusion d'espèces cohabite, côtoie et interagit périodiquement avec les personnages. Certaines apparitions se montrent ponctuelles et visent à transmettre une atmosphère, le trait de caractère d'un personnage, ou une coutume de la communauté, comme c'est le cas pour les «salties» ou crocodiles d'eau salée (7), les tortues dont la viande fournit un plat de choix aux populations autochtones (460) ou à Will lorsqu'il est sur son île de

1. Les raies ne sont pas en reste et contribuent à brouiller encore un peu plus ces limites entre ciel et océan : «he noticed the strange shape of a giant stingray, as big as the boat itself, flying across the sea like a passenger of the wind» (234).

déchets (479). Si une liste exhaustive serait trop longue à compiler, hormis les mérous dont le sujet vient d'être abordé en détails, le lecteur peut se référer aux nombreux passages de pêche ou encore les descriptions des espèces conservées par Norm dans son atelier d'embaumeur, les crevettes, brèmes, dugongs et autres mulets, pour n'en citer que quelques-uns. D'autres espèces encore fournissent un repas au protagoniste, tels les crabes de mangroves (« mud crabs », 368), ou une comparaison propice, comme la danse de la grue brolga décrite comme un mirage les deux fois où elle est évoquée (154, 442).

En revanche, la prolifération d'autres animaux, faisant partie de la ménagerie des beaux quartiers, entraîne des dérèglements comiques, soulignant la dégénérescence de cette société, qui ne s'est toujours pas adaptée aux conditions climatiques ou qui cherche à contrôler la nature par le biais de rituels dont l'efficacité reste à prouver. Deux exemples permettent de se rendre compte plus particulièrement de ce combat acharné entre la nature et les Australiens blancs vivant dans les beaux quartiers (« Uptown »). Le premier concerne l'épisode des poules et de leurs œufs, pourris par l'humidité qui transforme tout en moisissure juste avant que la saison des pluies ne commence réellement. Ces changements climatiques semblent entraîner un dérèglement général, rendant les habitants fous, tout comme leurs poules (« air caused madness », 296). La perméabilité des environnements entre mer et terre se perçoit encore et est associée au changement de saison et à l'humidité pesante de l'air chargé d'eau. Cette humidité, qui ne peut être évacuée correctement, gorge d'eau tout ce sur quoi elle se pose et fait apparaître ces moisissures recréant le monde marin, sur terre :

> Meanwhile, mould of strange-coloured greens invaded every dampened premise, person or thing. The mildew, fed on moisture-laden air steaming up from the earth, spread a magical, sealike world above water, throughout Desperance. (296)

Sans autre explication, les habitants se tournent vers la magie pour expliquer ce phénomène dont ils ne comprennent pas la cause :

> For years it was believed that the hens of Desperance had become bewitched and purposely covered the eggs they laid in a putrid fowl-yard muck. It was like that when the build-up called into town like an enchantress whose prime motive was to saturate everything and cause creatures of domesticity to become demons. (296)

Ces phénomènes, dont les habitants ne peuvent croire que la cause soit naturelle, se transforment en événements magiques, comme le lexique le démontre : «bewitched», «enchantress» et «demons». Les habitants réintègrent ainsi une intention («purposely») derrière une cause, qui tout d'abord sert à les dédouaner, puis à nourrir une conversation superficielle. Alors que les trois jeunes garçons sont arrêtés pour le meurtre de Gordie, qu'ils n'ont pas commis, les habitants n'ont qu'une chose en tête, les œufs :

> Citizens protected by the net to keep trouble away – secure citizens, living in real houses with nice graded Uptown streets – needed to talk about ways of producing clean eggs from backyard hens, so they watched their pet fowl very carefully, to add to the conversation. Vogue was what vogue was. Nobody watched for the little boys down in the jail. (297-298)

Cette critique amère («Why had no one walked right down there to Main Street of Uptown, to bail out of jail any one of the little petrol-sniffer boys [...]?», 297) se ressent dans la répétition du verbe «watch», qui souligne là où se place l'intérêt et l'attention des habitants, ainsi que dans la phrase presque proverbiale «Vogue was what vogue was», qui semble clore le sujet, tout du moins celui de ces trois malheureux enfants, qui se retrouvent bien relégués en fin de paragraphe, hors de cette conversation et à l'abri des regards.

Le second exemple de cette confrontation entre habitants des beaux quartiers et nature apparaît à la fin du roman lorsque, pour tenter de régler le problème des roussettes, ils sortent une artillerie disproportionnée chaque année. Cet événement a pris une ampleur telle dans la vie de la petite ville australienne qu'il devient une occasion de faire la fête, «an annual ritual», avec son nom attitré, «*The Great Bat Drive*»[1]. Cet autre fléau («plague») les pousse à détruire les arbres dans lesquels ces chauves-souris se réfugient :

> Mango trees – Baaaarrrrrzip! Cedar trees – Raaaarrrrip! Poinsettia trees – Zipped. What would you give for this tree? Such magnificent trees, decades in the making, were once shade in long, bright, burning summers. Poof! No joke. Straight out, lying now, down without a lie, cactus-smacktus, holus-bolus, flat out on the ground. (445)

Illustrée par les onomatopées incarnant à la fois le rugissement des tronçonneuses, l'engouement de la population («Baaaarrrrrzip!» et «Raaaarrrrip!») ainsi que la vitesse à laquelle disparaissent ces arbres («Zipped» et «Poof!»), cette folie forestière concerne les espèces qui attirent les roussettes. Or, bien que ces arbres s'avèrent tous être

1. Il s'agit en français de la «grande campagne anti-roussettes» (trad. Furlan, 454).

exotiques, puisque les manguiers viennent du continent indien, les cèdres du Moyen-Orient et les poinsettias d'Amérique centrale, le narrateur se désole du sort qui leur est réservé. Si les roussettes sont bel et bien attirées par ces types d'arbres spécifiques, alors même qu'ils ont été implantés récemment par la population, cette destruction démontre déjà que certaines espèces naturelles importées, ici les arbres, peuvent contribuer à dérégler le reste de la faune et de la flore endémiques (voir partie suivante). Cette invasion de chauves-souris suscite une peur déraisonnée de la contamination par un virus qu'elles transmettraient :

> Nobody really saw bats anymore. Showers of bat piss caught the imagination instead. Nobody walked the streets at night during the mango season because nobody had any trouble visualising the deadly virus pissing on the town. (446)

Dans l'imaginaire des habitants, les animaux laissent place à une peur viscérale du virus, jusqu'à ce qu'il ait finalement une vie propre : cette transcription visuelle de la contamination par le biais des sécrétions animales («showers of bat piss») contribue à nourrir l'imagination des habitants. Les prémices de cette phobie générale apparaissent après l'incident de la morsure du chien de Midnight par une de ces roussettes, entraînant des histoires à n'en plus finir :

> In town though, the bats had made a reputation for themselves after the incident with the dog. All kinds of legends jumped out of the woodwork about bad bat bites. Elaborate stories circulated on paper from the Council about the effect of falling bat urine on human skin, of inhaling bat spit, or of bodily contact with bat fur, and with so many years passing since Will killed the dog, a little bit of suspicion had gone a long way. Bats were high on the town's list of *things that can go wrong with the world*. Everyone now believed bats carried a deadly disease. A disease which could spread to humans through the treasured fowl pens: *If you looked closely*. (446, emphases d'origine)

L'intériorisation populaire du discours municipal officiel, qui pourtant ne repose sur rien de concret, se perçoit par le changement de registre des termes désignant les sécrétions animales : «urine», terme neutre et biologique, se transforme dans la suite du texte en «piss», informel et argotique. Ces légendes et autres histoires complexes, publiées dans ce que l'on imagine être des mises en garde municipales, ont pris de l'ampleur au fil des ans jusqu'à former une expression consacrée «bad bat bites», dont l'allitération ainsi que les monosyllabes contribuent à souligner l'aspect presque essentiel et indissociable, bien que comique. Quant à la dernière phrase, elle lie cet épisode à celui évoqué précédemment, sans pour autant fournir de preuve ou d'explication : la voie de contamination par les poulaillers reste un mystère, ne fait qu'ajouter aux légendes et souligne l'aspect complètement délirant de cette peur générale.

e. Les oiseaux, à la fois gardiens et esprits

Dans *Carpentaria*, les vols d'oiseaux occupent une place privilégiée, parmi les descriptions les plus resplendissantes de la faune. Ils se confondent avec les nuages (« the low-flying feathered clouds that swarmed noisily through the skies », 367) et incarnent souvent la présence d'esprits ancestraux. Si le plus souvent, ils ne forment que des nuées d'oiseaux de mer (« sea birds »), parfois des descriptions plus précises se détachent de la narration, pour souvent se concentrer sur des mouvements colorés très visuels, et souligner par exemple des changements de temps auxquels ils sont associés. L'un des passages les plus remarquables souligne cette interconnexion entre les oiseaux (« weather birds », 283) dont les cris annoncent la pluie et le temps (« Birds squalls calling up the rain », 283). Des espèces particulières sont aussi parfois introduites dans la narration :

> Bird squalls calling up the rain could be heard coming out of the clouds [...]. It was the channel-billed cuckoo heralding its arrival from its long flight overseas [...]. [Norm] had to concentrate on the bird squalls warning of the drop of pressure in the atmosphere. Somewhere out at sea a swell was building and might turn into a tidal surge. Norm expected the incoming tide would be affected by the winds and the power of the storm. It would bring in the surge and it was going to be high. (283)

Les signes naturels permettent à Norm de savoir que l'orage arrive : la prédiction de « would » se change ensuite en certitude avec « was going to ». Ces signes ne laissent donc place à aucun doute.

Si ces oiseaux sont les messagers de l'orage et des pluies torrentielles, d'autres se font les messagers des esprits avec lesquels ils se confondent dans autant de nuages de plumes. Les nuées de frégates, ces oiseaux de mer tropicaux noirs dont les mâles se distinguent par leur incroyable gorge rouge, rejoignent le continent en prévision du mauvais temps, tout comme les coucous présageurs blancs (« channel-billed cuckoo »), qui se font bien les porte-paroles des esprits des anciens :

> [...] the low clouds of densely-packed white birds flying towards him as they made their way inland had assumed the supernatural appearance of the spirits.

> Norm had never seen anything so spectacular or beautiful as this flight of the ancestral beings of the sea. (284)

De même, les mouettes sont comparées à des anges, qui regardent Norm, tranquillement posées sur son bateau, « sitting there like angels staring at him » (245). Dans la mesure où ces oiseaux se font les « présageurs » de l'orage et des cyclones, ils deviennent les messagers du serpent ancestral, dont le cyclone et les éclairs sont un attribut :

> Frequently, in the flight overhead by flying foxes, seagulls, sea birds large and small flying inland, [Will] saw a cyclone bird, the spiritual messenger of the ancestral creation serpent. This big black bird was the ultimate signal that a big rain was coming. (448)

Si la connaissance de ces vols d'oiseaux, ainsi que de leur signification, témoigne davantage d'une connexion importante entre les personnages aborigènes et « sea country », il n'en est pas toujours de même pour d'autres épisodes où les animaux tiennent un rôle important dans le roman.

f. Fragilité des espèces et cohabitation avec l'humain : entre extinction de masse et renouveau

Les descriptions de la faune et la flore rappellent également la fragilité de l'environnement et l'équilibre précaire dus à l'occupation humaine. L'épisode de l'aigle pêcheur à poitrine blanche ou pygargue blagre (« white-breasted sea eagle ») en est l'exemple le plus frappant. Cet oiseau de mer peut se trouver un peu partout en Australie mais aussi dans d'autres pays comme l'Indonésie ou la Chine, ou encore en Inde. Cependant, le déplacement de cette espèce maritime loin dans les terres, sur le lagon où Will retrouve le corps sans vie d'Elias, permet aussi de souligner la fragilité de ces espèces liées à un environnement écologique particulier et qui ne peuvent survivre face à des migrations forcées ou si leur habitat venait à changer. Tout d'abord surpris de trouver dans le sac d'Elias des espèces de poissons d'eaux salées, Will remarque ensuite cet oiseau, dont la présence inhabituelle souligne l'anormalité de la scène. Will, surpris de sa présence si loin dans les terres, « yet another unfamiliar sight » (163), l'interprète tout d'abord comme liée à l'impossibilité pour cet oiseau, recueilli par Elias plus jeune alors qu'il avait été blessé, de se nourrir seul. Puis, peu à peu, Will découvre des indices et pressent sous forme de flashs que la mort d'Elias a été orchestrée. La présence de l'oiseau et des poissons dans le sac ne sont finalement que les premiers indices qui permettent à Will de comprendre qu'Elias a été tué ailleurs, en mer, avant d'être déposé au milieu du lagon, dans une volonté de camoufler le meurtre. Ces indices font partie des mauvais présages contre lesquels les anciens mettent en garde :

> He knew the old Uncles always said there were bad omens surrounding the lagoon in that heavy foreboding of the land before the Wet. They pointed to where the spirits had lain in the atmosphere, before moving freely in and out of the lagoon, while they turned normality into a nightmare. (164)

Ce passage permet au lecteur de réévaluer les différents indices étranges que sont l'aigle et les poissons de mer comme des mauvais présages («bad omens», «foreboding») : il ne s'agit plus de considérer cette mort comme naturelle ou accidentelle («normality») mais de l'insérer dans un autre récit de meurtre cette fois-ci («a nightmare»). Cependant, Will ne fait pas tout de suite le lien :

> If he had not been so preoccupied with his thoughts about the mystery of the fish and why the boat was in this particular lagoon, he might have recognised there were sinister undertones to this unusual situation which had been designed to look so ordinary. (165)

Cette situation ne peut qu'avoir été mise en scène («designed to look so ordinary»), mais les indices macabres et étranges auraient dû mettre la puce à l'oreille de Will qui n'entend, que trop tard, l'hélicoptère des hommes de la mine revenir sur place. Effrayé, l'aigle de mer s'envole mais se prend dans les pales de l'hélicoptère :

> The sea eagle's blood sprayed over the lagoon like early rain when the bird took off in fright and hit the rotor blades of the helicopter descending at high speed over the spearwood. Will dived under the mud as the helicopter bubble, coated with blood, roared down towards him as the pilot tried to regain control and ascend the other side of the lagoon. (165)

La description de la mort violente de l'oiseau permet au lecteur de ressentir la même surprise que Will en proposant le visuel, la conséquence (les éclaboussures de sang) avant la compréhension de la cause (l'envol précipité de l'oiseau) – tout comme pour le meurtre d'Elias. De fait, la mort de l'oiseau montre en filigrane les coupables du meurtre d'Elias, les éclaboussures dénonçant les meurtriers. Ce passage met aussi en lumière les conséquences néfastes de l'industrie minière implantée dans le golfe et l'impact des actions humaines sur des écosystèmes déjà fragilisés puisque l'oiseau de mer n'aurait pas pu survivre quoiqu'il arrive sur le lagon.

Le récit met en garde contre la prolifération et l'extinction de masse des espèces, rappelant à quel point l'équilibre écologique est fragile et que tout interventionnisme de l'État, par le biais de certaines politiques visant à recréer cet équilibre par exemple, peut aussi avoir des conséquences néfastes. Dans *Carpentaria*, ces politiques environnementales et leur efficacité sont remises en question par le traitement ironique qui en est fait tout d'abord avec l'échec de l'extermination des cochons sauvages qui se transforme en élevage (51), puis avec la prolifération de millions de crapauds-buffles («cane toads»), implantés par Joseph Midnight, dans le but de récolter l'argent promis par l'État pour les chasser :

> Well! How do you think the cane toads got into this pristine environment? Joseph Midnight brought them in his port from Townsville, smuggled them in, not that anyone was there to stop him. Now, shine a torch around outside and you will see nothing but a plague of cane toads all over the place. (52)

Les politiques environnementales s'avèrent vouées à l'échec, comme avec les Wangabiyas qui finalement décident de faire ce qui leur profite le plus, entre élevage de cochons et chasse aux crapauds, qu'ils ont eux-mêmes importés dans le golfe. À tel point que ces vermines, «plague», en sont venues à infester cet environnement originellement immaculé («pristine environment»).

Au contraire, d'autres animaux peuplent des lieux où l'homme n'est pas le bienvenu et doit finalement se décider à les laisser tranquilles. Lors de son arrêt sur l'île peuplée de pélicans en train de nicher, Will ne s'attarde pas sur cette plage où règne le chaos, «the chaotically crowded beach» (368) :

> The island had been overtaken by nesting pelicans, watching him with angry-looking eyes, and wherever he tried to cut a path through their nests, their necks lunged out and he saw wobbling up to their mouths, little lumps of sound, travelling and stalling, until breaking out of their beaks into a long, deafening screech. Thousands of the white ghostly birds hovered over the islands, moving like noisy clouds as they filled the next part of the air space while abandoning the last. (368)

La saturation visuelle n'a d'égale ici que le vacarme assourdissant des petites boules de son («little lumps of sounds») auquel la narration donne corps, jusqu'à presque avoir une volonté propre comme le démontre l'utilisation des verbes à la voix active «wobbling up», «travelling and stalling, until breaking out [...]». Cette décomposition du mouvement sonore contribue à créer une tension jusqu'à ce que le son explose bel et bien en fin de phrase, «into a long, deafening screech». Enfin, la comparaison synesthésique «noisy clouds» confirme la fusion entre vision et son, qui envahit le récit jusqu'à ce qu'en résulte une impression de transgression et d'aliénation. D'ailleurs, ce passage rappelle la même peur de transgression («trespassing», 256) éprouvée par Norm après avoir célébré la cérémonie funéraire d'Elias en mer avec la sensation que la raie le punit de s'être introduit sur son territoire en le rendant aveugle (243). Au contraire, Will retirera de ses rencontres avec les oiseaux des estafilades sur les jambes : «He went back for the boat and moved to the next island and then the next, collecting nothing but gashes on his legs from the strikes of angry birds» (369). Par conséquent, Will reste peu de temps sur cette île, tout comme sur les autres qu'il visite ensuite pour s'assurer que sa famille n'y a pas trouvé refuge.

De manière similaire, au début du roman, bien qu'associés à la colère d'Angel Day, ce sont les grillons qui font fuir la délégation des gens des beaux quartiers qui venaient se plaindre de la situation autour de la décharge et de la rivalité avec le clan de Joseph Midnight :

> Then, to cap it off, the crickets were stirred into wakefulness, and began their choice of music. Ears pricked and prickled to hear the foreign, shrilling sounds of Handel's oratorio in full orchestra. The delegation listened for a short time, and this strange and severe sounding improvisation must have taken the cake, because there was a mad rush to leave [...]. (39)

Les cris et autres sons émis par les animaux rythment la vie des habitants, qui s'arrêtent tout autant pour écouter un silence anormal : «In the Pricklebush, everyone stopped to listen when the bush creatures became silent. Crickets and frogs were the guardians of the night for generations of Pricklebush folk» (80). Il s'avère que ces deux espèces très présentes tout au long du roman ponctuent régulièrement l'action de leur chant, tout en laissant entrapercevoir une autre réalité ou un autre monde. Ainsi, les grillons contribuent presque à faire penser que la maison et l'atelier d'embaumeur de Norm sont hantés :

> The crickets, part of the fishroom's metamorphosis, lived in the dark, musky, fish-smelly environment. Packs of these creatures had moved into the room in magic droves, having come out from under a maze of stubby grass and leaf litter in the bush, to live in the nooks and crannies of dark places inside the walls, behind jam jars full of chemicals, or under benches groaning with the weight of plastic baths full of fish-skin tanning fluid. Dozens of the gleaming fish hanging off the rafters sang eerie songs in shrilled, mezzosoprano voices

> that floated out of their mouths from the crickets' hidden nests, from deep inside the fishes' horsehair bellies. (200)

Les grillons envahissent le royaume de Norm et font le lien entre le monde organique vivant et celui, chimique, de l'embaumement des espèces de poissons : leur habitat n'est plus naturel, mais ils restent toujours dans l'obscurité. Ces grillons contribuent malgré tout à réinstaurer de la vie dans ces recréations marines, prêtant leur voix aux poissons suspendus dans l'atelier, et ne faisant plus qu'un avec eux, comme le montre la répétition de la structure soulignant l'origine de ce son à la fin de la phrase : «out of their mouths *from* the crickets' hidden nests, *from* deep inside the fishes' horsehair bellies» (je souligne). De plus, cette imbrication complexe se retrouve dans la syntaxe de la phrase, où les grillons se retrouvent bien dans l'antre des poissons : la phrase commence par introduire le sujet «gleaming fish», pour ensuite se concentrer sur les nids des grillons («the crickets' hidden nests»), et finir de nouveau sur l'évocation des panses de ces mêmes poissons remplies de crin de cheval, «deep inside the fishes' horsehair bellies». Cette invasion de grillons se retrouve visuellement dans cet entre-deux syntaxique, alors que la phrase précédente visait quant à elle à mimer leur invisibilité, en évitant de les mentionner directement («packs of these creatures»). Cette pseudo-ellipse du sujet portait plutôt l'attention sur l'énumération de leurs cachettes, toutes plus chimiques les unes que les autres, des parois murales aux bocaux remplis de produits d'embaumement. Ces grillons forment un chœur immense («mass choir», 200), tant et si bien que Norm s'interroge sur la possible évolution de leur chant à cause du trou dans la couche d'ozone : «'Could mere crickets, normally a curse to mankind, have developed the ability to chirp through the noise barrier?'» (201), tandis qu'Angel Day est persuadée qu'ils ont muté à cause des inhalations chimiques de l'activité de conservation de poissons de Norm : «She said the crickets were mutants addicted to inhaling those chemical fumes he used for tanning [...]» (201). Enfin, alors que leur chant donne vie à des poissons embaumés, ces grillons créent une connexion entre vie et mort puisque c'est d'abord leur silence tout aussi assourdissant qui alarme Norm, juste avant qu'il ne découvre le corps d'Elias dans son atelier. Ensuite, ce sont eux qui chantent le premier requiem pour la mort de son ami :

> Another requiem was being chanted when Norm discovered the body of Elias in the fishroom. In fact, it was the intensity and loudness of the sounds made

> by the crickets that had brought Norm running through the house, down the long corridor, with a million wild thoughts running through his mind. Scenes of death surrounded him. The music was so strange. The sound tumbled through his heart, mingling pulsing blood with the music for the dead. (204)

Leur chant emmène Norm dans une autre réalité peuplée de cauchemars et de pensées obscures, entremêlant toujours vie («pulsing blood») et mort («music for the dead»), jusqu'à ce qu'il se détache de la réalité, l'entraînant dans un tourbillon de souvenirs, «the noise whirling him into a vortex of blue-black clouds, spinning with his memories» (205).

Les grenouilles forment l'autre chœur animal peuplant tout autant le golfe que le roman : «countless million frogs croaking in the ecosystem» (83) ou encore «the frogs croaking on top of a mud pile every fifty centimetres, for hundreds of kilometres, around the Gulf of Carpentaria» (113). Les grenouilles reviennent lors de la saison des pluies et sont ainsi le signe soit du retour à la vie normale de ses habitants – «rebuilding the life of the love nest» (325) – soit du renouveau de la terre :

> The world was no longer under the spell of the monochrome grey-coloured Dry season. The land was covered with flood plains alive with frogs calling to each other in waves of sound running across the atmosphere [...]. (231)

Leur chant entendu en pleine mer signifie que la côte s'approche et entraîne la joie du retour à la maison pour Norm. L'intensité de leur chant lui permet de déduire leur prolifération exponentielle grâce aux pluies diluviennes de l'année passée :

> In this utter quietness of becalmed waters, he heard the distant sounds of frogs all calling together from the land. He listened more intently and was surprised how these amphibians could be heard so far out at sea. Even though he remembered how densely the frogs populated Desperance, it seemed to him as he listened more carefully, that there must have been an extraordinary explosion in their numbers in town this year. Ah! The good rains, he thought. (496)

Enfin, ce symbole clôt également le roman, dans une description du renouveau du territoire, après le cyclone dévastateur, qui paradoxalement apporte avec lui cette renaissance, annoncée et chantée par un chœur immense de grenouilles. Elles prennent le pas sur tout le reste, jusqu'à prendre la place des personnages, Norm et Bala, qui deviennent silencieux comme pour leur laisser le dernier mot :

> Neither spoke, because neither would have heard the other. It was much better to listen to the mass choir of frogs – green, grey, speckled, striped, big and small, dozens of species all assembled around the two seafarers, as they walked.

> It was a mystery, but there was so much song wafting off the watery land, singing the country afresh as they walked hand in hand out of town, down the road, Westside, to home. (499)

Ainsi, elles chantent aussi le renouveau de «sea country» ou, ici, «watery land». Selon Anne Le-Guellec :

> The appeasement and renewal, which do occur at the end of the novel, are not a gift from above; they can only be achieved through multi-vocal, multispecies harmonisation, represented by the 'mass choir of frogs–green, grey, speckled, striped, big and small, dozens of species all assembled [...] singing the country afresh' (*Carpentaria*, 499, qtd in Le Guellec-Minel, online)

Il ne s'agit pas du fait d'un élément ou d'une entité transcendante, mais bel et bien d'un renouveau qui provient de la terre elle-même, de «sea country» et de l'harmonie sur laquelle cette conception du monde repose et qu'elle recherche.

IV | POÉTIQUE DE LA POLLUTION ET TRANSFORMATION DU DÉCHET, LAURA SINGEOT

a. Écocritique et rôle de l'écrivain

De par la grande attention portée à l'environnement et aux différents tropes de la pollution, *Carpentaria* s'impose comme un roman propice aux lectures inspirées par l'éco-critique, définie ainsi par Cheryll Glotfelty :

> [...] the study of the relationship between literature and the physical environment. Just as feminist criticism examines language and literature from a gender conscious perspective, and Marxist criticism brings an awareness of modes of production and economic class to its reading of texts, ecocriticism takes an earth-centred approach to literary studies. (Glotfelty, xix)

Selon Greg Garrard, une telle approche ne peut se départir d'une visée fondamentalement politique, s'efforçant d'apporter si ce n'est des réponses, tout du moins une attention et une sensibilité particulière à la crise environnementale :

> Ecocriticism is, then, an avowedly political mode of analysis [...]. Ecocritics generally tie their cultural analyses explicitly to a 'green' moral and political

> agenda. In this respect, ecocriticism is closely related to environmentally oriented developments in philosophy and political theory. (Garrard, 3)

Par conséquent, en littérature, cette branche de la critique s'appuie entre autres sur l'étude des environnements littéraires comme commentaire social et environnemental. Elle s'intéresse tout autant à la reconnaissance du lien à la nature qu'à sa destruction par les actions humaines, ou encore à la consommation galopante et aux déchets ainsi engendrés.

Ces lectures éco-critiques, reliant les domaines de la politique, la culture et, ici, la littérature, sont d'ailleurs revendiquées par Alexis Wright, pour qui l'enjeu climatique doit être nécessairement l'un des principaux thèmes abordés par les auteurs contemporains :

> The world is becoming more in need of writers who can think far more deeply and bravely than ever before, to tell of the complexities, scope and connectiveness of our existence, to find the words and ways to express how we will live through the massive changes of global warming, in stories that can capture the imagination of far more people in the world, and in the hope that literature — these stories of ourselves — will have a role to play in helping to shape the future of our combined humanity. Call it survival literature [...].
> I absolutely believe that we need deep thinking and deep imagination in our literature to shock the daylight out of us, to make us see what is happening in the world, to make us think, and if we teach how to read more deeply, think more, then perhaps, perhaps, we might stop harming ourselves and the planet. (Power)

La littérature a un rôle prépondérant à jouer dans la construction du futur : elle fait réfléchir et ouvre les yeux sur les défis contemporains, qui ont déjà des conséquences sur l'avenir. Pour Wright, les écrivains doivent relever les défis environnementaux par un développement de l'imaginaire et de la littérature, contrebalançant ainsi quelque peu la perte et la destruction par un processus de création :

> Yet one day we will eventually meet the challenges of imagining how to live in worldwide catastrophic times because, if anything, global warming is expanding our imagination, and it is already eclipsing all normality in our current literary concerns. We will be left to create from the new normalities rupturing the country of the soul. (Oodgeroo)

Ce développement de la créativité et de l'imagination en réponse aux défis environnementaux se retrouve déjà dans les deux derniers romans d'Alexis Wright, *Carpentaria* et *The Swan Book*. Au-delà de la destruction, une création – ou re-création – est possible, ce qui ne va pas sans rappeler le traitement du déchet dans *Carpentaria* : tout un système de valeur est porté par le roman qui dénonce les dérives de l'activité humaine – notamment la pollution des océans et les abus de l'industrie minière.

b. La subjectivité au cœur du processus de création

Dans *Carpentaria*, la première image signifiante de pollution est la décharge à l'orée de la ville, royaume d'Angel Day sur lequel elle règne, jusqu'à déclencher une guerre. La description de la décharge fait écho à l'épisode de création du Serpent ancestral qui ouvre le roman[1], renfermant cette fois-ci «the haunting spirits residing in the smelly residue, deep down in the gloomy, slime-dripping serpentine caverns of the dump» (16). Depuis la naissance de Norm, cette décharge a fourni la matière première pour la construction du camp de la communauté aborigène qui est décrit comme «a human dumping-ground next to the town tip [...]. All choked up, living piled up together in trash humpies made of tin, cloth, and plastic too, salvaged from the rubbish dump» (4). Pourtant, Angel Day donne tout son sens à l'expression «one man's trash is another man's treasure», puisqu'elle récupère ce qu'elle peut de la décharge afin de construire sa maison. Le déchet devient trésor, «waste» devient «wealth», comme le montrent les oppositions et inversions constantes, telle l'expression oxymorique utilisée pour décrire son «igloo» (15) fait de bric et de broc, «rubbish dump palace», ou encore lorsque Mozzie se rappelle d'elle ainsi : «a woman [...] who spun gold from the rubbish dump» (135). Le récit propose plusieurs descriptions très visuelles de ce palais de déchets, dont elles soulignent l'hétéroclisme :

> Angel was on her way to the rubbish dump palace where her seagull sentinels sat in the thousands on **dead** foliage, **cardboard** **box**es, rus**t**e**d** iron, slash**ed** **t**yres, **pink** **p**las**tic** **p**urses and chea**p** wha**t**no**t**, **g**uar**d**ing for nothing a hum**pt**een amoun**t** of un**t**ol**d** **t**reasure. (17)

L'énumération des matériaux en illustre la diversité, tandis que les allitérations de plosives (/p/, /b/, /t/, /d/, /k/ et /g/) soulignées en gras dans l'extrait insistent sur leur profusion : l'amalgame d'objets et

1. Un parallèle se crée notamment avec le passage où le serpent creuse le sous-sol et façonne les méandres des fleuves : «Picture the creative serpent scoring deep into – scouring down through – the slippery underground of the mudflats, leaving in its wake the thunder of tunnels collapsing to form deep sunken valleys» (1).

l'amoncellement de sons forment l'image tout aussi sonore que visuelle d'un entrelacs complexe.

Ce processus créatif comprend une dimension subjective très importante, qui se perçoit dès la toute première description de la maison :

> Behold the sight of welcome home, embedded in the never-ending rattling corrugated-iron shanty fortress, built from the sprinklings of holy water, charms, spirits, lures acquired from packets of hair dye, and discarded materials pinched from the rubbish dump across the road. This was Number One house. (12)

Cette construction n'est pas seulement matérielle mais aussi spirituelle et émotionnelle comme le montre l'accumulation de mots à forte dénotation matérielle («corrugated-iron shanty fortress») et ceux qui décrivent des éléments moins tangibles («holy water, charms, spirits, lures»). Pour l'écrivain Alai, dans le passage cité précédemment, ces deux dimensions s'associent logiquement dans la définition même de ce qu'est une maison :

> If a house was just a dwelling for the body, then the house was only physical, one made only with materials picked up from the dump. For some people in this world, however, a house is also where you rest your spirit and emotions. [...] This kind of combined description and expression of the objective and subjective world is a tour de force of the book, like the most splendid cadenza in a symphony. (Alai, 49)

Cette dimension subjective se retrouve finalement à la fois dans l'action de jeter et de se débarrasser d'objets, et dans celle d'en récupérer et réutiliser à d'autres fins. Aussi, le roman n'offre pas exclusivement une critique de la société de consommation australienne blanche, mais met davantage l'accent sur l'aspect subjectif et personnel de cette relation au déchet, puisqu'elle implique forcément une sélection ou une prise de décision[1]. Ainsi Angel Day devient à son tour celle qui doit choisir

1. Nicoli Finn crée également tout un mur de bouteilles de verre récupérées sur la plage : «He created a foil by collecting all of the empty bottles lying about the water's edge. These he would neatly and painstakingly stack until they produced giant-sized walls of amber glass at the back of the Fisherman's Hotel. Anyone could go and watch him sitting at the plastic table on a chair in front of the walls of bottles» (63). Ici, le processus créatif et subjectif offre également la possibilité de créer un leurre («lures» dans la description de la maison d'Angel Day) : par exemple, cette dernière se prend pour la reine de la décharge dans son palais de détritus («queen herself», 23) mais cette auto-proclamation est remise en cause par la communauté et fournit l'une des causes de la bataille des clans sur la décharge.

entre les objets à conserver et ceux dont elle doit se séparer afin de prendre avec elle la grosse horloge : «Angel Day now had to choose what she could discard from her potato sack. Decisions, decisions, she mumbled to herself, sorting tins and bottles to make room for the big shiny clock» (21). Concernant cette action de jeter, Stephen Muecke explique :

> In the interval between finishing a drink and throwing the can out the car window there is a fundamental human decision to be made about purity, about what is connected with our body and what is not. Waste has that kind of magical liminal status of both being and not being in a relationship with our bodies. (Muecke, 2003, 122)

Angel Day doit ainsi faire des choix difficiles pour le recyclage et la récupération des déchets et trouver des stratégies efficaces pour éviter qu'on ne lui vole ses trouvailles (21) : toute récupération et collection implique un acte de sélection et de valorisation, c'est-à-dire l'attribution d'une valeur selon une échelle purement subjective. Cette revalorisation est tout aussi significative de la subjectivité du pilleur-glaneur de poubelles que ne l'était l'acte de jeter pour le premier utilisateur de l'objet.

Dans cette optique, la restauration qu'elle entreprend de la statue de la Vierge, transformée par ses soins en une «Marie aborigène» («Aboriginal Mary», 38) démontre à la fois une réappropriation culturelle ou un syncrétisme culturel et un rapprochement entre sacré et profane selon Peter Minter, dans «Rubbish Palaces, Islands of Junk: On the Function of Tropes of Pollution in Alexis Wright's *Carpentaria*» (Minter, 206-208). La restauration devient finalement une recréation, ou «reconstruction» dans le récit :

> She had torn herself away from the statue of Mary, which she had now repainted in the colour of her own likeness. She had examined pictures in the children's prayer books and after considering every detail of what needed to be done, she believed she knew how to restore the statue. Every bit of her time and attention had been given in its *reconstruction, which had now departed from that of its familiar image, to one who watches over and cares for the claypan people in the Gulf country*. Improvisation with Norm's fish colours and textures resulted in a brightly coloured statue of an Aboriginal woman who lived by the sea. (36-37, je souligne)

Cet épisode révèle un autre attribut du trope du déchet et de la pollution, décrit par Minter comme «an essentially productive figure» (Minter, 197) : «pollution always functions as a rhetorical object that is organizing and constitutive, and which can be appreciated as a medium that is systematically structuring and embodying» (Minter, 197). Angel Day a su se réapproprier la statue et la modeler selon ses besoins et ceux de sa communauté, dont elle est désormais la protectrice. Ainsi, cette statue de la culture australienne blanche se voit réintégrée dans la culture aborigène, à des fins précises.

Il en va de même pour les réparations automobiles opérées par les hommes de Mozzie lorsqu'ils sont sur leur «route spirituelle» :

> [...] the life of these vehicles had been refashioned many times over. In an astonishing modern-day miracle of recycling by those spiritual men of Fishman's convoy who had artisan hands and the minds of genius, using tools and parts found only in nature, all of these vehicles survived over thousands of kilometres of the country's hardest rock and gravel. (115)

Lynda Ng en propose une lecture spirituelle, tout en notant l'absence de l'utilisation du terme «recycling» sauf dans cet épisode :

> Wright's deliberate avoidance of the term 'recycling' therefore has significant political implications, for in certain cases the act of omission may be the only means available to shift the underlying basis of valuation. (Ng, 2018, 187)

L'absence presque totale de ce terme permet donc d'opérer une revalorisation des objets ainsi réutilisés, sans pour autant leur attribuer un statut de «seconde main», mais en les hissant au même niveau d'importance ou d'utilité que lors de leur première vie. Ici, on peut dire que recyclage devient synonyme de bricolage, et rejoint en quelque sorte la notion de réappropriation culturelle ou de syncrétisme mentionnée plus haut. Les hommes de Mozzie associent des éléments naturels à ceux de la mécanique[1], suivant un processus de sélection, qui fait écho à celui d'Angel Day sur la décharge, mais aussi d'adaptation à leurs besoins. Dans *Reading the Country*, Stephen Muecke *et al.* évoquent cette manière de vivre comme «créative et économique» (Muecke *et al.*, 1984, 169) et en donne cette définition : «*Bricolage* could be called the activity of roaming in the ruins of a culture, picking up useful bits and pieces to keep things going or even make them function better» (Muecke *et al.*, 1984, 168). Cette pratique

1. Plus loin, encore : «The motors were pieces of modern art held together with rusty wire and leather belts or whatever it took to keep the cars on the road. [...] Out on a lonely dusty road of the never never, Mozzie's bush mechanics would have picked up enough man-made rubbish to fancy-dress a car, or do a complete engine rebuild, gearbox overhaul, the upholstery and welding done to suit» (137-138).

illustre un mode de vie flexible et peut aussi être interprétée comme une subversion de la culture dominante (Muecke *et al.*, 1984, 169). Pourtant, les parties rapportées et recyclées sont toujours visibles et détectables :

> [...] the *bricoleur* never exchanges one set of meanings completely for another. He or she leaves the two representations half complete. [...] *Bricolage*, in any form, sets up a double vision, it forces a juxtaposition of forms, and new meanings must emerge. (Muecke *et al.*, 2004, 171)

Il ne s'agit pas d'opérer une homogénéisation complète, un mélange où il ne serait plus possible de reconnaître les éléments qui forment ce tout. Au contraire, un ensemble se forme à partir d'éléments individuels qui sont toujours distincts, ce qui ne va pas sans rappeler l'entreprise littéraire de Wright dans *Carpentaria* : « The idea of the novel was to build a story place where the spiritual, real and imagined worlds exist side by side » (Writing, Kindle).

c. L'île de Will : abondance et croissance personnelle

Dans l'avant-dernier chapitre, l'île sur laquelle accoste Will[1] fournit une réécriture en miroir de la décharge d'Angel Day au chapitre 2[2] : le trope de la pollution structure ainsi le roman de bout en bout. L'île flottante fonctionne tel un parangon de la fonction créatrice, comme le démontre l'évocation du serpent (« not knowing if [Will] was crawling onto the body of a sea serpent », 475) qui fait écho à la scène de création au début du roman, ou encore la comparaison à une naissance : « He felt like he was an intruder to be clinging to a foetus inside the birth canal, listening to it, witnessing the *journey of creation*

1. Wright revendique une écriture, voire même une pensée, de l'insularité : « All the main characters of this book are like islands of self-sufficiency that act alone. They are islands created from their own ideas. The book asks what becomes of the islands we have created, of communities, our places and ourselves. An island can easily destroy and remake itself from its own debris » (Writing, Kindle).

2. Ce n'est pas la première fois que de tels amas flottants sont mentionnés dans *Carpentaria*, puisque Will en avait déjà aperçus, petit, alors qu'il pêchait avec Norm et Elias. Cette répétition propose donc un autre écho structurant le récit : « [...] they had seen roaming armadas of the world's jetsam in flotillas that were like moving islands that you could walk on. As they had passed by, Will had seen thousands of screeching sea birds fishing off these sea-made apparitions which creaked and rattled as they moved along the circling currents of the Gulf. Norm and Elias ended the fishing and headed home to tell of what they had seen. The mysterious flotillas washed around in the Gulf for months » (370-371).

in the throes of a watery birth» (475, je souligne). Si la base de l'île se forme grâce aux débris de l'activité humaine («a tightly jammed composition of barges, ship's hulls, fishing boats, prawners, plastic containers, timber and whatnot», 476), les déchets organiques prisonniers de cette structure en deviennent à la fois l'engrais et l'humus :

> The nests [the birds] constructed with the bones of dead fish and droppings eventually covered the entire surface in a thick fertilising habitat, where over time, astonishing plants grew in profusion. [...] A single rotting tomato containing an earthworm settled in the newspaper-lined base of a plywood fruit box, and grew. Within a season, tomato plants inhabited the island like weeds. The worm multiplied into hundreds and thousands of worms. The worms spread like wildfire into every pokey hole of rotting rubbish and soon enough, a deep, nutrient rich humus covered the entire island. (476–477)

L'image de l'abondance se perçoit distinctement au cœur de cet extrait grâce aux termes dénotant l'idée de croissance mais aussi au passage du singulier au pluriel («a single rotting tomato» et «tomato plants»). Cette profusion se double d'une prolifération presque monstrueuse, excessive, que l'on ne peut contenir («like weeds», «hundreds and thousands», «spread like wildfire»). De manière paradoxale, cet attribut de la pollution est souvent laissé de côté mais est bien présent ici et, pour Lynda Ng, pollution et production ne doivent pas être considérées séparément :

> Alexis Wright's *Carpentaria* (2006) recovers and reasserts a second, often overlooked, definition of waste, this time as 'a profusion, [a] lavish abundance of something' that is life-sustaining and malleable – the territory of multiple and overlapping organic networks [...][1]. (Ng, 2018, 175)

L'assemblage et la décomposition d'éléments à la fois organiques et structurels se combinent pour recomposer un nouvel habitat, considéré comme une terre à part entière pour les oiseaux qui s'y posent (476). Tel un Robinson Crusoé («a practical man on a practical man's paradise», 477), Will y survit puisque la nature s'auto-génère et semble fournir assez de nourriture pour qu'il y vive en autarcie : la nature a intégré dans son cycle de régénérescence les déchets, brisés, compactés et compostés de l'activité humaine, qui forment la base sur laquelle elle prolifère et prospère. En cela, il s'agit bien ici de la valeur créatrice

1. Cette idée rejoint notamment la notion de «reproductive dimension of living ecosystems» mentionnée par Stephen Muecke. Voir Muecke, 2003, 125.

et productrice du déchet, de la pollution, qui est mise en avant et célébrée.

Sur cette île, Will développe aussi une sensibilité particulière envers sa culture, même s'il devient par la suite mélancolique et qu'il doute de sa survie, en pensant à la possibilité que l'île ne se désintègre[1]. Ce mouvement d'introspection et de retour à un savoir ancestral s'explique selon Aidan Tynan par la nature même de l'île : «an island is an aporetic place, a place with no escape routes, [...] by means of which all historical, onto-theological or anthropological being is revealed» (Tynan, 149). Will se retrouve prisonnier de l'île[2], et le lecteur ne sait pas à la fin du roman si Hope a finalement réussi à le retrouver et à l'en libérer. Pourtant, Will développe un savoir auquel il n'avait pas accès auparavant. Au début, ce ne sont que des hypothèses, transcrites par la valeur modale de «would», et des perspectives de compétences à acquérir en vue de sa survie sur l'île :

> He would have to learn about all of them [=the fish] if he were to survive. He would have to chart nautical routes in his mind. He would have to start remembering the journey of the heavens, all of the stars, breezes, just like his father, Norm Phantom. He would have to comprehend the feeling of water beneath the weight of his island and make its currents his map. In order to know, he would have to become a scholar of the sea, then one day, he would set off to find her [Hope]. (476)

Ensuite, l'apprentissage a bel et bien été effectif, comme le démontre le passage de la valeur modale de «would» à sa valeur fréquentative :

> When the rhythm changed with the seasons, he would stop measuring star movements for the current flow, or move through endless days of charting the flight of birds. Then, like these changing rhythms, he would switch the activities of his daily life. Sometimes, he would concentrate solely on the measurements [...]. After he had completed his measurements, he would spend the remaining hours of the day working on the boat [...]. (478)

La notion d'introspection et de développement d'un savoir culturel rejoint donc la dimension «onto-théologique» mentionnée précédemment par Aidan Tynan ; bien que l'île soit un lieu aporétique, elle mène vers d'autres

---

1. Selon Lynda Ng, la peur de Will concernant la relative stabilité de l'île dénote ici la difficulté de se détacher de la culture dominante et de son système de valeur : «Wright makes it clear that it is Will's own psychological barriers that make it impossible for him to trust in the thriving, alternate culture represented by the island of junk. Will has internalized the criticisms of White Australian culture» (Ng, 2018, 190).
2. «[...] [T]he island became a dungeon» (481).

chemins, intérieurs ceux-là : «His mind grew with the information he stored inside his brain. Unflinchingly, he ordered the patterns of water beneath him. Daily his mind sifted the information» (477). L'île de déchets devient ainsi le lieu privilégié de la croissance personnelle, cognitive et culturelle de Will.

d. La décharge comme archives et archi-texture

Dans *Carpentaria*, l'archive et l'écrit subissent un traitement particulier, que ce soit les archives du conseil municipal ou la saga des Smith, qui pourrit au fond d'un abri de jardin. En revanche, Angel Day récupère les livres pour enfants lorsqu'elle fourrage la pile d'immondices pour compléter son palais, car elle leur accorde de la valeur, en tant qu'histoires :

> Angel paused for a collection of well-used children's storybooks, and sat down on the ground to gather them up into a pile, all of the little picture books, pages flung open halfway through the adventures of Mickey Mouse, Donald Duck, Peter Pan, Cinderella, Alice in Wonderland. She flicked through the books with her thin childlike fingers. The blue-eyed gulls hovering, watched with disdainful interest, over her shoulder. They were just as engrossed as she was with the fantasy lands created in faraway places, of icy winters, cool forests and the paradise land of the rich people. Eventually, she placed the books carefully into the bottom of her sack so they would not become damaged. She had more to do. Ahead of her there were many mysteries to be discovered in the piles of fat green bags. (18-19)

L'intérêt d'Angel Day pour ces livres d'histoires se perçoit tout d'abord par le rapprochement opéré dans la description entre «children's books» et «thin *childlike* fingers». Tout comme les détritus sur la décharge transcendent leur condition lorsqu'ils sont récupérés et recyclés, ici les livres d'histoires emmènent le lecteur dans des lieux principalement inconnus et fantaisistes, sauf le dernier («the paradise land of the rich people»), tout aussi inaccessible pour Angel Day, bien que réel. Enfin, cette dernière reprend sa chasse au trésor, telle une exploratrice en mal de «mystères à découvrir».

Or d'autres écrits n'ont pas cette chance et leur abandon s'avère symbolique. Par exemple, les décisions du conseil municipal se voient délaissées par Angel Day :

> All there was were sheets of white paper which she thought had probably come from the Council office. She did not read them because she was not interested to waste her time examining the rates and whatnots other people owed to

> Uptown. [...] If she had scant interest, just enough to flick through leaf by leaf, even taking a cursory glance at the contents, she may have been fortunate to stumble eventually across correspondence relating to her own family and how their poor state of wellbeing was becoming an issue, for the Council at least. Especially 'the house' the mother built. (20)

La valeur des déchets est établie par l'intérêt porté par le fourrageur et doit surtout surpasser le temps perdu («waste time») à les extirper de la pile d'ordures et ensuite à les examiner, même si ces papiers traitent de sa propre famille. Au-delà des comptes-rendus des conseils municipaux qui sont ici délaissés, il s'agit aussi du discours administratif et officiel qui est dénoncé, «gammon» ou encore «what they had blabbered to each other» (20). Ici, l'accent est mis sur les différentes échelles de valeur entre les deux communautés («Uptown» et «Pricklebush people») : tout d'abord, la division de l'espace coïncide avec la distinction entre ces deux systèmes de valeur. Les communautés aborigènes occupent la périphérie de la ville, et vivent sur la décharge, pour pouvoir bénéficier de ses «trésors». Il s'opère un inversement de valeurs, ou plutôt une revalorisation du déchet, qui est récupéré et réutilisé à bon escient. Cette revalorisation se retrouve notamment dans le lexique précieux qui apparaît dans des oxymores qui soulignent la transformation du déchet en richesse ou trésor, comme par exemple dans l'expression «dump palace», qui apparaît plusieurs fois au chapitre 2. La politique urbaine de Desperance échoue puisque cette volonté d'invisibiliser le déchet en le reléguant symboliquement à l'orée de la ville, et donc en l'excluant de cette dernière, se voit annihilée par la construction des cabanes autochtones. Si le conseil ne juge pas nécessaire de parler de la décharge odorante à ciel ouvert entreposée aux portes de la ville, il s'inquiète pourtant de l'apparence esthétique de la maison d'Angel Day, une «horreur» (an eyesore), au lieu de la féliciter pour son «indépendance économique». En effet, elle n'aura pas bénéficié d'aides de l'État, et elle a donné l'exemple aux autres membres de sa communauté qui lui emboîtent le pas et construisent à leur tour leurs maisons de tôle[1]. Cette économie alternative s'impose hors des sentiers officiels et des aides, rejetant toute dépendance et tout contrôle qui pourrait s'établir par ce biais.

---

1. Quant à Joseph Midnight, il a également construit sa maison et il continue d'y vivre malgré la construction d'une maison neuve par l'État, entièrement gratuite, en remerciement pour le rôle qu'il a joué dans l'installation de la mine (357).

Une autre interprétation possible serait d'assimiler ces déchets au traumatisme intergénérationnel sous-jacent de la colonisation[1], dont les symboles jonchent la pile d'ordures : les archives du conseil municipal, la statue de la Vierge (22) et l'horloge. Ces trois objets renvoient aux trois piliers de la société blanche : l'administration, la religion et l'éducation. Dans *Culture and Waste*, Gay Hawkins et Stephen Muecke soulignent la dimension temporelle du déchet, ce qui favorise déjà une telle interprétation historique :

> Waste is a product of time, since it is literally an end product and the end of all living things. But it is a temporalizing effect, since the inevitability of waste is a repetitive and qualifying event. Events erupt and stay with us; others, as the saying goes, are consigned to history's proverbial waste bin. (Muecke, 2003, xiv)

Si les papiers municipaux, représentant l'administration, restent dans les poubelles de l'histoire, Angel Day récupère les objets représentant les deux autres piliers : l'horloge, dont ses enfants se serviront pour être à l'heure à l'école, et la statue de la vierge, bien qu'elle la répare et la peigne à sa façon. Dans « Rubbish Palaces, Islands of Junk: On the Function of Tropes of Pollution in Alexis Wright's *Carpentaria* », Peter Minter offre une lecture sacrée et spirituelle de l'activité d'Angel Day, mais cette activité pourrait également être entendue comme une remise en cause de l'Histoire, dont l'écriture est réservée aux blancs. Selon les mots de Patricia Yaeger, « [history is] a trash heap that reeks: a mess with a message » (Yaeger, 114). Yaeger comprend l'utilisation du trope du déchet comme « [an] archive or catalogue of trauma » (Yaeger, 105) :

> [...] trash turns into an instrument for refashioning or rediscovering an unassimilable past; it becomes an archive or instrument of historical reinscription. (Yaeger, 109)

L'exemple le plus frappant de cette volonté de se réinscrire dans l'histoire, notamment en exposant aux yeux de tous les torts qui ont été commis envers sa communauté, est celui de l'Oncle Micky et des cartouches et autres objets ou témoignages qu'il a récoltés concernant l'histoire oubliée et sanguinolente du massacre des tribus locales. La

1. Lynda Ng interprète de cette façon cette reconfiguration de la signification du déchet dans l'œuvre de Wright : « [it] is tied closely to the historical treatment of Aborigines by mainstream White Australian culture as marginal, valueless, unwanted excess » (Ng, 2018, 175).

collection et les archives de cassettes de Micky («Micky's museum», 10) prennent le statut de preuves, même si elles ne suscitent pas l'intérêt de la population blanche. La valeur des objets n'est pas seulement rattachée à leur utilité – comme toutes les montres qui ne fonctionnent plus et qui sont jetées sur le tas d'ordures (43) – mais aussi à l'intérêt des personnes pour les histoires qu'ils racontent. En décrivant le glanage d'Angel Day, ses explorations et reconfigurations créatrices, ainsi que l'entreprise d'Oncle Micky, Wright suggère que c'est l'interprétation qu'on donne des objets, des restes, et l'importance qu'on leur attribue qui établit leur valeur.

e. Du local au global : réseaux d'échanges

Tout comme les descriptions de la décharge, celles du monde marin procurent des images très architecturées : entre les labyrinthes de tunnels («labyrinth of maritime tunnels», 256), les palais des mérous («sea palace», 239), ou encore les trous profonds creusés par l'éruption d'un volcan (246). De manière similaire, les courants d'eau contribuent à cette architecture sous-marine dans l'imaginaire des deux personnages navigateurs, Will et Norm. Si l'on se rappelle de la carte nautique imaginaire de Norm qui visualise les courants marins en des figures géométriques complexes («polygon structure», 244), il en va de même pour Will qui rêve de la mer, «navigating the atmosphere» :

> Half dreaming of the sea, he saw the water circulating in huge masses hundreds of kilometres wide and as many fathoms deep, become moving columns of water passing over and under each other. Nothing stopped. Not a single drop. He was breathless from the simplicity of all that he saw, and continued, finding his path through the machinery of water. (443)

Les descriptions des courants marins structurent autant le texte que l'espace mental des personnages. L'eau se fait architecture («huge masses», «columns») : elle recouvre et relie tout, de long en large mais aussi en profondeur («hundreds of kilometres wide and as many fathoms deep») par un maillage habile («over and under each other»). La métaphore finale, «the machinery of water», souligne ce processus complexe de mouvements et d'échanges qui s'opèrent par le biais de tubes ou de colonnes dans ce grand ensemble bien huilé qui fonctionne sans jamais s'arrêter («nothing stopped») ni fuir («not a single drop»). L'eau prend corps mais devient aussi processus ou moteur. Will se retrouve au milieu de mouvements plus grands que lui, qui englobent tout et remontent à des temps anciens qu'il n'a pas connus et qui le poussent pourtant vers Desperance.

Or cette macro-structure aqueuse, qui porte par ses courants aussi bien une vision globale que ses conséquences locales, s'enraye lorsque les déchets plastiques l'envahissent, jusqu'à créer l'île de déchets que va occuper Will pendant un certain temps[1]. Ponctuellement, les sacs ou autres conteneurs flottent au gré des vagues jusqu'à se confondre avec des éléments de la faune ou de la flore, pointant la place grandissante que prennent de tels objets, puisqu'ils vont parfois même jusqu'à les remplacer visuellement. Ainsi, les oiseaux blancs perçus par Will se transforment en bouteilles de plastique : plus il y a de déchets, moins il y a de faune. La prolifération de déchets dans l'océan est comprise comme un mauvais présage le prévenant d'un danger imminent :

> [...] he started to notice in the shallower waters breaking onto the beach, an unusual amount of rubbish. Glistening in the sun amidst flocks of seagulls, there were dozens of white plastic cordial containers bobbing along the coastline. Will recognised these as an ominous message from the guardian spirits of the place. It was not a sign he had expected. Midnight had not warned him of any of the dangers associated with his old ancestor's land. (367)

Ces bouteilles se confondent avec des mouettes, posées sur l'eau, ou bien avec de gros fruits étrangers («large, alien fruit», 370) lorsqu'elles sont échouées sur la terre. Cette vision équivaut à un signal d'alarme pour Will, lié à la nouvelle activité minière dans la région, dont Joseph Midnight n'a pu le prévenir. Puis ces déchets de plastique semblent même entièrement remplacer la faune, qui se fait de plus en plus rare :

> There were fewer nesting birds to bother him [...]. He saw a lot more of the puzzling plastic bottles bobbing along the shoreline. He thought they might have come off a ship, a loose container from Asia perhaps, fallen into the sea. Once opened, the container had released thousands of bottles which floated to the surface and drifted, until they had been driven onto the islands. It could have happened a long time ago, or it could have been only a few months. It could be that simple, the bottles were caught in the waters running around the islands between the foreshore and the breakwater over the reefs. (369)

Les oiseaux de mer laissent place aux bouteilles plastique qui flottent le long de la côte et se retrouvent prisonnières des courants marins,

---

1. Cette île ne va pas sans rappeler le septième continent, l'amas de détritus qui dérive au nord-est du Pacifique et qui s'est formé à cause des courants océaniques qui s'y rencontrent.

« between the foreshore and the breakwater over the reefs ». Le message écologique est sans appel : si les conteneurs viennent d'Asie[1], ces mouvements globaux marins les entraînent à des milliers de kilomètres et ont des conséquences dramatiques pour les populations insulaires, dont la vie dépend de l'océan. L'attention portée à ces changements d'échelle rejoint ce que Ursula Heise développe dans *Sense of Place and Sense of Planet*, c'est-à-dire la nécessité de considérer l'interconnexion entre global et local pour agir pour l'environnement. Heise appelle à considérer « how local ecological and cultural systems are imbricated in global ones » (Heise, 11) : cette « déterritorialisation » selon Heise est le seul moyen de favoriser une justice socio-environnementale qui va de pair avec le concept d'« eco-cosmopolitanism », qu'elle définit comme « environmental world citizenship, building on recuperations of the cosmopolitan project in other areas of cultural theory, [including] environmentalism » (Heise, 10). Comme le dit Mozzie Fishman : « Now, even we [...] are talking globally. [...] I says, [...] we mobs got to start acting locally. Show whose got the Dreaming. The Laaaw » (392). Ces échanges constants, entre local et global, forment l'un des principes structurants de la pensée et la vision écologique de *Carpentaria.*

f. Valeurs annexes du déchet et limites poreuses

La notion de déchet prend parfois une valeur ontologique : la décharge reléguée en bordure de la ville témoigne déjà de l'exclusion et de l'ostracisation de la communauté qui a décidé d'y vivre afin d'en récupérer les objets. Ainsi cette séparation géographique se teinte d'une considération sociale, et même morale à cause de l'ambivalence du terme « rubbish ». Après la division de la communauté aborigène en deux clans, ceux qui appartiennent à l'autre camp sont eux-mêmes des déchets, et leur sang en devient contaminé :

> It was unfortunate to have to say it, but those Eastside people of old Joseph Midnight were just a lot of nuisance dogs, which was only natural to expect because *they were nothing but rubbish.*
> They lived among a hundred and one pussycats with pigs. This was how the old people on Westside *rubbished* those people on Eastside who, they claimed,

1. Pourtant, quelques pages plus loin, Will se rend compte que ces bouteilles n'ont pas été déversées par accident, mais qu'elles sont les vestiges de l'occupation de l'île par les hommes de la mine (370). La pollution n'est jamais accidentelle mais bien l'une des conséquences néfastes de l'activité humaine.

> knew nothing about culture if every one of them had been derived from the *genes of trash*, from Joseph Midnight. They saw his *rubbish blood* running through the lot of them so-called Wangabiyas. (51, je souligne)

Si le clan de Midnight est ainsi méprisé, c'est qu'ils ont cédé une terre à l'entreprise minière Gurfurrit qui ne leur appartenait pas à l'origine. Dans le passage cité précédemment, un déplacement de sens s'opère par la transposition du nom «rubbish» ensuite utilisé comme verbe, signifiant aussi bien «dénigrer» que littéralement, semble-t-il ici, «reléguer quelqu'un au rang de déchet». La virulence de ce dénigrement est mise en lumière par la redéfinition biologique et même ontologique («genes» et «blood»), liée au manque de culture[1] et de connexion au pays («country») qui imprègne le passage cité.

En outre, «rubbish» définit les balivernes que l'on raconte, comme lorsque Bala parle de son grand-père, Joseph Midnight («[my grand daddy] is one smart man, even if he is not talking to us, and sometimes he only talked rubbish anyway», 278) ou lorsque Norm ne comprend pas la peur irrationnelle de Hope qui ne peut regarder certaines étoiles et qu'elle a transmise à son fils : «Norm believed she must have told a different version of this same story a million times to Bala. He could not look at the evening star or any *jinkiji*. Rubbish! What a load of bullshit» (486). «Rubbish» ici est utilisé comme synonyme de «bullshit». Par conséquent, ce terme offre tout un panel sémantique, qui démontre bien son importance au sein du récit, ainsi que l'interconnexion des différents niveaux de perception sur lesquels il joue : que ce soit par rapport au langage («bullshit»), à la nature (polluée) ou aux communautés (ostracisées et dénigrées), l'utilisation de ce même terme montre que ces trois pôles sont toujours étroitement liés. Le traitement du déchet fonctionne comme un prisme selon lequel le lecteur se voit proposer une vision du monde et de ces relations fluctuantes au gré des courants.

À travers l'écriture du déchet dans *Carpentaria* se lit une critique sociale : il est généré par les blancs, tandis qu'il est récupéré, recyclé, et revalorisé par la communauté autochtone. Vestige du capitalisme, dénué de valeur marchande ou instrumentale selon l'échelle de valeur des personnages blancs, il n'est pourtant pas dénué d'intérêt pour l'autre partie de la population. Dans le temps, d'ailleurs, les Aborigènes

1. Lynda Ng propose une lecture plus culturelle de l'utilisation de ce terme, en expliquant notamment que ces communautés ont internalisé un système de valeur imposé par la culture australienne blanche (Ng, 2018, 180).

s'occupaient de transporter les ordures : « they worked the dunny cart in the old days, carted the rubbish and swept the street » (4).

La mobilité du déchet dans le roman révèle donc l'échec des limites que tentent d'imposer les gens d'Uptown : un réseau complexe d'échange et de transformation naît de la décharge, perçue comme « a region of flexibility » (Ng, 2018, 183). Ces limites ainsi transgressées ne sont pas seulement géographiques (entre le centre de la ville et la périphérie), politiques (Angel Day s'impose comme la reine de la décharge), culturelles ou religieuses (avec l'épisode de la vierge Marie qu'Angel Day rend aborigène en la repeignant). La circulation des déchets souligne aussi le passage d'une sphère à une autre, entre collectif et individuel (entre les archives municipales et la sélection d'objets pour le bénéfice personnel), matériel et immatériel, ou entre extérieur et intérieur (la construction de maisons dans lesquelles se retrouvent toutes les espérances et les émotions des habitants). Enfin, le motif récurrent de la pollution ne tend pas seulement vers la destruction, comme lors de la guerre des clans pour régner sur la décharge, mais laisse entrevoir également une possibilité créatrice, comme lors de la construction des maisons ou de l'éco-système sur l'île où échoue Will, dont la beauté et la croissance deviennent hypnotiques.

PART TWO

WRITING AND LITERARY TECHNIQUES

1

ALEXIS WRIGHT ET LA LITTÉRATURE

Laura Singeot

I | ALEXIS WRIGHT ET *CARPENTARIA*

Alexis Wright est une auteure engagée sur bien des fronts, qui convergent pourtant tous vers une réflexion inclusive et globale, revendiquant comme inspiration primordiale son attachement à son pays waanyi, « Country », et à l'importance des histoires qui créent les liens nécessaires entre Country, ancêtres et peuples. Cette vision l'a guidée dans sa quête d'authenticité lors de l'écriture de *Carpentaria* :

> I was determined to create a work of authenticity to honour my traditional homeland, and in the writing I began to understand more fully how the powerful spirits of our ancestral homeland were imbued in the soul of our people, who are country itself. This was where true sovereign governance lay, with the ancestors. We are governed by the stories of the ancestral spirits of place in our traditional country. Their strength is in our sovereignty of the mind and spirit [...]. (Self-governing)

Ce lien aux ancêtres résulte également en une conception particulière du temps, puisque l'intention de Wright était d'écrire « a novel capable of embracing all times » et ainsi de montrer « the reality of the Indigenous world » (Writing, Kindle).

Pour ce faire, temps et espace s'entremêlent au sein du récit, dont la fondation est l'authenticité récréée par « [a] constant opposition between different spaces of time. Time is represented by the resilience of ancient beliefs overlaying the inherited colonial experience [...] » (Writing, Kindle). Ainsi, il ne s'agit pas tant de parler d'une réalité que de toutes les réalités qui prennent racine dans les possibilités d'autres mondes : « *Carpentaria* imagines the cultural mind as sovereign and in control, while freely navigating through the known country of colonialism to explore the possibilities of other worlds» (Writing, Kindle).

Il en va de même pour les histoires racontées par le récit, défini comme « a spinning multi-stranded helix of stories. The helix of divided strands is forever moving, entwining all stories together [...] » (Writing, Kindle). Différentes réalités mais aussi différentes voix et différents mondes[1] cohabitent au sein du texte, se heurtent pour enfin entrer en dialogue. Dans « The Ancient Library », Wright développe un peu plus cette vision particulière et inclusive de la réalité, qui englobe différents temps et lieux :

> I have created [...] a story line that resembles a truthful reality, and that will become the sum total of an imagined reality. [...] This is how I believe Aboriginal people see time and place as being interconnected and related, and encompassing all times and realities [...]. (Ancient Library)

II | REFONDATION DU RÉCIT NATIONAL

Wright affirme que l'un des principaux problèmes à régler est que les Aborigènes n'ont jamais pu raconter leurs propres histoires sur le plan national, mais que ces dernières ont toujours été racontées et, par conséquent, appropriées par d'autres (What Happens) :

> In the history of failed policies still governing the lives of Aboriginal people and controlling the national narrative, the belief is that others will better articulate and tell the Aboriginal story on behalf of Aboriginal people; better than we can tell it ourselves. (Self-governing)

Cette tendance, Wright la rapproche d'un sentiment d'aliénation :

> Alienation is what happens when people feel that they are not in charge of their stories, either locally or in a globalised world. This is the problem of censoring, of silencing, amputating parts of the story, or having stories stolen, or writing official scripts, or having your story told on other people's terms. (Untold)

Face à un récit national qui les a invisibilisés et a souhaité les vouer au silence, Wright demande :

> What do we make of the foundation stories millennia in age, that have survived since ancient times through the care and responsibilities of the custodians of

1. Wright explique : « The idea of the novel was to build a story place where the spiritual, real and imagined worlds exist side by side » (Writing, Kindle).

> these stories? Do we know what these stories can mean for Australian literature, or to the literatures of the world? (Power)

Pour les auteurs autochtones, la littérature permet de dépasser le sentiment d'aliénation, se réapproprier leur histoire, réécrire l'histoire même, en y incluant cette fois-ci la leur.

Par l'écriture et par la revendication de ces histoires, l'intention de Wright est de modeler un paysage littéraire souverain (« self-governing literary landscape »), qui en retour modèle par ces histoires chaque membre de la communauté. Par conséquent, la conception de l'écriture selon Wright contient toujours un mouvement réciproque. Ainsi, elle transcrit l'histoire que raconte son pays waanyi (« Country »), tout en s'adressant à lui, « as if the land was telling a story about itself as much as the narrator is telling stories to the land » (Writing, Kindle). Pour ce faire, l'auteure puise dans « l'ancienne bibliothèque » (« the ancient library, the oldest surviving library on Earth »), dont les fondations reposent sur le savoir ancestral de la Loi. Cette voix qui s'exprime et fut passée sous silence lors de la colonisation et par les tentatives de réécritures au sein d'un récit national australien homogène, se fait la garante d'une souveraineté de l'esprit et de l'imagination, « the sovereignty of the mind and the sovereignty of imagination » (Oodgeroo ; Migration). C'est ainsi que les écrivains et la littérature seront à même d'explorer et de façonner un futur commun, tâche sans fin pour Wright :

> [...] literature—these stories of ourselves—will have a role to play in helping to shape the future of our combined humanity. Call it survival literature, works that make you think, or food for the mind. This is why I believe that the task of literature is endless. (Power)

III | ENTRE VISION LOCALE ET VISION GLOBALE

Tout en rappelant que les cultures autochtones australiennes partagent le même lien culturel et spirituel avec la mer et la terre que d'autres cultures autochtones du Pacifique et d'Asie [1], Wright prône un

---

1. Elle écrit : « In the broader region, we have shared connections through cultural understandings of ancient spiritual relationships and knowledge of the land and sea with our closest northern neighbour, Asia, and our brothers and sisters of the Pacific Islands, and Maori in the south. The broader neighbourhood widens our imaginings of our regional geographical sense of our home in the world » (Self-governing).

sentiment à la fois d'ouverture mais aussi d'appartenance au monde («global sense of belonging») (Self-governing), entre ancrage profond au monde et liberté absolue de le parcourir par l'imagination. Cette littérature qui s'auto-gouverne doit simultanément repousser les limites trop souvent imposées aux écrivains tout en incluant cette vision du monde où toute chose fait partie d'un tout, et où l'interconnexion est ce qui crée ce sentiment d'appartenance. En cela, la vision de Wright s'étend à une échelle planétaire. Pour elle, tout est lié et il est du devoir des auteurs de questionner ce monde et ces réalités :

> These are some of the most important issues that writers of the world need to grasp—to transform the science into the known, to figure out how to describe these realities, to get into the habit of asking big questions about their homelands, their region, and the world of others on the planet. Think what the Earth needs. What makes a good ancestor? How to think in planetary terms, since scientists warn that we require global cooperation as never before. (Self-governing)

Dans «The Power and Purpose of Literature», cette vision planétaire ancrée dans le local est illustrée par le concept de «Aboriginal cosmopolitanism» (Power), soit de «cosmopolitisme aborigène». Le local ne prend plus le pas sur le global mais ces deux échelles sont intrinsèquement liées : il convient de partager ce sentiment d'appartenir à un monde «total» qui, pour autant, ne rejette pas les mondes des autres[1], tout en ayant toujours la possibilité de revenir à son héritage culturel. Cette pensée s'avère tout aussi vraie pour ce qui est de la littérature, puisque Wright considère que la littérature a vocation de raconter l'humanité dans sa globalité et d'embrasser une portée aussi bien planétaire que locale (Ancient Library).

1. Alexis Wright l'expose ainsi : «This holds the most importance to me, of belonging to this total world, yet one that relates to the worlds of others» (Power).

2

GENRES AND LITERARY INFLUENCES

Susan Barrett

"a spinning, multi-stranded helix of stories" (Wright, Writing, Kindle)

1 | INTRODUCTION

The word "genre" in French literally means "a kind" or "a type," but it has been adopted to designate categories of literature, music or art that can be characterised by their style, form or content. It is thus "primarily nominological and typological in function" (Chandler, 1) since its aim is to sort literature into different types and to give those types names. However, as David Chandler reminds us, determining what constitutes a genre is "not a neutral and 'objective' procedure. There are no undisputed 'maps' of the system of genres within any medium (1). It is important to think about whose genre it is, particularly when discussing works that lie outside the Western canon. There is a danger of attempting to shoe-horn such works into an existing genre with the risk of missing their originality, or conversely of dismissing them precisely because they do not fit preconceived ideas about what a work of literature should or should not be. When reading and analysing postcolonial and Indigenous literatures it is important to bear in mind the questions raised by Wai Chee Dimock:

> What would literary history look like if the field were divided, not into discrete periods, and not into discrete bodies of national literatures? What other

> organizing principles might come into play? And how would they affect the mapping of "literature" as an analytic object? (85)

This is not to say that individual works exist in a vacuum. It is more an invitation not to think about them as being in rigid categories but to think of them as individual works which are interconnected; to think of "kin" rather than "kind," not necessarily a "genealogical relation, but [...] a remote spectrum of affinities" (Dimock, 86).

II | ABORIGINAL REALISM

> *"I felt literature, the work of fiction, was the best way of presenting a truth – not the real truth, but more of a truth than non-fiction which is not really the truth either" (Wright, Politics, 12)*

The term "realism" is used to describe forms of art that supposedly accurately reflect the real world. When realism refers to fiction, it tends to be associated in particular with novels written in the nineteenth century which focussed on everyday life, and whose protagonists were ordinary people rather than extraordinary heroes. The idea that any work of art can be an exact, neutral reflection of the real world is of course problematic. Even if we lay aside the solipsistic argument that nothing exists outside of our own minds, which means that objective knowledge is a philosophical impossibility, what an artist decides to include or to leave out invariably influences the perception of reality the work presents. Moreover, what is ordinary to one person may appear extraordinary to someone else with a different life experience. This is complicated still further in works of literature since words themselves do not have a fixed meaning because of the gap between the signifier and the signified.[1] This is exacerbated when the language of one country becomes the dominant language in another since the original language, born out of one reality, does not have all the words necessary to describe another.[2]

With these caveats in place, it is, nevertheless, possible to argue that *Carpentaria* does contain some elements that a reader would expect to

---

1. See the work of Ferdinand de Saussure. For a discussion of these ideas relating to *Carpentaria*, see Part two, 3. I. « Les différentes langues ».
2. See chapter 2 "Re-placing language: textual strategies in post-colonial writing" in Bill Ashcroft, Gareth Griffiths, Helen Tiffin, 2015.

find in a realist novel. The everyday life of Aboriginal people in a small rural Australian town is described with a level of detail that draws white readers' attention to the poverty and racism faced by many Aboriginal people in their everyday lives. The Aboriginal inhabitants of Desperance live on the edge of the town rubbish dump in makeshift shelters; racism is rife; when their children leave school, their only future is a dead-end job with the mining company with its poor safety record; teenage boys sniff petrol, live in abandoned cars and die in custody; women have been raped by the Mayor. There are some grounds for thinking that the detailed descriptions of Aboriginal life are examples of hyper-realism, not in the sense in which it was initially used in the art world to designate paintings and sculptures whose level of detail was derived from photography in an attempt to create a sense of heightened reality, but as a form of resistance:

> [...] to make the real more real, when the real is itself what is at risk, at stake: namely, Indigenous history, language, presence, silenced, denied, ignored. To put it crudely, it is a hyperreal of survivance. (Biddle and Lea, 6)

For European readers, however, the inclusion of what appear to be supernatural elements, such as Norm's ability to "fly through storms like an angel" (468), the land, which at times seems to act of its own volition, and the appearance of the *yinbirras* and the devil woman *Gardajala*, raises the question of whether the term "magic realism" would be a more appropriate classification. The expression "magic realism" originated in 1920s Germany where it was used by the photographer and art critic Franz Roh to describe:

> [...] a new post-expressionist art, where the art would give representation to a subjective experience of reality, a reality that is amplified until its own so-called magic appears in the work of art. (Ravenscroft, 2010, 196)

When talking about literature, works of magic realism are characterised by the incorporation of "fabulous and fantastical events [...] in a narrative that otherwise maintains the 'reliable' tone of objective realistic report."[1] The term is generally associated with the work of Central and South American writers such as Miguel Angel Asturias, Alejo Carpentier, Gabriel Garcia Marquez and Carlos Fuentes. It is considered to be a subversive form of writing because such works challenge the realism found in colonial literature. Automatically assuming that the term can be

1. *Oxford Dictionary of Literary Terms.*

applied to work by Aboriginal Australians is, however, problematic since Australia is not a postcolonial nation and colonisation is still a reality for its Indigenous inhabitants.

Critics who read *Carpentaria* as a work of magic realism justify their interpretation in several ways, all of which are open to question. Ben Holgate, for example, states that the liminal setting between land and sea forms an ambivalent "in-between" setting common in many magical realist works (634). This is not an Indigenous vision of the world because it sees the land and the sea as separate. For Aboriginal people, the sea is simply an extension of the land. Norm Phantom is described as a "salt-water man" (386) who is just as at home on the sea as he is on the land, while Will is able to go in search of Hope because the songlines criss-cross both land and sea.

For Frances Devlin-Glass, Wright "uses a method in *Carpentaria* which is typical of that genre [magic realism] in defamiliarising the commonplace" (2008, 393). Again this seems to be a white interpretation of the text. The world Wright describes *is* the "commonplace" for Aboriginal inhabitants of towns like Desperance; if what she describes seems unfamiliar to white Australians, it is simply because they have never taken any interest in what life is like for many Aboriginal people. As the narrator makes clear very early on in the novel, for the Pricklebush mob it is the white world of children's storybooks that is defamiliarising: "the fantasy lands created in faraway places, of icy winters, cool forests and the paradise land of the rich people" (18).

Wright has said explicitly that, although she has been influenced by Caroles Fuentes' ideas, she does not consider that the Dreaming stories have anything to do with magic: "such stories could be called supernatural and fantastic, but I do not think of them in this way" (Writing, Kindle). The Dreaming stories are a part of Aboriginal life, and just as "real" for Aboriginal people as the world they perceive with their five physical senses. It is therefore important not to forget that the novel tells a story not of white reality but of Waanyi reality "born of Waanyi times and place" (Leane, 2015, 161). Estelle Castro-Koshy suggests that we should perhaps borrow the term "ancestral realism" from the Tahitian Kareva Mateata-Allain who coined the expression in her work on Ma'ohi women writers of French Polynesia (126). Mateata-Allain describes ancestral realism as being a way of: "giv[ing] life to the Ma'ohi voice too often drowned out by tendentious accounts of explorers, navigators, European authors, and British missionary chroniclers" by using "collective memory passed down by the ancestors (§ 22).

Arguably the main problem with the term "magic realism", however, is the fact that the term consists of two words each of which refers to a different vision of the world. In postcolonial works, magic realism is often considered to be a subversive form of writing since such works present two oppositional and irreconcilable elements: the magic/supernatural (associated with the Indigenous inhabitants) and the realist/natural (associated with the colonisers) which are locked in a dialectic, either as a 'fight' for superiority or as equals.[1] It is subversive because neither one is shown to be superior to the other. However, as numerous critics have pointed out, the fact that the term "magic" refers only to the Indigenous world is a way of undermining Indigenous beliefs. Colonialism is built on a series of binary opposites in which the colonisers are portrayed as strong, rational, intellectual and logical while the Other is presented as weak, irrational, emotional and illogical. By relegating Indigenous beliefs to the mythical, the Western world becomes the only possible form of reality.

III | INTERTEXTUALITY

Wright has stated that she "started writing simply for the pleasure of writing" because she loves "the rhythms that can be created in sentences" (Politics, 10). Such a statement runs the risk of undermining how much thought she puts into her writing and how well read she is. Even before she started her creative writing degree at the Royal Melbourne Institute of Technology, she was familiar with a wide range of Australian authors including Colin Tatz, Lorna Lippman, and Kevin Gilbert (Politics, 11). Australian literature, however, did not offer her the "words [she] was searching for," and she turned to the literature of Indigenous writers of other countries, trying to find "somebody to speak to [her]", somebody who had been colonised and who could show her how to write about her people, their

1. One of the most influential people to have written about postcolonial magical realism is Stephen Slemon, 1995. For a critical discussion of his ideas, and an analysis of to what extent they can be applied *to Carpentaria* see Alison Ravenscroft (2010) and Ben Holgate (2015).

lives, their lands and the "agelessness" of their culture. Among the writers who influenced her she cites the names of:

> Keri Hulme the Maori writer, South American writers and poets — Fuentes, Marquez, Eduardo Galeano, [...] Pablo Neruda [...] Octavio Paz, Salman Rushdie the Indian writer. [...] Irish writers, African writers, Gunter Grass the German writer. Holocaust writer Elie Wiesel, Black American writers such as Ralph Ellington's *Invisible Man*, James Baldwin's *Go Tell it on the Mountain*, Richard Wright, Toni Morrison, Alice Walker. Amis Oz the Israeli writer, the Martinique writer Frantz Fanon [...] and many others. (Politics, 12)

The term intertextuality was invented by Julia Kristeva in the late 1960s as a way of describing the relationship that any given text has with other texts.[1] Kristeva's ideas about intertextuality were part of the French post-structuralist movement, which argued that the meaning of a text is generated not by the author when they write the text, but by the reader at the moment of reading. The fundamental idea behind the term intertextuality is that no work of literature can ever be entirely unique but is rather "a tissue of inevitable and to an extent unwitting references to and quotations from other texts" (Allen, n.p.). Although over the past fifty years, the term has come to have a much wider meaning, and has been used to refer to both the conscious influence of one writer on another and to intentional allusions to existing works, literary theorists such as Graham Allen argue that this is a mistaken use of the term and that it should be used only about what Kristeva and Barthes called the "the *between-ness* of the text", a way of describing the idea that "meaning exists between texts rather than inside" a specific text.

Intertextuality can be a particularly fruitful way of analysing work by authors who do not belong to the majority culture since reading in this way draws attention to the cultural system within which the work exists. As Kristeva points out: "in literary language there is always more than a singular meaning [...] the text is always addressed to an Other and always emerges from a previous text, a previous utterance, a previous Other" (qtd in Allen, n.p.). Kristeva's definition is, however, insufficient for works by Indigenous writers that draw not only on written sources but also on oral sources. This has lead Tahitian author Flora Aurima Devatine and French scholar Estelle Castro-Koshy to coin the term "interorality" (§73). In works by authors from previously

1. See in particular her 1969 essay translated into English as "Word, Dialogue and Novel."

colonised countries, intertextuality and interorality become a way of creating a specific literary space which is influenced by, but very different from, European and American literature.

a. Australian Literature

Although explicit allusions to existing texts are not strictly speaking examples of intertextuality, it is nevertheless important when studying *Carpentaria* to think about the authors and texts that are specifically mentioned as well as what appear to be intentional, conscious allusions to other writers.

Norm's youngest son Kevin is described as the child "who inherited all the brains" (104), for whom both his family and his school have high hopes. Specific reference is made to his school essay on Tim Winton that "scored A plus" (102). Tim Winton is the only novelist who is named in *Carpentaria* and therefore merits some consideration. Although the first Australian novels were published in the nineteenth century, Australian literature was not widely taught in Australian universities until the 1950s, and only became part of the school syllabuses in the 1960s and 1970s. Tim Winton, who was born in Perth in 1960, published his first novel, *An Open Swimmer*, in 1982. He has become one of the most widely studied contemporary Australian novelists in Australian schools and universities.[1] Alongside his work as a writer, Winton is actively involved in the environmental movements in Australia. The landscape of Western Australia plays a major role in his work. In interviews he has spoken about how the land is "a form of spiritual inspiration, of enchantment" (Ben Messahel, 2012, 12) and that when he spent two years touring Europe he felt "almost, like torn out of the soil from home" (Arizti, 176). Nevertheless, as a white Australian his relationship to the land is different from that of an Aboriginal Australian's and his writing is ultimately meaningless for Kevin. The narrator comments about Kevin's A plus, "but you tell me, who on earth cared?" (102). While he was busy reading Winton's novels, Kevin was isolated from his friends and "became the silent non-participant" (102) in life around him. School fails to prepare him for the workplace and when he finally takes a job down the mine, he is

1. For a discussion of how and why Tim Winton's work has risen to prominence both in Australia and overseas see Robert Dixon, 2005.

injured in an explosion on the first day and left permanently brain-damaged. The message could not be clearer: focussing on white Australian literature is not just irrelevant but dangerous.

Although Winton is the only named Australian author in *Carpentaria*, there are echoes of other Australian books. A few reviewers compared the novel to the novels of Patrick White (1912-1990), who was awarded the Nobel Prize for literature in 1973 for what the Swedish Academy described as: "an epic and psychological narrative art which has introduced a new continent into literature."[1] Several reviewers saw a parallel with Xavier Herbert (1901-1984).[2] For Frances Devlin-Glass there is a similarity between *Carpentaria* and *Poor Fellow My Country* (1975) in the way the different Aboriginal groups are depicted, and in the use of satire, although she concedes that the vision of Aboriginal life in *Carpentaria* is different since Wright, unlike Herbert, is an "insider" (2007, 82).

More interesting parallels are perhaps to be found with Herbert's earlier novel *Capricornia* (1938) a long novel spanning the life of several generations and set in the fictional region of Capricornia, which is based on the Northern Territory. *Capricornia* is a nationalistic novel and contemporary reviewers described it as "thoroughly, completely, brilliantly Australian!" and "the novel of the Spirit of the Land". *Carpentaria* and *Capricornia* are similar as titles, and both are set in a fictional place. Both novels use satire to denounce the brutal nature and underlying racism of life in northern Australia. *Capricornia* also has a town that is swept away several times during the wet season, and one of the main characters shares a very similar first name with Normal Phantom. Nawnim/Norman Shillingworth has a white father and an Aboriginal mother, but unlike Norm Phantom, Norman Shillingworth constantly fails to 'read' the country, relying instead on maps drawn up by white settlers, which inevitably prove to be inaccurate. *Carpentaria* is thus different from Herbert's work not only because the point of view from which Aboriginal life is described is different, but also because in doing so it presents the Aboriginal world as normal and the white world as defective.

Comparisons have also been made concerning the treatment of Aboriginal characters in *Carpentaria* with the work of the socialist-realist writer Frank Hardy (1917-1994), and in particular *The Unlucky*

1. https://www.nma.gov.au/defining-moments/resources/patrick-white-wins-nobel-prize
2. Martin Renes, Frances Devlin-Glass, Alison Ravenscroft (2010).

Australians (1968), which tells the story of a strike by Gurindji stockmen on a cattle station in the Northern Territory. Hardy, like Herbert, is portraying Aboriginal people from the "outside." Perhaps the greatest similarity with *Carpentaria* lies not so much in the style of the two books but in the fact that they both drew white Australian readers' attention to the living conditions of Aboriginal people in the rural north.

Similarities can also be seen between *Carpentaria* and the Tasmanian author Richard Flanagan's novel *Gould's Book of Fish: A Novel in Twelve Fish* (2001). This is a historical novel based on the life of William Buelow Gould, who was transported to Australia in 1827 for stealing a coat. He became one of the most important early colonial artists, painting the local flora and fauna. His *Sketchbook of Fishes* contains thirty-six watercolour sketches which he completed at Macquarie Harbour (Tasmania).[1] Twelve of these are reproduced in colour in Flanagan's novel. The *Sketchbook* is the first European record of a number of species and was inscribed on the UNESCO Australian Memory of the World Register in 2011. Flanagan's novel retells Billy Gould's story, with the last pages written at the bottom of the sea as he slowly turns into a fish. There is an obvious parallel between Gould's delicate watercolours and the beautiful taxidermy fish that Norm creates, since by their actions both men are preserving in their own way the fish for posterity, but there are also stylistic parallels which include the presence of non-realistic elements and the use of metafictional devices[2] to criticise the colonisation of Australia.

b. European Literature

It is not only works of Australian literature that are incorporated into *Carpentaria*: the novel also contains allusions to European literature. In postcolonial studies, rewriting works of literature from the Western canon has come to be seen as a way for Indigenous writers in countries that were once colonised to position themselves at the centre.[3]

1. Libraries Tasmania has made an animated version of the sketchbook available on Youtube: https://www.youtube.com/watch?v=vRle_ym5llQ
2. *The Oxford Dictionary of Literary Terms* defines metafiction as: "Fiction about fiction, more especially a kind of fiction that openly comments on its own fictional status." *Carpentaria* and *Gould's Book of Fish* are both consciously telling a story.
3. One of the best-known works that does this is Jean Rhys *Wide Sargasso Sea* (1966), which tells the story of how Bertha Mason, the "madwoman in the attic" in Charlotte Bronte's novel *Jane Eyre*, came to marry Rochester.

Daniel Defoe's novel *Robinson Crusoe* (1719) is often considered to be the prototype of the colonial novel as it contains all the themes that are to be found in later colonial works such as the innate ability of an Englishman to survive whatever the circumstances in which he finds himself, the sub-ordination of a non-European Other, the imposition of Christianity and English "civilisation" on a "new" world, the importance of economic trade, and the spiritual awakening that can happen when a civilised man finds himself away from civilisation and in contact with the natural world. It is therefore perhaps not surprising that *Robinson Crusoe* appears to some degree in the work of many postcolonial writers.[1]

Like Robinson, Will finds himself marooned on an uninhabited island in the middle of the ocean. Will's island, however, is not pristine but formed of the detritus of capitalist society, and reminiscent of his mother's house built and furnished with what she found in the town dump. Although initially on the island "everything was bountiful" (476), instead of increasing his wealth as time passes by exploiting the island's natural resources, first the boat he builds, and then the island itself, begin to disintegrate beneath him before finally being taken over by seagulls, over which he has no control. The longer he spends on the island, the more unsure he becomes of his own identity: "he felt stranded and claustrophobic" (480), and feels like a "prisoner grown old with incarceration" (481).

An interesting example showing how the same story can be rewritten multiple times can be seen in the name of the cyclone that brings Elias to Desperance. The cyclone is called Leda. In Greek mythology, Leda was an Aetolian princess who became a Spartan queen through marriage. One of the stories about her tells how Zeus took the form of a swan to seduce her, resulting in the birth of several children including Helen of Troy. In Yeats' sonnet "Leda and the Swan" (1923), Leda is quite clearly raped and Agamemnon's death is specifically mentioned. The poem thus raises questions about power, agency and the extent to which we are in control of our destiny – themes absent from the original myth. In Yeats' poem Leda the queen has been reduced to a "girl." Zeus can rape her because his powers as a god are more powerful than her powers as a queen. This can be seen as a comment on the colonisation of Australia, and the fact that the

1. Derek Walcott's *Pantomime* (1978) and J.M. Coetzee's *Foe* (1986) are two works in which *Robinson Crusoe* is central to the whole plot.

white colonisers were able to rape the land because they possessed superior weapons.

c. Tales and Films

Carpentaria also has echoes of much earlier European forms of literature such as fairy tales and folk tales, and offers an unsettling parody of them. Chapter 3, which focuses on Elias Smith, begins as all fairy tales do with the expression "Once Upon a Time" (42). The first paragraph contains many stylistic elements found in fairy tales: superlatives ("the blackest of midnights"), old-fashioned language ("voyaging"), and references to the supernatural ("a wizard of many oceans"). However, it also subverts the expectation of the genre by taking place "not *even* so long ago" (italics mine). The expression "not even so long ago" undermines the significance of fairy tales, whose roots cannot be compared to those of the Dreamtime stories, which have existed since "time immemorial."

There are brief references in the novel to a number of specific fairy tales. Angel Day is described as "a woman so magnificent in every way, who spun gold from the rubbish dump" (135), which comes from the story of Rumpelstiltskin. Unlike the original fairy tale, in which the woman is powerless and relies on the goblin to save her, Angel has no need of anyone else's magic.

After Gordie's murder there is a brutal parody of the Prince in "Cinderella" when Bruiser says: "One of them little black bastards left his red thong behind right there on the spot [...] whoever it fits [...] Well! You work it out" (315). In this Australian version, not only are the genders inverted – it is a tale about a boy, not a girl – but all three boys are condemned. There is no fairy godmother, and no prince to take any of them away to a better life. The three boys are arrested, beaten up, imprisoned without a trial, and eventually killing themselves appears to them to be the only way out. The "beautiful rose gardens" (69) that Truthful grows around the police station, and the *Ficus elastica* and *Monstera* that he cultivates inside the cells, which have grown into "jungle proportions of twisted vines" (69), are reminiscent of the hedge in "Sleeping Beauty" that the Prince has to hack his way through to save the princess, but Truthful is no prince and the boys' sleep is the literal sleep of the dead. This suggests that the morals European fairy tales are supposed to teach children have no place in the brutal life of Aboriginal children. As the narrator wryly remarks:

> Children in this [Uptown] world belonged to the thinking of fairy tales which came out of books, or else, the happy life of children's television. Theirs was the quiet world where murder was not a child's toy. (302)

The character of Lloydie George is a reworking of European myths about mermaids. Although Lloydie meets his death by drowning after falling in love with "the spirit of the beautiful fish woman, locked inside the timber planks of the bar" (328), the mermaid does not drown him by seducing him and tricking him into jumping into the water; she is a prisoner until the cyclone releases her. Ben Holgate interprets Lloydie's death as the mermaid's spirit taking revenge for the way Lloydie seduced an Aboriginal woman and then failed to recognise either her or their son (637). Martin Renes reads the mermaid story rather differently. He argues that as a hybrid form, half fish, half woman, the mermaid symbolises the "antagonistic world views of European and Indigenous Australia" and the impossibility of reconciling them (53). The mermaid is unable to survive on the land and yet is fatally attracted to it. Lloydie can never have an equal relationship with his mermaid – either she is imprisoned in the wood of the bar rendering her powerless but keeping him safe, or she is set free and becomes a destructive force which kills him. Renes goes on to suggest that the mermaid can also be read on a "metatextual level" in which Wright takes on the role of the siren, seducing her readers with the chant of the Gulf Country and luring them away from Herbert's *Capricornia* (54).

For Ben Holgate, *Carpentaria* also offers an inversion of the vampire myth. Norm is said by Mozzie Fishman to be one of those powerful people who "must have swapped their blood for magic [...]. They only got magic running through their veins" (*Carpentaria*, 468). Holgate sees this as referring to vampires, since vampires no longer have their own blood flowing through their body. However, in this case the image is inverted because it is not Norm who is the vampire but the white settlers who are draining away the life-blood of the country through their destruction of the land and its people. The magic in Norm's blood is an affirmation of the strength of the Aboriginal people, and a refutation of the colonialist belief that the 'impure' blood of the Indigenous inhabitants could contaminate white bloodlines[1] (Holgate,

1. A common racist belief held by white colonisers throughout the British Empire in the 19th and early 20th century, and also in the Southern States of the United States of America, was the idea that mixed-race people were "tainted" by their Indigenous blood. Attempts were made in many countries to control who Indigenous people could marry in order to "preserve" the "purity" of the white race. Kim Scott tackles this issue in his novel *Benang* (1999).

639), an idea which was evoked earlier in the novel by Aaron's uncle after the boy was arrested for Gordie's murder:

> [...] he spoke plain about what other people liked to think. Miscegenation was the word, he said, for interbreeding: 'was treated as though good white sperm had been falsely procured by a lesser kind and produced a snake'. (317)

Carpentaria does not only rework written and oral tales. The character of Libby Valance appears to be a reference to the film *The Man Who Shot Liberty Valance* (1962). This is a classic American western directed by John Ford and starring John Wayne. In the film, Liberty Valance is a gangster who terrorises the local community. In *Carpentaria* Libby Valance is the town clerk, an outsider recruited from the South (313), "a man accused of neither being local, nor understanding the region and its values" (35), whom Bruiser considers to be "useless" (68), constantly making "a balls-up of a job" (70). He is the polar opposite of the tough American cowboy; his name has been feminised and he has "baby blue eyes" (309); he is unfit with a "tubby body" (309) and is not a "drinking man" (313). The film hinges on the idea that Tom Doniphon eventually does the honourable thing and owns up to the murder of Liberty Valance. Libby Valance, on the other hand, knows that he should stand up to Bruiser but lacks the moral courage to do so. This seems to suggest that the white Australians in positions of power in rural areas are even more reprehensible than the whites in America: not only do they kill the Indigenous inhabitants but they are not even capable of respecting each other.

d. The Bible

The book that occurs most frequently in *Carpentaria* is the Bible. In most British colonies, Christian missionaries played an important role in shaping the encounter between the colonisers and the Indigenous population and Australia was no exception. As early as the 1820s, missionaries had started trying to Christianise and "civilise" the Aboriginal population. Some missionaries made an effort to learn Aboriginal languages, and to find out something about Aboriginal culture, although this was usually done in order to undermine it rather than to understand it. When the missionaries found that the adults showed little interest in Christianity, they concentrated on the children, sometimes separating them from their parents. Missions were not set up in the remote areas of northern Australia until the beginning of the

20th century, when it was seen as the missionaries' last chance to civilise Aboriginal Australians before they 'naturally' died out.[1]

Although Mozzie Fishman dismisses the Biblical stories because they were "lived in somebody else's desert" (136) and says "he believed Christian beliefs had indoctrinated Aboriginal communities like grog" (136), allusions to the Bible abound in *Carpentaria.* To give just two examples, Norm, Bala and Hope are at sea for forty days and forty nights, which corresponds to the temptation of Christ in the desert, while Fishman's convoy has thirty-three cars, the age Jesus was when he was crucified.

It is a mistake, however, for Western readers to interpret the stories purely in Christian terms. Chester Eagle, for example describes the beginning of the novel as "the Waanyi people's equivalent of the *Book of Genesis*" (357). Although the story of the ancestral Serpent is indeed a creation story about the origins of the Gulf of Carpentaria, interpreting it as a simple equivalent of the *Book of Genesis* gives greater importance to the Bible and occults the fundamental difference between the two stories. As Jane Gleeson-White points out Genesis gives Man dominion over Nature whereas Aboriginal Law sees human life as enmeshed with the natural world (1).

For Louise Loomes, Biblical themes play a very prominent role in the novel, although her argument that the story of the rainbow snake is the secondary plot (125), and it is the apocalypse story which forms the "arching plot [...], there has been a sin against God, which results in destruction of the people," seems not to take into account Wright's own explanations about the origins of the novel in "On Writing *Carpentaria.*" Loomes claims that the sentence "ARMAGEDDON BEGINS HERE" (1), at the end of the capitalised passage, is a clear statement that the novel is going to be about Armageddon (the last battle of the Apocalypse) during which forces of good and evil are opposed and that, whilst the two opposing forces are never openly named in the novel, it seems clear that it is the Aboriginal population that is to be liberated from the forces of evil (125).

---

1. The information in this paragraph is from Richard Broome's work, *Aboriginal Australians*, in particular p. 34-39, and Chapter 7 "Mixed Missionary Blessings" p. 105-123. Broome quotes Bishop Frodsham who in 1906 said "The Aborigines are disappearing. In the course of a generation or two, at the most, the last Australian blackfellow will have turned his face to warm mother earth [...] Missionary work then may be only smoothing the pillow of a dying race" (105).

Much of Loomes' argument centres on the character of Mozzie Fishman and the parallels that can be drawn with Moses. After stating that the name Mozzie is "phonemically similar to the Hebrew Moseh" (127),[1] she points out a number of parallels with the story of Moses: they both have impaired eye-sight, live in the desert, and have water-divining abilities. The apocalyptic ending, with the destruction of the town of Desperance, can be read as the Passover, and it is therefore highly significant that Mozzie's car is marked with a cross (Loomes, 127). Even though Mozzie rejects Christianity, Loomes suggests that Wright has deliberately "constructed a character Christian readers should recognise from their own stories: a prophet who leads his people out of slavery" (127).

Angel Day's obsession with the statue of the Virgin Mary, which she finds in the rubbish dump and takes home to paint in her own colours, is a symbol of the power that missionaries once held over Aboriginal Australian's lives. She believes that "with the Virgin Mary in pride of place, nobody would be able to interfere with the power of blessings it would bestow on her home. [...] Mrs Angel Day, now owned the luck of the white people" (22). Her view is similar to Norm's who, towards the end of the novel, tells Hope that he "believed in the Bible because the white people had prospered by believing in what the Bible had told them" (491). This makes it quite clear that the Bible holds no real spiritual meaning for the Aboriginal characters and is primarily a way of trying to understand white power.

In an interesting reversal of colours, while Angel uses Norm's "fish colours and textures" (37) to turn the Virgin Mary from a Christian icon into "an Aboriginal woman who lived by the sea" (37), Hope is almost always seen in a blue dress, which is the colour associated with the Christian Virgin Mary. Being dressed in the colour of innocence, however, does not save Hope from the violence of white men, just as the church did not save the "innocent little black girls" (1) in the epigraph to the first chapter.

While the biblical references in the novel are undoubtedly a way of recognising the impact that Christianity had on the Aboriginal population of the Gulf, they are nevertheless just one aspect of the spirituality of the novel. In her interview with Kerry O'Brien, Wright said: "I've often thought about how the spirits of other countries have

1. Birns suggests that his surname "Fishman" reflects his role as a prophet "fishing" for men's souls (Kindle).

followed their people to Australia, and how those spirits might be reconciled with the ancestral spirits that belong here" (219).

Will is saved by both Mozzie Fishman and the Irish Priest Father Danny who both turn up to take him away in their cars at critical moments. Although Will is aware that there is some competition between them: "Will knew the priest was on his way to visit Norm, to compete with all of his godliness to win the old man's devotion against the zealot Mozzie Fishman and his devotees" (176), Father Danny's existence in the novel is, as Estelle Castro remarks, symbolic of the fact that different spiritualties are not antagonistic (2015, 6). Father Danny is something of an atypical Priest. He is "an ex-heavyweight fighter" (180), who teaches Christianity "through the art of boxing" (181) and is not averse to swearing: "I have been travelling like a bloody donkey up and down these roads for years" (179). Will notes that "his dexterity and control over the steering wheel belonged to an inhuman kind of power" (183), suggesting that he is being helped by the spiritual powers of his own religion, while the description of him being "wet to the gills" (182), is perhaps a sign that he is being accepted by this country of water people; something which seems to be confirmed by Will's thought that "the land was full of spirits which might help the heavenly power of the Irish to tilt flat land and push the Valiant home" (183-4). Father Danny forms a stark contrast to the supposedly Christian white inhabitants of Desperance who "don't even remember their own religion" (47), suggesting that it is not necessarily Christianity itself that is problematic but the use that people make of it.

e. Sounds of the natural world

> *"One of my intentions was to write the novel as though it was a very long melody of different forms of music" (Wright, Writing, Kindle)*

The protagonist in one of the novels by the South African writer Nadine Gordimer says: "What I say will not be understood," drawing attention to the unreliability of words as a means of communication. Gordimer's novel explores visual art as an alternative medium of communication in a society in which the use of the English language has become complicated for political reasons.[1] In *Carpentaria*,

1. See Susan Barrett, 2004.

something similar happens with non-verbal sounds, although it is not so much an alternative medium to human language as a complementary one.

In the Dreaming, all animals have language, even if we as humans cannot understand it (Rose, 1992, 45). In *Carpentaria* it is not just the animals such as crickets, frogs and birds who have a voice but also the wind and the land. Out at sea Will can hear "the wind play[ing] ancestor music" (441), and in the build-up to the cyclone the narrator tells us "the earth murmured" (453). The combined sounds of the natural world are compared to "Handel's oratorio in full orchestra" (39). By comparing the sounds not to an orchestral work but to a choral work, the text emphasises the idea that the natural world has its own language and can speak to those who know how to listen.[1]

As Norm approaches the coastline, not yet aware that Desperance has been destroyed, he is "surprised how these amphibians could be heard so far out at sea" (496). His realisation that it is the "sweet" sound of the "song of frogs" he "had missed the most in all the time he had been away" (496), underlines the importance of the sounds of the natural world for the Aboriginal characters. Significantly at the end of the novel, the "shock of the cyclone" has left the dogs abandoned by the white inhabitants "speechless, dumbfounded, unable to crack a bark" (498). Symbolically white Australians have been silenced. Or perhaps the white imported animals have been turned into native ones since it is generally believed that dingoes,[2] the Australian native dogs, cannot bark. Without the noise of the foreign dogs, the native animals can finally be heard properly, suggesting perhaps that Aboriginal people too will finally be able to make their voices clearly heard.

It is beyond the scope of this book to analyse all the textual references in *Carpentaria*. This chapter has focussed on the works that are particularly important in understanding the novel and also on those that are unlikely to be familiar to students preparing the Agrégation exam.[3] Wright has spoken and written extensively about the writers who have influenced her. The readers of *Carpentaria: The Law of the*

1. For a detailed discussion of the language of animals, see section Part one, 3. III. f, «Fragilité des espèces et cohabitation avec l'humain : entre extinction de masse et renouveau»

2. This is in fact scientifically incorrect. https://theconversation.com/dingoes-do-bark-why-most-dingo-facts-you-think-you-know-are-wrong-68816

3. For those who are interested in finding out more about works of literature set in the Gulf Country, see Richard Martin, Phillip Mead and David Trigger, 2014.

Land are encouraged to read her essays, and also to draw on their own literary knowledge, to form their own interpretation of the novel. As Lynda Ng has said, "Wright's depth of knowledge of various literary traditions [...] is in itself an assertion of power" (2018, Kindle). The multiple allusions to existing works both in Australia and in Europe are one of the ways in which Wright creates a unique voice to tell her people's stories to the world.

IV | SUBGENRES

Carpentaria has been regularly described as a "saga,"[1] and Wright uses the term about the novel in her essay "On Writing *Carpentaria*." While there is no doubt that the length and the complexity of the family story that the novel tells, together with its focus on action rather than psychological reflection, mean that it fulfils the criteria for a saga, seeing the novel only in this light is a reductionist way of reading it. Elements of many other subgenres can be found in the novel, including the Ancient Greek forms of tragedy, comedy and the epic.

a. The Epic

> *"The everyday contemporary Indigenous story world is epic" (Wright, Writing, Kindle)*

The idea of the epic dates back to Ancient Greece where it referred to a long narrative poem derived from an oral tradition of recitation. The best-known early examples are Homer's *Iliad* and *Odyssey*, which were written in the eighth century BC. In the Ancient world, an epic was expected to recount heroic deeds in a ceremonious style with a hero, either protected by the gods or descended from them, who would be called upon to perform superhuman exploits. The hero's actions were often associated with saving or founding a nation (Virgil's *Aeneid*) or even, in later epics, the human race itself (Milton's *Paradise Lost*).

---

1. "Saga" is the Norse name for prose tales composed in medieval Scandinavia and Iceland, most of which recount the exploits of heroic leaders. Many of the sagas focus on feuds and family histories, which has led to the term being used in English to describe any long family story which spans two or more generations. See *Oxford Dictionary of Literary Terms*.

Typically, epics started with the invocation of a muse and began in medias res.[1]

The first known written description of the epic is found in Aristotle's *Poetics* where he opposes epic and tragedy to history. According to Aristotle, history's aim is to describe everything that happens within a given time period, or to a given people, whereas epic and tragedy have a unity of action, and focus on one particular element of a longer story; he gives the example of the *Iliad* which is not about the whole Trojan war but concentrates on the last few weeks. Two important considerations separate the epic from tragedy. The first is its length (an epic can be considerably longer than a tragedy), and the second is the metre in which it is written. Obviously metre is not relevant in a discussion about a novel but the idea of greater length is important because, according to Aristotle, the greater length makes it possible to present different sides of the same story by jumping back and forth between events happening at the same time in different places.

It is easy to draw some formal parallels between the Greek epics and *Carpentaria*. The novel is based on the oral tradition of Indigenous storytelling, it starts in medias res with the invocation not of a muse but of the ancestral Serpent, it lacks a linear plot, continuously interweaving the stories of the different characters, and it focuses on the resistance against white invasion in the small town of Desperance rather than in Australia as a whole. Wright has stated clearly that the Aboriginal protagonists are to be seen as heroes:

> My hope was that the novel would allow a space where Indigenous heroes are celebrated. I also wanted to portray Indigenous heroes caught up in monumental situations such as I have seen practically all of my working life, so I went looking inside the full box of complexity of the contemporary Indigenous world. (Writing, Kindle)

It is also possible to argue that the ancestral beings take the role played by the gods, although, as has already been seen, the Dreamtime stories, which are such an integral part of the novel, are much more than foundation myths and legends. Arguably one of the aims of the novel is to help non-Aboriginal readers to understand how the Dreaming stories have been, and always will be, a central part of Aboriginal life, which is something quite different from the role played by the gods in the Greek epics.

1. *Oxford Dictionary of Literary Terms.*

Thinking of *Carpentaria* as an epic is one way of analysing the different battles that take place in the novel; it gives weight to the idea that the Aboriginal people have been waging war against the whites since their land was first invaded, and undermines the idea, found until recently in Australian history books, that the colonisation of Australia was peaceful with little Aboriginal resistance.[1] The word "war" recurs frequently in the novel; for example "Wars were fought here. If you had your patch destroyed, you'd be screaming too" (11), "[Will] was going to create his own race war" (337), "Life had no meaning in this new [mining] war on their country" (363).

In terms of physical force and the possession of weapons, Aboriginal people were, and often still are, at a disadvantage compared to white people. This is clearly shown through the multiple examples of gratuitous white violence that occur in the novel. Sometimes the reader witnesses this directly when, for example, Bruiser beats up the three young boys or Kevin is attacked by the hooded white men. These descriptions are deliberately brutal and show that there is nothing heroic about white behaviour. At other times the violence happens 'off-stage' and is left to the reader's imagination. This is the case with the description of the empty bullet-cartridges that Uncle Micky collects, and the rape of the Aboriginal women. Both approaches form a stark contrast with the stories in white colonial novels where the 'plucky' white man massacres 'treacherous' blacks as a form of entertainment.[2]

One of the reasons that makes the epic in *Carpentaria* unusual is the intervention of the natural world in the battle between the Aboriginal inhabitants and the whites. It is Will, with Fishman's men, who light

---

1. Henry Reynolds offers this extract from the late 19th century Historian Edward Curr's work as a typical example: "In the first place the meeting of the Aboriginal tribes of Australia and the White pioneer, results as a rule in war, which lasts from six months to ten years, according to the nature of the country, the amount of settlement which takes place in a neighbourhood, and the proclivities of the individuals concerned. When several squatters settle in proximity, and the country they occupy is easy of access and without fastnesses to which the Blacks can retreat, the period of warfare is usually short and the bloodshed not excessive" (1981, 62).

2. The work of Henry Rider Haggard, who was one of the most commercially successful British colonial adventure novelists at the end of the 19th century, contains numerous examples of this sort: "Our people fought magnificently, hurling themselves upon the dark mass of Elmoran, hewing, thrusting, slaying and being slain. [...] I myself did not go into the mêlée but hovered outside like the swift 'back' in a football scrimmage, putting a bullet through a Masai wherever I got a chance" (*Allan Quatermain* (1887) London: Puffin, 1990, 80).

the initial fire that leads to the explosion of the mine, but the massive destruction happens only because they are helped by the land. Initially the land encourages the men, "the whole world cheered them" (390), but later the roles are reversed and it is the men who encourage the fire: "calling out with no shame, *Come on, come on*, willing the little flame not to fizz" (394). As it burns, the fire becomes a snake, "throwing long red tongues" (387), "roaring like a fiery serpent" (393), becoming "a monster cut loose from another world" (393), which can only be the world of the ancestors. The cyclone at the end of the novel, which completely washes away the town of Desperance, is a further illustration of how the land is a participant in the battle. The narrator states that the land is angry and wants to do something: "Everyone clearly saw what the spirits saw. The country looked dirty from mining, shipping, barges spilling ore and waste. Something had to run a rake across the lot" (385). It is quite clear that the final cyclone is not an event that happened by chance:

> The earth murmured, the underground serpent living in the underground river that was kilometres wide, responded with hostile growls. This was the old war of the ancestors making cyclones grow to use against one another. (453)

The white population fail to understand that the Aboriginal characters and the land are working together. The authorities start by broadcasting "a badly composed identikit picture of Will Phantom" (373) in an attempt to arrest the man they hold responsible. When this fails, they come up with a "scientific explanation" (398), blaming it all on natural causes and analysing in detail how "the fire at Gurfurritt mine initiated from a grass-fire" (398).

In 1941 the Russian literary theorist Mikhail Bakhtin wrote an influential essay entitled, "The Novel as a Literary Genre"[1] in which he attempted to define the characteristics of the novel by comparing it to other literary forms, in particular the epic. He concluded that the novel was superior to the epic because it allowed for greater flexibility and a greater engagement with the modern world. Bakhtin's ideas have given rise to many discussions and debates that are beyond the scope of this book. Wai Chee Dimock is one academic who takes issue with what she sees as Bakhtin's restrictive definition of the epic. Dimock returns to Aristotle's definition in *Poetics*, focussing on the idea that the epic is "spurred by cultural contact" (94). She notes that there are a

1. Also published under the title "Epic and Novel".

number of non-Greek words in the *Iliad* and suggests that by including these words the epic has become "a kind of linguistic sponge [...] super-responsive to its environment" (93). She argues that in epics written in areas where two cultures are in contact, the inclusion of non-standard forms of the dominant language, or even words from the non-dominant language become "a map, not only of space, but also of time [...] testimonies to a receding but still active past" (94). Dimock's definition of the epic seems particularly useful when thinking about *Carpentaria* as an epic since the novel was very clearly born out of contact between two cultures. It contains many examples not only of Australian-English but also Waanyi words, although as has already been noted, the past in the novel is not portrayed as "receding" but as intimately linked to the present in a cyclical repetition.

b. Tragedy

In contemporary society, "tragedy" has become a very over-used word that is employed to talk about any situation in which a living being (not even necessarily a human) dies in an unnatural way or is subject to extreme suffering. As a literary term tragedy, like the epic, has its origins in Ancient Greek literature where it referred to a serious play depicting the downfall of a central character. Aristotle's definition in *Poetics* is generally accepted as the first detailed description of what constitutes a tragedy both in terms of form and content. For Aristotle, the aim of tragedy was for the audience to experience catharsis – the play would arouse feelings of pity and terror in the people watching, as a consequence of which they would be purged of their emotions. Character was secondary to plot and, although the audience needed to be able to identify with the hero, the plot focussed primarily on matters of cosmic importance rather than on the individual. Much has been written since Aristotle about the literary characteristics of tragedies, with Bertolt Brecht famously declaring that it was an obsolete and bourgeois genre that had no place in the modern world. This is not the place for a detailed literary history of the term, but it is nevertheless important to briefly mention a few other definitions that can be helpful when thinking about whether or not *Carpentaria* should be considered a tragedy.

In his *Aesthetics* (1820-29), the German philosopher Hegel argued that the suffering of the tragic hero is a way of reconciling opposing moral claims. The tragic hero does not have a "fatal flaw" as Aristotle believed, but rather the hero's own ethical system comes into contact with another ethical system and the tragedy arises because no compromise is possible. For David Scott, the Hegelian vision of tragedy, with its focus on the limits of an individual and its demonstration of how well-intended actions often have unintended consequences, can become a "powerful challenge to the teleologies of history" (800) whose aim is not to offer "some final postcolonial truth" (806), but rather to explore conflict (both between individuals and between individual and community) and its sometimes catastrophic effects.

Wright has spoken many times of the suffering of Aboriginal people: "our people die young, too frequently, and many die badly" (Breaking, n.p.); their lives are a "living hell" (Politics, 14). There can be no doubt that in the everyday meaning of the word, the lives of many Aboriginal people *are* a tragedy. The story of Norm's youngest son Kevin is undoubtedly one of the saddest stories in the novel. He seems to offer the hope of a better future not only to his family, but also to the white inhabitants of the town and to his schoolteachers:

> None smarter than your Kevin, the white people used to say all the time about Kevin. [...] schoolteachers just about wore the road away, tramping down to the Phantom's place every other day just to make sure Kevin was alright. [...] He has to amount to something, the teachers wailed (101).

The white people's concerns for Kevin, however, turn out to be self-interested – they need him to succeed to prove that the policy of assimilation is working; talking to Norm about his son they are "biting their tongues, trying to make the family understand that Aboriginal people needed to succeed, and to succeed they needed to be educated" (101). Despite all his promise, Kevin is the unluckiest child in the family. Not only is he left permanently brain-damaged after an accident on his first day down the mine, but he is also the victim of a brutal racist attack that leaves him fighting for his life. Sad as it is, however, Kevin's life is not a tragedy for it has no cathartic effect on the reader.

The same is true of the deaths in custody of the three boys who are wrongly arrested for Gordie's murder. The reader is left shocked and appalled by what happens to both Kevin and these boys. This is a deliberate stylistic choice, for the aim of the novel is not to allow readers to purify their emotions by feeling pity for the boys. Instead it aims to force readers to open their eyes to Aboriginal suffering in the hope that it will galvanise them into taking action to change Australian society: "Que dire de toute cette souffrance? La réponse est une silhouette solitaire qui crie 'Non!' Puis une autre et une autre encore, jusqu'à ce que la nation entière se soulève" (Wright, *Croire en l'incroyable*, 38). Something has to change, because what future can there be for a country that kills its own children?

At first glance it seems that it might be possible to think of *Carpentaria* more as a Hegelian tragedy since the novel shows two ethical systems that are in contact with each other, and for whom compromise seems impossible because of the white inhabitants' reluctance to recognise even the most basic human rights of Aboriginal people. The question then arises, however, as to who the tragic hero might be. The only other important death in the novel is that of Elias Smith who is murdered by the mine workers, and his body left as bait for Will. Elias is certainly an in-between character, clearly not Aboriginal but not from Uptown either, and he is the victim of white intolerance. He is not, however, elevated to the status of a tragic hero because, like the boys, his story is not cathartic. Moreover, his death ultimately becomes a way of uniting Aboriginal and white culture. Elias's friendship with Norm was already a suggestion that a genuine friendship is possible between Aboriginal people and white people who have somehow managed to escape the prejudices of white Australian society, with Norm describing Elias as "his best fishing mate" (82) and "his one trusted friend" (243). Norm's decision to take Elias's body to the gropers shows that Elias's relationship to the sea is equivalent to the relationship Aboriginal people have with the land and the sea. This journey is one of the climatic moments of the novel and leads Norm to be reunited with his grandson, Bala.

Angel Day's story also has tragic elements as she too is a victim of the collision of two cultures. She builds her house from what white people throw away, but rather than feeling a sense of injustice about why they should have so much and she should have so little, she is in awe of the white people and their wealth. She is so intimidated by "official papers" that "she could never read them without her heart pounding" (20). She tries desperately to be like the people who live in Uptown, believing that owning a clock and a statue of the Virgin Mary will mean she "own[s] the luck of the white people" and that her family "would also be prosperous [...] like the white people" (22). The pathos that such a character might have created in the reader is, however, diminished in two ways. Firstly, she is not a helpless, passive victim, but is capable of defending herself should the need arise, throwing "a billycan full of boiling water" (41) towards Bruiser's voice when he is drunkenly telling Valance to rape her, for example. Secondly she is not somebody with whom the reader can easily identify. She "had no intuition about other people, none at all" (24). She gets into fights, abandons Norm and her children to go and live with Mozzie Fishman, accuses Kevin of having "destroyed his life for nothing" (430), and takes so little interest in him after his accident that she has "no idea why he was in hospital" (430).

Unlike Elias, Angel does not die but is picked up by a truck driver when she is trying to flee from Desperance, and becomes "lost on the long road to nowhere" (436). No one knows her exact whereabouts, only that she "lived unhappily in a devilish place. She would never see the bright starry nights of the Gulf country again" (436). Despite her very forthright personality, Angel is never the centre of anyone's life; like all the Pricklebush mob she lives on the outskirts of Uptown, and Norm abandons her for five years. Eventually she leaves Norm for Mozzie but still finds herself regularly alone when Mozzie is travelling the country. The narrator makes it very clear that she is of secondary importance in his life: "Mozzie Fishman, unable to leave his Dreaming road, never went after her. A spiritual man could not just go gallivanting around the world when he had his business to attend to" (436). And yet Mozzie still sees her spirit every day in the early morning light "fishing for snakes" (438). Hers is not a happy life, but her story is not turned into a tragedy. One way of understanding the character of Angel is as an attempt to show that not all victims are likeable and photogenic. White Australian policies harm all Aboriginal people; the drunks, the addicts and the physically violent are just as much victims as the babies and the young children.

Perhaps it is only white readers who think that the lives of Aboriginal people should be turned into tragedies. Nicholas Birns comments that there are "Western expectations that all Indigenous literature must be polemical protest novels [... and] every story of Indigenous identity [...] a tragedy" (Kindle). This assumption, that outsiders can tell people how to write, is relatively common in countries that are considered to have serious problems of social injustice. The South African novelist Nadine Gordimer spoke of the quite extraordinary expectations that Americans and Europeans had about her work:

> Those critics and readers who live safe from the realm of midnight arrests and solitary confinement [...] have their demands upon the writer from such places.

> [...] For them, his essential gesture as a social being is to take risks they do not know if they would. [...] When interviewed abroad there is often disappointment that you are there, and not in jail in your own country. And since you are not – why are you not? Aha ... does this mean that you have not written the book you should have written? (1989, 287)

The political situation in Australia is not as extreme as it was in apartheid South Africa, and writers do not risk prison for denouncing government policy, but nevertheless care should be taken to allow all writers their stylistic freedom.

c. Comedy

The term "comedy" also initially referred to a form of drama and was first defined by the Greek playwright Aristophanes.[1] Like tragedy, the exact meaning of the word comedy has changed over time, but it is generally used to refer to a play which is designed to amuse and entertain, and which has a happy ending. The fact that comedies are designed to amuse does not necessarily make them light-hearted. Very often comedies use humour as a way of criticising society and educating the reader, and this is very much the case for *Carpentaria*.

In novels humour can either be situational or stylistic. There is no slapstick farce in *Carpentaria* but comic effect is created by the gap between what is happening and the language used about it. One example of this can be found when Elias arrives in Desperance. Although clearly an old, amnesic, temporarily blind, unarmed man presents no threat whatsoever to the local inhabitants, they worry he may be a "violent maverick, or a murderer" (71). Their fears are so over-exaggerated that they become absurd. A similar effect is obtained when there is a deliberate mismatch between the register of the language and the event described; after the fire, "The whole mine, pride of the banana state, ended up looking like a big panorama of burnt chop suey" (395).

Images are used to create visually comic pictures in the reader's mind: Father Danny leaping out from under his car is described as having "the grace and noise of a wounded elephant" (183), an Aboriginal woman in a white dress looks like "the white cliffs of Dover" (24), while the little black flies go around in "fly squadrons" (25).

1. For a brief overview of the different types of comedy see the entry in *The Oxford Dictionary of Literary Terms*.

Using half of a cliché is another source of humour so that instead of being 'a fly on the wall' the journalists reporting on the mine explosion are "Unlike any fly" (397). Françoise Palleau-Papin analyses at length the way Wright plays with words to humorous effect, sometimes by mixing metaphors, "[Mozzie] fought like a rabid dog to maintain an octopus vision of himself, where all arms lead to great glory and success" (*Carpentaria*, 400), but also by changing words in a set expression, for example "stunned mullet", which she used literally in her earlier novel *Plains of Promise*, becomes "stuffed mullet" three times in *Carpentaria* (Palleau-Papin, 18).

Much of the humour around the Pricklebush mob is gently mocking. Midnight sees the three boys dead in the police cell but "Nobody heard what Midnight said, since nobody ever paid him any attention" (345); Mozzie comments on the way traditions have changed saying, "One time the spirit, he wasn't so greedy. He only used to go for fancy wagons and animals [...] but now he only eats cars" (140). The Aboriginal inhabitants in turn mock white ways of talking by adopting their vocabulary and turns of phrase:

> What a turnout. Gee whiz! We were in really serious stuff now. We were burning the white man's very important places and wasting all his money. We must have forgotten our heads. We were really stupid people to just plumb forget like – because the white man was a very important person who was very precious about money. (391)

What the white characters say is sometimes so outrageously racist that it provokes a wry laugh: "What does he look like? What do you mean? Don't they all look alike? I don't know" (379), while white political discourse is the subject of satire. Angel Day's home, built and furnished with what she finds in the rubbish dump, is held up as a successful example of the policy of assimilation:

> Those were modern days and Angel Day was a very rich woman. [...] She now possessed dozens of baked bean tins and pickle bottles full of nails, loose screws and bolts. She became a genius in the new ideas of blackfella advancement. [...] She became a prime example of government policies at work and to prove it, they came and took pictures of her with a Pentax camera for a report. (16)

The use of humour and satire can be seen as a way of inviting the reader to reflect on white behaviour rather than merely demonising it, and avoids turning the Aboriginal and the white characters into binary opposites. Anne Brewster argues that the combined effect of all of these elements is that the very concept of whiteness becomes "idiosyncratic and comic" (2010, 93), while for Estelle Castro-Koshy humour in the novel "assumes the same role as the explosion of the mine; it invites the reader to look for a humanisation beyond destructive clichéd expressions and unjust realities" (2018, 131).

Much of the humour in *Carpentaria* is black comedy.[1] Sometimes it becomes a way of coping with a reality that is otherwise too awful to contemplate; for example, when Kevin is described after the accident in the mine as "burnt and broken like barbecued spare ribs" (105). At other times it is used as a way to denounce white behaviour. A good example of this can be found in the names of the characters. In a reversal of colonial practice, the Aboriginal characters have both a first name and a surname (Normal Phantom, Joseph Midnight, Angel Day), while most of the white characters are referred to primarily by their surname, which is not a proper surname but an adjective describing their personality, often in an ironic way (Bruiser, Truthful, Danny Real). This is not a complete reversal of the white habit of naming Indigenous people with an abstract noun because the surnames Phantom, Midnight and Day still have what Nicolas Birns calls an "artificial quality" to them (Kindle). However, unlike the white characters, their names are not humorous. The name "Phantom" is thus symbolic of Norm's invisibility to the white population – or perhaps to all the characters in the novel since no one seems particularly troubled by the fact that he disappeared to sea for five years. It is the white characters' names, however, which cause a bitter laugh and can be qualified as grotesque.

The grotesque as a literary term is difficult to define precisely but it is usually used to refer to "anything that disrupts whatever is considered to be the norm at a particular place and time" although "the precise points at which the boundary into the grotesque has been crossed are always highly subjective" (Graulund, n.p.). The grotesque evokes ambivalence in spectators since it inspires both horror and laughter. Grotesque is the word that Wright chose herself to describe the lives of Aboriginal people in *Croire en l'incroyable*:

> Je peux regarder autour de moi n'importe quand, aller n'importe où, je ne vois que des Aborigènes qui meurent sans aucune raison, si ce n'est que ce sont des Aborigènes qui ont vécu toute leur vie dans une pauvreté si étrange, si absurde

1. *The Oxford Dictionary of Literary Terms* defines black comedy as a literary work "in which disturbing or sinister subjects like death, disease, or warfare are treated with bitter amusement, usually in a manner calculated to offend and shock."

> qu'elle en paraît grotesque à côté de l'insouciance et la sécurité de la société australienne dominante. Grotesque est le mot approprié, car cette réalité, les Aborigènes la vivent à deux pas de ceux-là mêmes qui ont volé leur terre ou hérité de cette terre volée. (20)

Most of the white characters in *Carpentaria* can be considered as grotesque. Bruiser, the mayor of Desperance, is "the epitome of the self-made man" (33) and embodies all the negative stereotypes of corrupt white power. He is a "prosperous cattle man" (33),"a big beefy, six-two, no-fuss man who liked to call chalk chalk and night night" (32). For "ten straight years" he has been voted "citizen of the year" (33) but there are rumours that the voting box "was rigged" (33), he made a lot of money on the stock market "after he picked up a hint one night on the radio" (33) and he drives around the "Aboriginal camps on pension day, selling the necessities of life for a profit of three to four hundred per cent after costs" (33). It is common knowledge that he has raped Aboriginal women and his motto is "If you can't use it, eat it or fuck it, then it's no bloody use to you" (34). The name "Bruiser" is an understatement for the violence of the character, but the accumulation of clichés used to describe him has, nonetheless, a comic element to it.

The ironically named Truthful, a "thug copper from The Valley in Brisbane" (70), becomes the town's new policeman following the death of Jay Smith who had been there for sixty-one years. Supposedly in Desperance "nobody had use for a policeman anymore" (69). However, this is due not to a lack of crime, but to the white inhabitants having their own "ways and means to deal with pub brawls, rape, robbery, assaults, family violence and fraud" (70). Although Truthful initially joins Bruiser in beating up the three young boys they arrest, puts pressure on Girlie to sleep with him, and is rumoured to have a possibly paedophilic interest in boys (334), his violence is, on the whole, more insidious than Bruiser's, and he is often guilty of collusion rather than outright violence. The black comedy around Truthful comes from the fact that he is the opposite of the white colonial hero. He grows roses in the police station gardens and Bruiser uses a homosexual insult after the deaths in custody, accusing him of being "off with the pixies" (346). In many ways his character is reminiscent of Gregory Rose in Olive Schreiner's novel *The Story of an African Farm* (1883).[1] Gregory Rose is the antithesis of the virile white colonist. He

1. *The Story of an African Farm* is generally recognised as the first novel written by someone born in a British colony to be published to critical acclaim and widely read in both Great Britain and the colonies.

uses pink, writing paper and, in an extraordinary scene for a nineteenth century novel, shaves off his beard and dresses as a woman in order to be able to nurse the dying woman he loves. The fact that Bruiser's actions are also responsible for Truthful's death seems to suggest that the lives of white people too are constrained by the current situation in Australia; their choice boils down to 'kill or be killed.'

d. The Carnivalesque

The grotesque is often considered to be part of another subgenre, the carnivalesque. Carnivals are a Western Christian tradition that originated in the Middle Ages. They took place in the runup to Lent and were a time of festivity before fasting during which people were allowed some freedom from the rules of the Catholic Church. As a literary term, "carnivalesque" was first defined by Mikhail Bakhtin in his study of Rabelais.[1] According to Bakhtin, during carnival time the normal rules of a hierarchical society are put aside. Rather than being a spectacle with performers and an audience, people of different classes mix freely with the lower classes being permitted an unusual freedom and culminating in the mock crowning, and then de-crowning, of a carnival king. Inhibitions and identities are abandoned allowing new possibilities to emerge. Laughter is an important element of the carnivalesque as it is a way of defusing the fear of the dominant, and often violent, authority. Lachmann *et al.* suggest that Bakhtin's theoretical ideas were influenced by his experience of living through the turmoil of the Russian Revolution with "the swirling up of meaning that it brought forth, the experience of the plurality of worlds, of the inter-crossing of cultures and languages, of texts, and genres" (117). They go on to suggest that the carnivalesque is therefore particularly suited to the writing by a minority group that emerges in situations when cultures collide. Bridget Haylock follows a similar line of thought and suggests that:

> One of the reasons that Wright employs this technique is that for many Indigenous people, daily life is an awful experience of traumatic repetition, the carnivalesque, in offering 'the temporary liberation from the prevailing truth of the established order,' provides a survival strategy. (95)

---

1. This was initially submitted as a dissertation in 1946 and published in book form in Russian in 1965. It was first translated into English in 1968 and is currently available in English in the following edition: Mikhail Bakhtin, *Rabelais and His World*, trans. Helene Iswolsky, Bloomington, Indiana University Press, 2009.

The Pricklebush mob are, without a doubt, a marginalised group in Desperance who are regularly excluded from community decisions about how the town is run; those who take up the offer to attend a council meeting "listened, stunned again by how they had been rendered invisible" (35). The mixture of languages, registers and genres used in *Carpentaria* also appears to be characteristic of the carnivalesque. It is therefore worth considering to what extent reading the novel as an example of the carnivalesque can add to our understanding of it.

For Diane Molloy, one of the interesting points about the carnivalesque is that it is associated with change and renewal. As she notes, change runs as a leitmotif throughout the novel: the land itself changes constantly alternating between being flooded and bone-dry, with regular cyclones which completely reshape the landscape and the river beds, while the arrival of the white people, with their animals and plants, modified both the vegetation and the lives of the Aboriginal inhabitants. She goes on to suggest that the Pricklebush mob live "permanently in carnival time" (3). Not only is the Aboriginal sense of time different from the Western concept of time,[1] but their position on the edges of Uptown means they are outside the normal rules of white society. She argues that the use of what she terms elements of the "supernatural" (3) – the Dreaming – are also characteristic of the carnivalesque, although this seems a reductive way of thinking about Aboriginal beliefs.

More interesting is her idea that the novel is written in such a way as to "confuse the "boundaries between memory, history, imagination and reality" (4). *Carpentaria* thus challenges multiple forms of white writing: standard English, traditional history books, realist novels, and the literary representation of Aboriginal people as the exotic Other (4-5). It is laughter that provides the levelling force in the novel as both the inhabitants of Uptown and the Pricklebush mob are mocked at various times. As Molloy says:

> Laughter releases social and political tensions and makes way for the little stories in between the lines of the larger, national narrative to help understand history from the Aboriginal people's point of view. (5)

This leads her to conclude that "Wright's use of the carnivalesque demonstrates that the dominant culture is vulnerable to change and renewal" (7).

---

1. See Part one, 2. III.

The limitation of the carnivalesque, however, is that the freedom from normal rules is only temporary. *Carpentaria* suggests that life could be different for the Aboriginal inhabitants in the future but it is not able to describe how. The ending of the novel with Norm and his grandson reclaiming the land where Desperance once was, suggests that the ancestral songlines and Dreaming stories will persist long after the whites have disappeared. The fact that Norm is with his grandson, and not his son, is perhaps an allusion to the hope that the problems Aboriginal people face will disappear with Will's generation, leaving the younger generation to live a better life.

Like the preceding section on "Genre and Literary Influences", this section is not an exhaustive discussion of subgenres in *Carpentaria*. It is also possible to analyse the novel in the light of more modern forms such as the rural apocalypse genre with the destruction of Desperance at the end of the novel[1] or as a political thriller when reading the description of the sabotage of the Gurfurritt mine.[2]

---

1. See Birns' discussion of the American rural Apocalypse genre (Kindle). A parallel can also be drawn with the apocalyptic fire at the end of the Australian writer Janette Turner Hospital's novel, *Oyster* (1996).
2. See Brewster, 2010, 91.

3

POLYPHONIE

Laura Singeot

I | LES DIFFÉRENTES LANGUES

À la lecture, *Carpentaria* se distingue d'autres romans par la variété des langues et des registres qu'il mobilise. Il se distingue en particulier par l'utilisation régulière du waanyi, langue de la nation aborigène d'Alexis Wright au sud du golfe de Carpentarie (voir Part three, 2, « Some notes on Australian languages and Waanyi in particular » de Mary Laughren). Toujours en italiques, ces mots ou phrases ponctuent le récit qui n'en propose pas toujours la traduction immédiate ou littérale. Le lecteur doit la plupart du temps en inférer le sens par ce qui suit. Prenant l'exemple de Joseph Midnight qui transmet son savoir à Will dans un mélange d'anglais aborigène[1] et de waanyi, Estelle Castro-Koshy explique ce parti pris :

> Le lecteur doit alors essayer de deviner le sens des mots waanyi, qui s'apparentent à des « effets de réel », ces « notations » par lesquelles le « réel concret devient la justification suffisante du dire » (Barthes, 185). L'accumulation de termes non traduits confronte le lecteur à son ignorance, et lui rappelle que l'anglais n'est pas la langue originelle du pays. (Castro, online)

Cette juxtaposition, à la fois politique et pédagogique, vise à transcrire la réalité polyglossique[2] australienne. Pour les lecteurs internationaux peu familiers du vocabulaire australien, d'autres mots en anglais

1. En voici quelques exemples : « You mob [...] talk all the time », « we got to fight each other », « you wrong at this » (364).
2. Dans *The Dialogic Imagination*, la polyglossie est définie comme : « The simultaneous presence of two or more national languages interacting within a single cultural system » (Bakhtin, 2008, 431).

australiens, tels «doona» (81, 375), «eskies» (373) ou encore «billy» (145), peuvent s'avérer ardus à comprendre. Enfin, le roman comprend aussi les noms latins d'espèces de la faune et de la flore : «*Promicrops Lanceolatus*» (mérou géant, 238), «*Pteropus scapulatus*» (chauve-souris, 445) «cycad palms – *Cycas angulata*» (367) entre autres. Ces termes se réfèrent au discours scientifique occidental et transfèrent au sein-même du récit ce contre lequel il met en garde, c'est-à-dire «becoming *scientify*» (96), l'italique soulignant ici, comme souvent dans le roman, une accentuation ironique. Mozzie Fishman se moque ainsi de la science occidentale, qui se distingue de la transmission intergénérationnelle du savoir autochtone de par la facilité de son acquisition : «All that scientify stuff is easy. You could learn it in a day. [...] The radio has been my education» (238). Le changement de typographie, souligné par l'absence d'italiques dans les paroles de Mozzie lorsqu'il utilise le terme «scientify», en souligne finalement sa trivialité.

Le récit reflète par son usage des différentes langues une relation complexe à l'anglais, langue du colonisateur. Le rapport ambivalent à l'anglais se perçoit à maintes reprises au cœur de la narration et à travers différents personnages. Par exemple, les «elders» qui tentent de comprendre la science («becoming *scientify*», 96) se sentent épiés par les satellites utilisés par les entreprises minières installées partout dans le monde, qui traduisent très certainement leur anglais aborigène en «bon anglais» afin de les comprendre :

> It was some kind of gadget that can take away all your myall words, transcribe what you say in better language so people can understand what you are talking about. And then the beam flies on orbiting through space, straight to the boardrooms of rich multinational mining people in Holland, Germany, the USA, even 'Mother' England, or who knows where, to listen to you, before you have even had a chance to end your sentence. *So, watch what you are saying. That's why,* they said, *a man had to stay quiet like a mouse while he snuck around getting his cheese in the big people's house.* (96)

Plus tard, pourtant, l'anglais semble si facile à assimiler que même les cacatoès de Desperance peuvent en inonder d'injures miraculeuses les rues :

> [...] large flock of resident cockatoos, thousands of them, flying over the town, scream[ed] in a spectacular, uncoordinated chanting, *What are you doing youse bastards?* It was thought to be a miracle of the English language, that simple birds had learnt to talk English too, just like everyone else. (100)

L'ironie mordante de ce passage ne passe pas inaperçue, puisque si «it was thought to be a miracle» traduit peut-être au départ ce qui est communément pensé par « Uptown », c'est-à-dire une vision plutôt positive de l'anglais comme langue universelle, l'expression clôturant la phrase, « just like everyone else », dénonce quant à elle l'anglais comme langue coloniale : l'anglais n'est pas la langue originelle du pays. De plus, loin de représenter effectivement l'anglais de tout le monde, l'expression « youse bastards » peut aussi être associée au stéréotype du « bogan »[1]. Cette expression n'est qu'un autre trait humoristique visant à apostropher et à insulter collectivement « Uptown », comme le prouve l'utilisation du « youse », terme qui n'est pas grammaticalement correct mais qui a pourtant été entendu assez régulièrement par les cacatoès pour qu'ils puissent le répéter.

Selon les définitions de Mikhail Bakhtin, cette polyglossie se double d'une hétéroglossie, propre au genre du roman, décrite comme :

> The base condition governing the operation of meaning in any utterance. It is that which insures the primacy of context over text. At any given time, in any given place, there will be a set of conditions—social, historical, meteorological, physiological—that will insure that a word uttered in that place and at that time will have a meaning different than it would have under any other conditions; all utterances are heteroglot in that they are functions of a matrix of forces practically impossible to recoup, and therefore impossible to resolve. (Bakhtin, 2008, 428)

Dans un roman, la langue va toujours plus loin que les mots et ne se réduit pas à eux seuls, dans la mesure où elle prend racine dans le contexte de la narration. Aussi, les différentes langues de *Carpentaria* doivent être considérées dans leur relation et leurs frictions ; le roman se caractérisant par son dialogisme, elles doivent être étudiées, lues et comprises les unes par rapport aux autres :

> [...] languages are dialogically implicated *in* each other and begin to exist *for* each other (similar to exchanges in a dialogue). It is precisely thanks to the novel that languages are able to illuminate each other mutually; literary language becomes a dialogue of languages that both know about and understand each other. (Bakhtin, 2008, 400)

Ces langues font donc partie d'un tout et ne peuvent s'en détacher. Les différentes voix qui cohabitent dans le récit, ou qui « s'inter-animent les unes les autres »[2], montrent également que celui-ci se fait dialogue.

1. À l'origine, les « bogans » étaient ces Australiens qui vivaient dans les banlieues défavorisées des grandes villes et faisaient partie de la classe ouvrière. Ce terme hautement dépréciatif est souvent utilisé pour souligner un manque de culture flagrant et une ignorance sans limite. De nos jours, certains se réapproprient ce terme, qui a pu perdre de son caractère insultant.

2. Bakhtin utilise les expressions « interanimated each other » ou « mutually animating each other » (Bakhtin, 2008, 65).

II | POINTS DE VUE ET POLYPHONIE

Dans «On Writing *Carpentaria*», Wright rapporte que sa volonté était la suivante : «to write the novel as though it was a very long melody of different forms of music, somehow mixed with the *voices of the Gulf*» (Writing, Kindle, je souligne). Cette affirmation offre deux indications importantes concernant le traitement spécifique de la voix dans le roman : cette voix se veut plurielle et liée à «Gulf Country». Wright poursuit cette analogie avec ces voix du pays du golfe, qui forment le cœur – si ce n'est le chœur – du roman : «the story [...] does not only come from colonisation or assimilation, [...] but is sung [...] from those of our ancestors who wrote our stories on the walls of caves and on the surface of weathered rock» (Writing, Kindle). Dès les premiers mots, cette voix collective apparaît, pour finalement ne plus jamais disparaître : ce sont ces voix qui tissent les fils de cette histoire, que Wright définit comme «a spinning multi-stranded helix of stories» (Writing, Kindle).

Dans la définition qu'il donne de la voix, Mikhail Bakhtin évoque la subjectivité derrière chaque voix : «This is the speaking personality, the speaking consciousness. A voice always has a will or desire behind it, its own timbre and overtones» (Bakhtin, 2008, 434). Cette voix est liée à un processus d'identification importante, puisque «cette action verbale est considérée dans ses rapports au sujet, ce sujet n'étant pas ici seulement celui qui accomplit ou subit l'action, mais aussi celui (le même ou un autre) qui la rapporte, et éventuellement tous ceux qui participent, fût-ce passivement, à cette activité narrative», selon la définition qu'en donne Gérard Genette dans *Figures III* (Genette, 226). Le terme de voix englobe à la fois la voix narrative du narrateur mais aussi l'ensemble des voix «narrées» tout au long de la narration : le roman offre une polyphonie d'autant plus complexe dans *Carpentaria* que les voix des différentes communautés ne cessent de se faire entendre, et ce très distinctement. À lui seul, ce roman illustre parfaitement ce que Bakhtin disait des œuvres de Dostoievsky, perçues comme «a plurality of independent and unmerged voices and consciousnesses, a genuine polyphony of fully valid voices» (Bakhtin, 1984, 6).

Carpentaria se caractérise par cette polyphonie de voix, même si elles restent très distinctes. Il ne s'agit pas seulement de voix autochtones puisque le contrepoint des voix de «Pricklebush mob» ou de celle des anciens est celle de «Uptown», que l'on entend fréquemment tout au long du récit. Ces instances de voix collectives (ou «chorus of voices», 288) s'inscrivent dans la lignée des mots sur lesquels s'ouvre le roman, «A NATION CHANTS», et en déclinent effectivement le chant au fil des pages. En sus de ce qui a été dit précédemment concernant les changements de langues, la typographie – plus particulièrement les italiques – fournit généralement une aide précieuse pour suivre ces changements incessants de voix. L'un des exemples les plus frappants de l'enchevêtrement polyphonique apparaît lorsque, après avoir proposé le changement de nom de la rivière, les réactions de la communauté autochtone et de Norm sont décrites :

> Traditional people gathered up for the event mumbled, *Ngabarn, Ngabarn, Mandagi*, and so did Normal in a very loud and sour-sounding voice over the loudspeaker in his extremely short thankyou address, although those who knew a fruit salad full of abuse in the local languages knew he was not saying *Thank you! Thank You!* and belly-laughed themselves silly because the river only had one name from the beginning of time. It was called *Wangala.* (9)

L'usage des italiques, primordial ici, met en exergue la parole qui se fait entendre («mumbled», «say»), la langue aborigène («*Ngabarn, Ngabarn, Mandagi*»), mais aussi l'ironie latente lorsque le discours de Norm est mal interprété par la population blanche présente, qui ne comprend pas un mot de ce qui se dit. Au lieu des remerciements de rigueur, Norm profère des insultes[1] («a fruit salad full of abuse in the local languages»), et ce certainement sous les applaudissements de la population blanche et des autorités présentes[2]. Ces changements de voix, entre celle des «traditional people» et celle de Norm, et l'utilisation régulière d'italiques, soulignent tout autant la polyphonie du roman que l'ironie qui le constelle, tandis que le rire est littéralement retranscrit, comme pour donner une dernière indication du ridicule de la situation au lecteur («belly-laughed themselves silly»).

1. On peut également souligner ici les différents registres de langue, notamment le recours aux injures, qui en viennent parfois à définir certains personnages comme le Père Danny et les «joyaux irlandais» qu'il profère à l'encontre des hommes de la mine : «the words he uttered through a mouthful of dirt were Irish jewels best left lying on the little known roads of the outback» (182).

2. Pour plus de détails concernant la parodie des cérémonies très répandues lors de la période coloniale où les autorités nommaient ainsi les lieux, sans se préoccuper des noms locaux, voir Arnaud Barras, «Mapping Carpentaria: Voices, Stories and Journeys of the Gulf Country».

L'auteure défie ainsi les schémas narratifs et discursifs occidentaux, qu'elle dénonce aussi en ayant recours à l'humour et à l'ironie.

Dans le roman, le narrateur est principalement hétérodiégétique[1] selon la distinction de Gérard Genette, puisqu'il « est absent de l'histoire qu'il raconte » (Genette, 252). Le récit repose notamment sur une diversification des discours ou des focalisations par exemple. Un repérage exhaustif serait bien sûr impossible à faire ; cependant, ces variations peuvent apparaître dans des passages très condensés, faisant à peine quelques lignes et témoignant bien de « l'énergie » que l'auteure voulait transmettre dans son roman, « the energy of Gulf Country » (Writing, Kindle). Les épisodes où Norm se retrouve seul sur son bateau en compagnie d'Elias, avant de célébrer sa cérémonie funéraire en mer, offrent tout un panel de ces mouvements narratifs, désignés par les chiffres entre crochets :

> Norm carefully watched [1] the green form spiralling around the boat, once, twice, each time as if it wanted to land and attach itself to him. With his arms flailing aimlessly at the plastic thing in the night, he told her straight: 'Don't you come here.' [2] Oh! Yes! What a thing. [3] He was convinced [1] this was a sorceress of a wife. [...] It was the change coming and he told Elias, in a low steady voice to get ready. [4] (236)

Ce passage montre bien toute la richesse des discours utilisés alors que la focalisation est interne, puisque le lecteur suit le point de vue de Norm [1]. En effet, les guillemets signalent une instance de dialogue et donc un discours direct [2]. Ensuite, le discours passe à l'indirect libre [3] puisque les guillemets ont disparu mais des marqueurs de dialogue sont toujours présents, cette fois-ci intégrés à la narration, comme les interjections et les points d'exclamation. Enfin, ce passage se clôt sur du discours indirect [4], introduit par le verbe « to tell ».

Ces changements narratifs et vocaux donnent un rythme particulier à la narration de *Carpentaria*, et résultent de l'intention d'Alexis Wright de transcrire ces voix au plus près de la réalité des vieux conteurs de son pays : « I chose to try to recreate the voices and tone of the old storytellers of the Gulf » (Writing, Kindle). En effet, le tour de force de ce roman, selon Anne Brewster, réside dans ce changement de paradigmes narratifs, lié très fortement à ce traitement spécifique de la voix : « The narrative point of view positions [the Indigenous

---

1. Pour plus de détails sur la narratologie, notamment concernant les narrateurs intra et extra-diégétiques dans *Carpentaria*, voir Rodoreda, 7-9.

characters] as central to this cosmology and renders indigeneity the default position for humankind» (Brewster, 2010, 87). *Carpentaria* raconte l'histoire, non pas de la nation, puisque celle-ci est rejetée dès les premiers mots du roman («A NATION CHANTS, *BUT WE KNOW YOUR STORY ALREADY*», 1, emphase d'origine), mais d'un ensemble plus grand et plus signifiant encore selon Jeanine Leane : «The nation becomes a part of a bigger story – that of Country» (Leane, 2018, 222). Alexis Wright va encore plus loin et revendique une sorte de réciprocité narrative selon laquelle le pays, dans le sens de «Country», raconte à la fois son histoire et l'écoute tout autant : «I wanted the reader to believe in the energy of the Gulf country, to stay with a story as a welcomed stranger as if the land was telling a story about itself as much as the narrator is telling stories to the land» (Writing, Kindle). Ce lien à la terre et aux ancêtres l'a donc guidée jusque dans la manière d'écrire *Carpentaria*, qu'elle revendique également comme une adresse aux esprits ancestraux : «I thought it was a book trying to tell a story to the ancestors. How do you speak to the ancestors?» (Brasch, online).

III | L'IRONIE COMME CONTRE-DISCOURS

Dans son interview avec Jean-François Vernay, Wright parlait ainsi de la place de l'humour dans la communauté autochtone, ainsi que dans ses romans :

> There's a lot of humor in Aboriginal society. It relieves a lot of energy and strain. It's a good weapon to have, otherwise you just despair and melt away, waste away. You have to see the world as a funny place, a wonderful world and that's good. We deal with hard issues but we have the ability to laugh it off, to laugh at ourselves, but we do not forget who we are and what is happening around us. Humor is very strong in *Plains of Promise*, and there's lots of humor in *Carpentaria*. (Vernay, 2004, 121)

Dans *Carpentaria*, l'ironie participe à cet humour, très présent. Tous deux doivent être compris comme des «armes» («weapon») et font partie intégrante de la vie et de l'expérience quotidiennes autochtones, en aidant à surmonter ou dédramatiser les problèmes. Sans pour autant effacer ces difficultés, l'humour permet de les tenir à distance, mais dans le récit en tout cas, l'utilisation de l'ironie sert principalement à les exposer aux yeux du lecteur et à démontrer une certaine forme de résistance face aux discours dominants. Cette utilisation de l'ironie insère différentes strates de sens dans le texte, le rendant à la fois difficile et ludique à appréhender puisque le récit navigue entre différents réseaux de sens. En tant que double discours, l'ironie repose sur la contradiction entre ce qui est dit et ce qui est pensé, prenant souvent la forme de commentaires à visée moqueuse et humoristique. Ce caractère double impose l'ironie comme contre-discours dans *Carpentaria* dans la mesure où elle questionne et dénonce les discours dominants, avec lesquels elle prône une prise de distance.

De ce fait, l'ironie sert à dénigrer principalement les figures d'autorité : des allusions ponctuelles mais régulières parsèment ainsi le roman. Une ironie mordante se perçoit par exemple dans l'évocation des gens des beaux quartiers («big, righteous Uptown», 307) ou encore dans l'éloge des qualités de déduction d'un détective, dont le seul exploit est de déceler la ressemblance, même infime, des membres de la famille Phantom, alors qu'ils sont tous en rang d'oignon devant le bâtiment de la police :

> There was no strong family resemblance running through them, anyone could see that, but the senior detective saw smidgens of familiarity, and *must be credited for his exceptional detective skills.* (355, je souligne)

L'utilisation de l'ironie s'avère critique et politique, surtout lorsqu'elle s'attaque principalement à la soi-disant volonté de «réconciliation» affichée par le gouvernement australien, et envahit les descriptions qui incarnent le plus les représentants d'un pouvoir répressif, comme le gendarme Truthful ou bien le gouvernement, «an infamous State government» (58), qui échoue à changer le nom de la ville en Masterton. Cet échec se voit d'abord illustré par l'incapacité flagrante des agents envoyés pour effectuer ce changement, «those government workers who were full of nonchalance, sat around and did nothing until it was time to go away again» (58), mais aussi par le refus catégorique des Desperanians, qui détruisent leur travail et enlèvent tous les panneaux de signalisation, «to make sure no one would mistake Desperance for the name of some past his use-by-date Southern politician who wanted to plant his ego in the minds of the future generations» (58). Ce genre de politique est perçue comme inutile mais aussi dépassée, assujettie au bon vouloir des politiciens qui espèrent en tirer profit, et elle n'entraîne qu'une seule et même réaction des habitants de Uptown : «a two fingers V shaped in the air – *Go and get stuffed*» (58).

Lorsque l'ironie n'est pas langagière, elle se distingue dans les événements eux-mêmes, dans certains «coups du destin». Ainsi, ce sont les déchets des hommes blancs qui mettent le feu à la mine, comme un juste retour des choses – ou de boomerang. L'incendie est le fruit de cette mondialisation tant recherchée par la compagnie internationale minière Gurfurritt puisqu'il prend peut-être à partir d'un carton de Pizza Hut et fait tout brûler comme du Chop Suey, mets américano-chinois (395). De même, lorsque les entrepôts prennent feu et que Chuck et Cookie poursuivent Will et ses sauveurs, la nature semble aider les fugitifs aborigènes, qui s'abritent derrière les rochers, symboles d'une nature protectrice[1], tandis que Chuck se tue en trébuchant et en se heurtant la tête contre l'un d'eux :

> Fate and precious moments are tied up together, and as the saying goes, *What goes around comes around*: the yellow-haired man tripped. Instantly, his head was split open at the temple by a rock that had, up to that moment, lain on the ground, embedded in soil that was thousands of seasons old, untouched by humankind since the ancestor had placed it in this spot, as if it had planned to do this incredible thing. (389)

L'ironie trouve sa traduction littérale dans la locution adverbiale « *What goes around comes around*», et devient le synonyme d'une juste rétribution, du «destin» même : la nature s'est justement retournée contre les figures qui participent à l'exploitation des populations et des ressources autochtones.

L'ironie devient un acte de résistance transposé dans le langage mais reflétant une prise de position réelle par les écrivains, selon Jana Ščigulinská :

> Critical voices from the Aboriginal community of writers, having reacted to all the wrongs done to Aboriginals, very slowly found another way of expressing feelings of injustice. Instead of attributing ineffective direct blame, the writers started to use more creative methods of exposing and reflecting the behaviour of the white population with roots in the colonial past by depicting attitudes based on relationships with Aboriginals and other minorities. Humour and irony have become among the most effective means of resistance against the remnants of colonialism which had caused such harmful consequences seriously influencing, even today, relationships between whites and Aboriginals but also relationships within Aboriginal communities themselves. (Ščigulinská, 174)

L'utilisation de l'ironie souligne un déplacement dans le langage, une mise à distance du discours dominant ou hégémonique, ainsi que de

1. « [T]hey were thrown down for shelter behind the boulders, in the fold of the ancestral spirit who governed the land. » (391)

ses représentants, comme par exemple Graham Spilling, le patron de la mine. Lors de l'incendie, le chaos règne et les voix semblent également se confondre, notamment celles des hommes de Mozzie dont l'enchevêtrement au sein de la narration en vient à mimer le discours colonial :

> What a turnout. Gee whiz! We were in really serious stuff now. We were burning the white man's very important places and wasting all his money. We must have forgotten our heads. We were really stupid people to just plumb forget like – because the white man was a very important person who was very precious about money. Well! He was the boss. We are not boss. He says he likes to be boss. He says he's got all the money. Well! We haven't got the money neither. And now, all it took was a simple flick. (291)

Ce mimétisme vise à ridiculiser le discours australien blanc et ses représentations des populations autochtones, qui deviennent ici internalisés dans la narration : des expressions comme «the white man's very important places», «we were really stupid people» font penser par exemple à l'infantilisation de ces populations qui perdure depuis la période coloniale. De plus, l'utilisation de répétitions («very important», «very precious») et de structures en miroir («be boss», «have got all the money») fait ressentir la vision paternaliste et condescendante caractérisant cette retranscription du discours de l'homme blanc, qui se transforme en modèle ou en archétype à la fin du passage :

> Straight out we should have been asking ourselves – Why are you not hanging your head in shame to the white man? We were supposed to say, Oh! No! You can't do things like that to the, umm, beg your pardon, please and thankyou, to the arrr, em, WHITE MAN. (391)

La mise à distance ici se perçoit dans la narration qui grommelle, toussote, se reprend pour finalement éructer en majuscules : «WHITE MAN». Le langage, notamment à travers les phrases toutes faites «beg your pardon, please and thankyou» (*sic*), dénonce à la fois la domination coloniale et l'internalisation de la hiérarchie sociale au sein du discours et de la société autochtone. Les onomatopées, tels des sons parasites, «umm, [...] arrr, em», interrompent et entrecoupent la phrase, acte de résistance linguistique s'il en est. La parole se refuse à reconnaître cette hiérarchie héritée des temps coloniaux et fait transparaître cette réticence, cette résistance, par son refus d'une expression sans accroc.

Ces instances ironiques n'épargnent pas la politique australienne, qui tente de contrôler chaque aspect de la vie des communautés autochtones, au contraire :

> Living in harmony in fringe camps was a policy designed by the invader's governments, and implemented, wherever shacks like Angel Day's swampside residences first began to be called a community. (26)

L'expression «living in harmony in fringe camps» prouve que parfois l'ironie frise l'euphémisme et vise à dénoncer la langue de bois des politiciens : loin d'être une décision politique altruiste favorisant la vie en harmonie avec la population autochtone, il s'agit en réalité de leur voler leur terre et de les reléguer là où ils ne dérangeront pas la nation australienne blanche, comme le fait comprendre l'utilisation des termes «invader's governments». Si dans l'extrait ci-dessus la ségrégation qui se dit «volontaire» est évoquée, d'autres exemples parsèment le récit et font souvent écho à des politiques plus sanguinaires, comme l'entrée du registre municipal statuant «Camels removed» (6), qui ne va pas sans rappeler les entrées de journaux à l'époque coloniale titrant par exemple «Natives dispersed» (c'est-à-dire, le plus souvent, «massacrés»), ou encore lorsqu'apparaît l'expression «Harmless coercing of the natives», dont le pendant colonial était également plus sanguinolent. De manière générale, le récit se moque des gens des beaux quartiers et de ce qui est appelé le «savoir-faire australien» : «Invisible things in nature made no sense to Uptown because of their savoir faire in being Australians» (75). L'ironie souligne souvent l'opposition entre une perception du monde qui se veut hégémonique et la vision autochtone qui, elle, s'attache aux choses invisibles de la nature, et dont la sensibilité et la délicatesse contrastent fortement avec ce «savoir-faire» aveugle et peu compréhensif, mais dont le devoir est de «soutenir la bonne société dans la nation tout entière» (trad. Furlan, 14), «maintaining the decent society of the nation as a whole» (4). L'ironie et son double sens participent également au dialogisme du texte (théorisé par Bakhtin) et à son ouverture, puisqu'ils tendent vers autre chose que ce qui apparaît effectivement sur la page, au-delà de la signification littérale du texte : ils insèrent par le biais de ce pli du langage un double sens, une autre vision, qui à son tour devient un outil avec lequel critiquer, ridiculiser et résister.

PART THREE

GOING FURTHER/ PERSPECTIVES

1

THE CONTEMPORARY RELEVANCE OF ABORIGINAL SPIRITUALITY AND THE CREATIVE POSSIBILITIES IN RELATEDNESS

Victoria Grieve-Williams

We are really sorry for you people. We cry for you because you haven't got meaning of culture in this country. We have a gift we want to give you. We keep getting blocked from giving you that gift. We get blocked by politics and politicians. We get blocked by media, by process of law. All we want to do is come out from under all of this and give you this gift. And it's the gift of pattern thinking. It's the culture which is the blood of this country, of Aboriginal groups, of the ecology, of the land itself.

– David Mowaljarlai, senior Lawman of the Ngarinyin people of the west Kimberley, addressing a gathering of white people in his country (Mowaljarlai 1995)

Aboriginal spirituality or philosophy is not generally understood well but many westerners who begin to understand Aboriginal lifeways become intrigued. The truth is, Aboriginal philosophy is extremely foreign to the western materialist values that predominate in the world today. It is also complex, so at first glance may not seem to make sense at all. David Mowaljarli echoed the sentiments of Aboriginal cultural leaders Australia-wide when he expressed a deep desire to be able to share this spirituality with westerners. The aim is to have them live well in the country known as Australia. What is becoming clear over time is that Aboriginal philosophy and cultural values can teach the people of the world a great deal about how to live well in a future that looms as very short on material comforts.

David Mowaljarlai speaks of the importance of "pattern thinking" and he drew a map of Australia that was connected by criss-crossed lines illustrating the connections and the relatedness of all things. This is the core of Aboriginal philosophy and it demands of human beings that we support and sustain this relatedness. The reward for this is a sense of wellbeing. A state of being in concert with all that is around you – of having fulfilled your responsibilities and enjoying certain rights – of being in balance, of being "level" as expressed in Aboriginal English.

Indigenous Australian spirituality has been described as embodying a reverence for life as it is – it does not promise a life after death, salvation, nirvana or similar. Thus life is as it is, a mixture of good and bad, of suffering and joy, and it is celebrated as sacred (Grieves, 2009). The remarkable resilience of Aboriginal people is partly explained by the legacy of a spirituality that demonstrates "an enthusiasm for living, a readiness to celebrate it as it is, a will to survive and to pass the baton of life to the next generation" (Stockton, 1995).

As Uncle Bill Neidjie from Kakadu said, "this is a story about feeling" (Neidjie, 1989). While feelings may be discounted in this commodified world, they are the stuff of human wellbeing and resilience.

***

Aboriginal society as it existed before first contact with Europeans was marked by an absence of materialism, of surplus and of accumulation of anything much at all. The question remains: What was it that could sustain human sociality and lifeways for so many thousands of years without material appropriation?

The answer lies in the rich intellectual traditions of the many interrelated clans and language groups across the vast land mass that is Australia. These traditions and belief systems were built on the necessity to have little in the way of material goods but a great deal by way of spirituality and connectedness or relatedness. This important principle in itself was acting to support the natural world rather than plunder it. If you understand the deep relatedness between humans and the natural world, then you do not tend to destroy that which sustains you. Aboriginal traditions and lifeways are marked by deep intellectual and complex knowledge of place, of species and the nature of human beings as part of this natural world.

The abundant traditions of song, dance, mimicry, theatre and art for which Aboriginal culture is celebrated, have been founded in these observations and relationships: to honour them, to explain them and to uphold them.

⁂

My late friend and colleague Dr Joseph Gumbula explained that "everything is making me who I am", a seemingly simple statement that belies a deep complexity born of relatedness. The exhibition he developed at the University of Sydney in 2009-2010 was an autobiographical work including artworks, cultural objects, historic photographs, natural history specimens and his own *manikay* (songs). He framed this show as approaching a *garma* (open) ceremonial performance. His work contributes to an understanding of how Aboriginal philosophy/spirituality explains the complexity of a human being as a part of the landscape, the natural world, the species, family and kin. This relatedness also implies a responsibility that reflects principles, values and ethics that are also embedded in the creative lifeways of the people.

Aboriginal spirituality prescribes a living intellectual tradition that is in the stories of the people as expressed through a huge range of creative mediums. The stories holding these spiritual values are held in a panoply of expression and performance. Imagine the spectacle of the landscape and the movement of people and animals within this landscape against a rich backdrop of the movement of clouds, the drama of the weather and the movement of the night sky. The stories held in the night sky and constellations, in the movement of hot and cold air producing rain clouds and also of the meeting of salt and fresh water, can be allegories for desirable human behaviours, especially in navigating the processes of change.

⁂

Walpiri senior law man Steven Wanta Jampijinpa Patrick has developed a bi-annual festival at Lajamanu called *Milpirri*. The visually spectacular performances include the natural panorama of the desert and the open night sky. Patrick says that the eve of the wet season when the hot and cold air meet to produce the rainstorms over the desert is an important learning time. The combination of the hot and cold air is a time for change, mirrored in the festival bringing together the young and old, the *yapa* and *gardiya*, the Walpiri and western ways of being to produce shared futures.

> As sacred beings transformed the landscape, their actions formed the connections between people and the rules for living that still underpin Warlpiri thinking today. Much of the ceremonial dance in Milpirri is more than a reenactment of the ancestral being's journeys. Through dance, the performers reconnect and channel the power of these sacred beings and reaffirm their strength and relevance to people today (Tracks n.d.).

A closer examination of the philosophy behind the Milpirri festival illuminates the ways in which Aboriginal lifeways are based on a deep understanding of the nature of human beings and their relationship to the natural world. Steven Wanta Jampijinpa Patrick says:

> Milpirri is a Warlpiri way to get country to express itself. Country is expressing itself all the time. All around Australia, Indigenous people, culture and art express (in various forms) what animals, plants and the elements, including weather and the seasons themselves—look like and speak like. How they tell history stories and knowledge that becomes history. This is how culture teaches us and cultivates us, as the soil is cultivated, and as if we are its cultivators. Who is the gardener ultimately and who is the garden? (Patrick, 2015).

Australia has been and is a Law-ful country. Aboriginal people share a similar philosophical, spiritual and cultural approach to being human when deeply interconnected with country. Understanding the Walpiri methodology is a way of gaining insight into the way this works within Aboriginal culture more generally.

The paradigms for human behavior, the right way to be, is given to Warlpiri people through the *Jukurrpa* that tends to be a fixed set of principles, values and ethics, not open to change. This is diametrically opposed to western law that is rather a set of rules designed and constantly modified by humans to regulate society. The difference between them is the issue of property that has grown out of the materialism of the west.

The Warlpiri ceremony *Jurntu Purlapa* teaches about Law and the primacy of Justice, Respect, Discipline, and Responsibility in human relations. This is how we can avoid conflicts, violence and bloodshed and in the case of the Walpiri, all are bound by the law and must face the consequences of their actions.

Kuruwarri is a mark or pattern identifiable with creative spirits associated with the Law. This Law or *Jukurrpa* explains the proper functioning of the world – essentially humans' relationships to each other, the species, the landscape and the universe. *Kuruwarri* was famously represented in the paintings developed by law men on thirty doors of the Yuendumu School in 1984. Known as the *Yuendumu Doors*, this event was the beginning of the desert arts movement whereby artists began to work in acrylic paint rather than the coloured sand and ochres of their sand painting.

Their aim? To educate the broader public about the *Jukurrpa*.

⁂

There are many terms in Aboriginal languages for the *Jukurrpa* but the concept remains the same. It is not a specific time in the past, it incorporates eternal time into the present. As the anthropologist W. E. H. Stanner coined it, it is everywhen.

Eternal time exists as the place where the ancestors are, where they go after a couple of generations. They become incorporated into the paradigms for proper human behaviour on Earth. We access the knowledge of the ancestors through the agency of the stories locked in the landscape and in the night sky.

Eternal time travels along beside us in normal time and it can erupt over into our consciousness or particularly into the consciousness of those with particular knowledge to read the signs. When this happens it is proof of the existence of the ancestors in our lives and is met with joy.

In Warraimaay country and Law, Seal Rocks and the Southern Cross connect us to the epic journey of Birrugun, an ancestral hero and also the Magpie Goose. Birrugun travelled down the coast from Gumbaingirr country to Seal Rocks and his journey exemplifies his manliness. He was hunting, proved he could fight and he was chosen by a young woman to be her husband. She and her sister travelled with him and at Seal Rocks they ascended into the sky to form the constellation the Southern Cross. The paradigm for the proper marriage exists in this story and in this constellation, connecting the people to the universe and eternal time.

Whenever the Southern Cross is viewed from that place the story is alive to the people and until relatively recently the people from tribes to the north followed those tracks. They sang the songs of Birrugun on their journey, they celebrated his life and emulated his feats. Then they were hosted by the Warraimaay to camp at Seal Rocks, to join in with the netting of the sea mullet. The people feasted, danced and sang, traded and exchanged ideas, songs and stories. They also negotiated upcoming liaisons through marriage law.

***

This is but a taste of what life is like living within the bounds of nature eschewing material goods and gaining meaning from the intellectual and creative possibilities of a rich natural world and natural Law. The relatedness of all things in the natural world, including people, has created breathtaking possibilities for drama, theatre, art, song and dance.

2

SOME NOTES ON AUSTRALIAN LANGUAGES AND WAANYI IN PARTICULAR

Mary Laughren

I | SOME BACKGROUND

It has been estimated that there were approximately 250 distinct languages with their several dialects spoken in Australia when the so-called *first fleet* carrying English settlers sailed into Botany Bay in 1788 (Dixon, 2002, p. 5). The indigenous population all over the continent and adjacent islands consisted of groups of kinfolk engaged in what has been generally described as a hunter-gatherer way of life conducted within relatively discrete geographical areas. This lifestyle was dependent on people's intimate knowledge of their local environment and their sophisticated methods of exploiting its resources, as well as their highly organised social organisation. Bilingualism or multilingualism was the norm and there is much evidence — including linguistic — of social and economic links between neighbouring groups.

The distribution of Australian indigenous languages presents an apparently paradoxical pattern in light of the long occupation of Australia that stretches back 50,000 years or longer, as revealed by archaeological and art dating evidence (Mulvaney & Kamminga, 1999, p. 223; Bradshaw *et al.*, 2021). However, the Pama-Nyungan (PN) language family which covers most of the continent shows a high degree of lexical and grammatical uniformity (Map 1). This linguistic similarity suggests a relatively recent expansion—possibly within the holocene. Alternatively the interactions of small language-speaking groups in close contact could also have led to this linguistic similarity. In northern Australia there are many families of languages referred to as non-Pama-Nyungan (nonPN); the genetic relationship between these nonPN language families is not fully understood. Similarly the relationship between PN and nonPN languages is unclear, although the general consensus among linguists is that all Australian languages are genetically related.[1]

Map 1. Distribution of Pama-Nyungan and non-Pama-Nyungan languages[2].

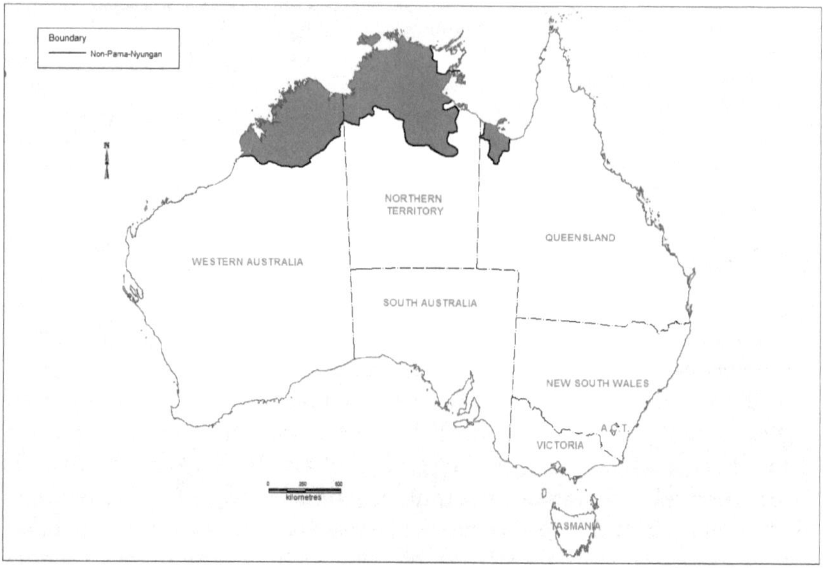

Typologically, the PN languages which combine both inflectional and agglutinating features marked by suffixal morphology, exemplified by the Warlpiri[3] examples in (1a, b), differ from nonPN languages which are mostly of a polysynthetic type in which whole clauses or simple sentences can be expressed as a single word, as in example (2a).[4] Furthermore, while PN languages are characterised by their suffixing morphology, nonPN languages such as Kunbarlang are characterised

1. The status of the PN family is questioned by Dixon (2002, 44-54).
2. The maps were prepared by Mark Harvey.
3. Warlpiri is spoken in central Australia, in the Northern Territory (see Map 2).
4. These typological traits were first discussed in detail by Capell (1956, 1962).

by prefixal morphology as in example (2b) in which the dative case morpheme *bi* is prefixed to the genitive pronoun *ngarrku* 'we'.[1] In both (2a) and (2b) the subject pronoun *kadda-* precedes the other morphemes in the verbal word in which the inflected verb is the final morpheme.[2]

(1) Pama-Nyungan: Warlpiri language

a.

Ngarrka	*ka-lu*	*ya-ni*	*ngurra-ngurlu*	*ngapa-kurra.*
man	PRES-they	go-NONPAST	home-from	water-to

'Men are going from home to the water.'

b.

Karnta-lu-jana	*ngarrka-ku*	*ya-nu*	*wangka-nja-ku.*
woman-they-them	man-DATIVE	go-PAST	speak-INFINITIVE-DATIVE

'Women went to speak to the men.'

(2) Non-Pama-Nyungan: Kunbarlang language

a. *Kadda-nganj-mulmul-kidanj.* (Kapitonov 2019: #4.106a)

they-hither-many-go.PAST

'A lot of people came.'

b.

Kadda-kalng	*mayi njunjuk*	*bi-ngarrku*	*ngob.*	(Kapitonov 2019: #4.108d)
they-get.PAST	CM.III water	DAT-we.GEN	all	

'They brought water for us all.'

Another feature of nonPN languages present in Kunbarlang is the marking of the class and/or gender to which a noun belongs. In example (2b) the noun *njunjuk* 'water' belongs to what Kapitonov has labelled class 3 which is marked by the form of the noun marker *mayi* which precedes the noun. While some Pama-Nyungan languages also

1. Kunbarlang is spoken in central-western Arnhem Land in the Northern Territory.
2. Abbreviations used in language examples are: ACC = accusative case, ASP = aspect, CM = noun class marker, ERG = ergative case (subject of transitive verb), GEN = genitive case, PRES= present tense, R = realis mood, SG = singular, TOP = topic.

distinguish gender and/or class distinctions these are typically not marked by prefixes, but by suffixes.

While the elements inside morphologically complex words are strictly ordered in both Pama-Nyungan and non-Pama-Nyungan languages, word order within a clause is relatively free and is mostly determined by pragmatic factors such as what is in focus, or the topic, whether new or old information.

II | THE POSITION OF WAANYI

The Waanyi language was spoken south of the Gulf of Carpentaria in a very linguistically diverse area where PN and nonPN languages meet. The closest genetic relatives of Waanyi are Garrwa and Gunindirri spoken to the north of Waanyi.[1] These languages form the Garrwan group of languages. The land traditionally occupied by speakers of these languages divides a PN group of languages known as the Ngarna languages (Breen, 2004, p. 223), so named because of their shared word for 'I' (first person singular nominative pronoun). To the north is Yanyuwa, spoken on the southwest side of the Gulf and adjacent islands, while the other members of the Ngarna group occupied land to the south of Garrwan-speaking country. The western side of Garrwan country was occupied by people who spoke nonPN Mirndi languages while their eastern neighbours also spoke nonPN languages, but of a distinct Tangkic family. The location of Waanyi in relation to the other Garrwan languages and to their neighbours is shown in Map 2.

Prior to European contact, which led to serious dislocation and loss of both kin and country, Waanyi people lived on fairly well-resourced land watered by the upper reaches of rivers such as the Nicholson (*Kanalanja* in Waanyi) (Trigger, 1982, 1987). Waanyi are fresh-water people as opposed to salt-water people such as the Yanyuwa (Ngarna language) to their north or the Ganggalida (Tangkic language) on their eastern side.[2] Other Tangkic languages are spoken on the South Wellesley Islands in the Gulf of Carpentaria.

1. For documentation of the Waanyi language see Belfrage (2003), Breen (2003), Laughren (2018a, 2018b), Osborne (1966).
2. Also known as Yukulta (Keen, 1983).

Map 2. Location of Waanyi

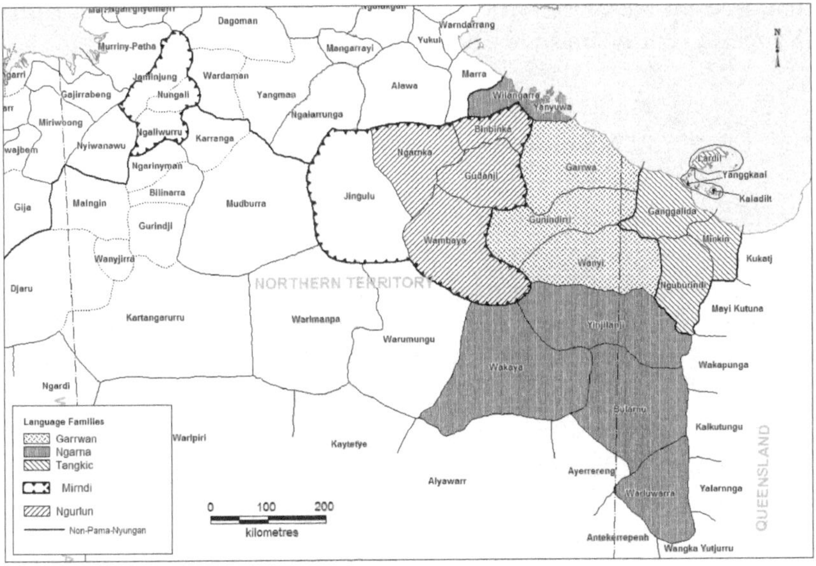

While the reconstructed forms of their ancestral pronouns is the principal evidence for Tangkic languages being classified as nonPN, their sentence structure or syntax is of the type most commonly found in PN languages. Conversely, Yanyuwa, the *stranded* northern member of the PN Ngarna language group, while retaining most features of its southern Ngarna relations, has acquired morphological and syntactic features mostly found in nonPN languages to its west. These include a system of noun classifiers marked by prefixes on nouns, adjectives and determiners ('this/that' words) as shown in (3a,b).

(3)	a.	*Nya-mangaji*	*nya-buyi*	*nya-ardu*	(Bradley n.d.: p. 46 #1)
		CM-that	CM-small	CM-boy	
		'That small boy.'			
	b.	*Wayi*	*ma-mangaji*	*ma-ngarra?*	(Kirton & Charlie 1996, p.31 #4.52)
		how	CM-that	CM-food	
		'How is that food?'			

A morpheme complex made up of a tense-aspect marker (*j* or *k*) followed by the object and subject weak pronouns is prefixed to the Yanyuwa verb as shown in examples (4) and (5).

(4)	a.	*K-al-anda-rama.* ASP-them-she-hit	'She hit them.'
	b.	*K-al-alu-rama.* ASP-them-they-hit	'They hit them.'

The overall tense, aspect and modal values are jointly marked by the form of the tense-aspect morpheme, *k* or *j*, and the verbal suffix, as illustrated by the verb *wingka* 'go' in (5a-e). [1]

(5)	a.	*K-arna-wingka.*	'I went.'
	b.	*K-arna-wingka-la.*	'I will go.'
	c.	*J-arna-wingka-yi.*	'I'm going.'
	d.	*J-arna-wingka-yani.*	'I'm about to go.'
	e.	*K-alu-wingka.*	'They went.'

The southern Ngarna languages are more typical of PN languages with cognate pronouns that are *not* prefixed to the verb, as seen in the Warluwarra sentence in (6). [2]

(6)	*Ngarna*	*yinya*	*garla*	*nguta-rna*	*yiwa*	*nganha*	*nhuwu-rna*	*nguta-rna-mi.*
	I	her	meat	give-PAST	she	me	honey-with	give-PAST-hither

'I gave her meat (and) she gave me sugar.'

Linguists differ in their assignment of Garrwan languages to a genetic grouping. Based on his comparative study of pronouns in Australian languages, Blake (1988) concluded that Garrwan languages were the only ones that showed a genuinely mixed set of both PN and nonPN forms. However he concluded that the pronouns most likely to

---

1. Yanyula examples (4) and (5) are from Bradley (n.d.), p. 46 and p. 87 respectively.
2. Warluwarra data is from Gavan Breen's unpublished *Warluwarra Grammar and Dictionary*, 1990.

be ancestral were of nonPN origin while the newer ones were most likely borrowed from PN languages, particularly from the Ngarna group. On the other hand, Harvey (2009), based on his analysis of pronouns, argues that Garrwan languages belong to the PN family.

Typologically the Garrwan languages are of the predominant PN type. They are suffixing languages: verbal suffixes mostly mark mood distinctions while nominal suffixes mark case distinctions. Pronouns also have distinct case forms. One aspect of their syntax which distinguishes Garrwan languages from their neighbours is the tendency to begin a sentence with the main predicate, usually a verb, to which the subject or object pronoun is added, so that it forms a phonological phrase with the preceding verb which is distinct from the rest of the sentence (or clause) as in (7a) taken from Alexis Wright's *Carpentaria* (452).[1] In sentences in which a word is in focus — such as a question word — then it is the first word of the sentence followed by the subject or object pronoun. Such an example is found in *Carpentaria* reproduced here as (7b).[2] The negation marker *budangku* in Waanyi must also occupy this sentence-initial position as in (7c).

(7)	a.	*Naj-ba*	*-ngamba-lanya*	*nana-ngkani*		*karrinja-na.*
		see-R	-us-ACC	that-ERG		stand-on
		'That one standing there is looking at us.'				
	b.	*Wanyi-ngkanyi*	*-ninji*	*nana-ngkurru*		*jila?*
		what-to	*-you* (SG)	*that-to*		*go*
		'What are you going to there?'				
	c.	*Budangku*	*-ngamba*	*laji-bi*	*nana yanyi*	*yalu-ngi.*
		not	-we	hear-R	that language	their-GEN
		'We don't understand that language of theirs.'				

Given the close proximity of distinct language groups to the Garrwan languages, it is not surprising that many words are shared between these languages. Interactions between peoples seem to inevitably lead to word borrowing the world over. Multilingualism may also lead to some syntactic and morphological levelling, so that

1. See Mushin (2012) for an in-depth discussion of Garrwa syntax which closely mirrors that of Waanyi.
2. Alexis Wright *Carpentaria* (2009), London, Little, Brown/Constable, p. 288.

languages in close contact may come over time to share features that make them grammatically more alike. We saw this with Yanyuwa assuming some nonPN characteristics, while the syntax of nonPN Tangkic languages is more like that of PN languages. The Garrwan languages such as Waanyi also have a more PN type of syntax: absence of noun class or gender marking, words inflections are suffixal, and verbs have no prefixes or proclitic morphemes as found in Yanyuwa and Kunbarlang.

Because European settlement and control in the Gulf area forced people of different language groups to live in even closer proximity that they would have traditionally — in missions, boarding schools, on cattle stations and government established settlements — one might expect extensive lexical borrowing between the language groups and even a certain levelling of phonological and grammatical differences would have occurred in the post colonial period. However, while there is some evidence of lexical borrowing, there seems to be few other signs of language mixing.

The colonial emphasis on learning English and the need to use it to communicate with the European bosses, the separation of children from their parents in strictly run English-only boarding schools, the movement of young people, especially men, out of their home areas to find paid work, the removal of so-called wrongdoers by the government to far-away places such as Palm Island, all of these factors contributed to the dominance of English and the adoption of English and an English-lexified Kriol over the indigenous languages. The settlement of Waanyi people and their neighbours into European controlled living areas followed an initial contact period which was extremely violent as Europeans took ownership and control over the land and its resources, and led to a large loss of life (Roberts, 2005; Trigger, 1982). While some distinctive Waanyi words and fixed expressions are still used by Waanyi people in their day-to-day conversations, the last generation of fluent speakers with a command of the complex morphology and syntax, has now passed away. The way that Waanyi words are used in passages of direct speech, and also in some descriptive passages in Wright's *Carpentaria*, well reflects the way in which Waanyi is spoken today.

III | AUSTRALIAN LANGUAGE PHONOLOGY

The phonological features of Australian languages are relatively uniform across the continent. Most languages have a series of stop (or occlusive) consonants showing a 5 or 6-way contrast. A first two-way contrast involves the *active articulator*: coronal (obstruction to outgoing breath is made with front part of tongue) and non-coronal consonants. The latter divide into two classes according to which part of the mouth moves to make the occlusion: lip versus the back of the tongue (*dorsum*). The former divide into two sets: apical (obstruction is made by the tip of the tongue), and laminal (by the blade of the tongue). A further division is made according to the *place of articulation*: the occlusion made by the tongue tip against the alveolar ridge as opposed to the palate, or the occlusion is made by the blade against the upper teeth as opposed to the palate. In languages such as Waanyi in which words all start with a consonant, the apical distinction is not made word initially; it is only made between vowels. Because of the very few Garrwa and Waanyi words in which this distinction is salient, the practical orthography used to write these languages only uses the letters in the alveolar column in Table 1. The dental versus palatal distinction is not made in Garrwan languages even though it is made in the surrounding languages.

In most languages, including Waanyi, the nasal consonants match the stop consonants. There are fewer *lateral* consonants since these are all coronal, and fewer glide (or semivowel) consonants. These four *manners of articulation* (stop, nasal, lateral and glide) plus a trilled 'rr', characterise most Australian languages. The distinction between voiced and unvoiced stops found in French as between p (*peau*) and b (*beau*), or t (*thé*) and d (*dé*), is rarely found in Australian languages and is often associated with a contrast between geminate and non-geminate consonants or tense versus lax stops. The distinction between stop and fricative consonants, as between p (*pour*) and f (*four*), or b (*beau*) and v (*veau*) is found in a very restricted number of Australian languages. A typical array of consonant sounds, written using a practical orthography that includes some digraphs (2 letters), is shown in Table 1. The bolded letters are those used in the Waanyi and Garrwa orthographies.

Table 1. Typical set of consonants in Australian languages

Active articulator	Non-coronal		Coronal			
	labial	dorsal	apical		laminal	
place of articulation			alveolar	post-alveolar	dental	palatal
stops	**b**/p	g/**k**	**d**/t	rd/rt	dh/th	**j**/ty
nasals	**m**	**ng**	**n**	rn	nh	**ny**
lateral			**l**	rl	lh	**ly**
trill			**rr**			
glide	**w**			**r**		**y**

The vowel inventory is limited to oral vowels, usually only three (a, i, u) as in Waanyi, although some languages, mainly nonPN, also have mid vowels (e, o). Some languages also distinguish vowel length. These include Waanyi in which the long 'a' vowel is written as a double vowel in the name of the language, in contrast with *wanyi* 'what' with a short vowel.

IV | WAANYI LANGUAGE IN WRIGHT'S *CARPENTARIA*

Most examples of Waanyi language in *Carpentaria* consist of single words or short phrases or sentences used alongside English words that give a clue to the meaning of the Waanyi words. In addition to the words listed in Table 2, two Waanyi words are used as names: *Gardajala* 'bogeyman, devil' and *Bala* 'sky; fork in tree'.[1]

1. The question marks in Table 2 do *not* indicate that the Waanyi word is wrong or that its meaning is incorrect; they mark a word that I have not found in my own recordings or in other sources, or where I am unsure of my own interpretation of meaning based on its use in *Carpentaria*.

Table 2. Waanyi words in Alexis Wright's *Carpentaria*, 2009

Waanyi	English equivalent	page	Comments
ngabarn	bring, carry	9	*ngaba-n* (verb) 'carry'; final *n* is emphatic
mandagi	whiteman, European man	9	
yidimil	?morning star	90, 486	Also recorded as *kambirriji*
walakuku	?	117	*wuluku* 'big'; *wululuku* 'old, elder'
maranguji	doctors	117	
binjuna	?	147	
malbu	old man	147, 269, 270, 271, 277-281, 288, 452	widely used term in Gulf area
kuluwuluku	?big balls	147	*kulu* 'testicle' *wuluku* 'big'
warri	first	150	
ngabaya	devil-man	150	Also recorded for 'whiteman'
damu	?	150	
kunbulki	?flat country	184, 185	*kunburrki* 'firestick'; *muwanbi and mangkurru* recorded as 'flat country, open grassland'
jurrbu	?hole	185	
jarrbikala	Wedge-tailed Eagle; policeman	189, 203,214, 298	
waydbala	whitefella	214	see also *mandagi* (p. 9); *waydbala jarrbikala* 'whitefella policeman'
kadajala	bogeyman, devil-devil	189, 264	Name Gardajala is a variant spelling
moonba	?	235	Garrwa *munyba* 'cover'
kangolgi	Morning Glory cloud	247	Garrwa *kangulki* 'dew'
wirriwidji	whirlwind	264	
gundugundu	scrub-devil lizard	264, 270	Also name of important ancestral being in Waanyi country

Waanyi	English equivalent	page	Comments
dandaayana	?on river bank (people)	271, 278	*dandaya* 'side of river (*rive*)'; *-na* 'on, in'
Wangabiya	name of people		
dumularra	running water, stream	286	
yinbirra	?fairy-like people	286	*yimbirra* 'debris carried by river in flood'
wawaru	?nothing	288	
malirriminji	?Pricklebush	288, 446	
wadara	?	288	Garrwa 'paperbark hut, humpy'
wanyimba	do something to	289	*wanyi-mba* (verb) what/something-causative verb 'do something to'
kurrkamarra	many	289	Also recorded as *kurrkamala*
bari	bad	289	
ngamiri	?	452	
najba	see, look	452	See example (7a).
ngambalanya	us	452	first person plural inclusive accusative pronoun
nanangkani	that one	452	'that' in transitive subject form; *nana* intransitive subject or object form
karrinjana	while standing	452	*karrinja* 'stand' *-na* 'in/on'
barrba	?go	452	Garrwa *balba* 'go'; Waanyi *bulubarrba* 'jump'
jayi	move away	452	*jayi* (verb) 'move away'
yurrngijbangka	?for good	452	*yurrngujbu* (verb) 'do permanently'
kayi	?	452	*kayi* (verb) 'shout, call out'
barraku	?talking	452	*barrawu* 'house, town'
warawara yanja	keep talking	452	*yanja* is imperative verb 'speak'

Waanyi	English equivalent	page	Comments
ngawu	I	452	*ngawu ninya lajib* 'I hear/ heard you' or 'I am listening to you'
ninya	you (singular, accusative)	452	
lajib	hear, listen	452	
damu	?daddy	452	
ninji	you	452, 288	Singular nominative pronoun
murriba	Father	452	
baki	?	452	*baki* 'and'
yarrbanji	youth, boy	452	
majinmaja	hawk	467	Also recorded as *majinmanya*
maliwi	?star in the west	477	
kudawedangire	Pleiades, or the Seven Sisters	485	*kudawudanngirri* 'group of young women; Pleiades'
jinkiji	star	486	Also recorded as *jinkirrji* 'star'

3

PLAINS OF PROMISE, ALEXIS WRIGHT (1997)

Mylène Charon

Plains of Promise est le premier roman publié par Alexis Wright en 1997 par University of Queensland Press (UQP). Salué par la critique en Australie – il a été sélectionné pour plusieurs prix : le Commonwealth Writers' Prize, The Age Book of the Year Award et le NSW Premier's Literary Awards –, il est dès 1999 traduit en français par Sabine Porte et publié par Actes Sud. L'ouvrage avait été retenu par Marc de Gouvenain pour sa collection Antipodes, en raison de « its beauty, its ability to convey emotions, a whole universe, and to mingle reality and the invisible » (Castro-Koshy, 2018, 119). Précédant *Carpentaria* de près d'une décennie, il annonce déjà son style et ses préoccupations. Les deux romans s'ancrent dans un même univers référentiel : l'Australie (post)coloniale du XXe siècle marquée par la coexistence de deux communautés, les Autochtones et les colons issus de l'immigration (« migrant/settlers »[1]).

Les deux ouvrages suivent une ligne généalogique : *Plains of Promise* suit quatre générations de femmes qui subissent la politique australienne consistant à enlever systématiquement des enfants d'ascendance partiellement autochtone, connus sous le nom des Générations Volées, tandis que *Carpentaria* se focalise principalement sur la famille Phantom, divisée sur la question des droits fonciers et de la manière de les exercer face à des entreprises internationales. Ce déroulement généalogique justifie que la notion de « postmémoire », c'est-à-dire de traumatisme intergénérationnel, puisse être évoquée au sujet des œuvres de Wright, comme le fait Sylvie Kandé, la co-traductrice de son recueil de nouvelles inédit en anglais,

1. Je reprends la terminologie d'Anne Brewster à propos du personnage d'Elias Smith (Brewster, 2010, 97).

Le Pacte du Serpent Arc-en-ciel, publié en 2002 par Actes Sud. Selon elle, le concept de postmémoire peut être emprunté à Marianne Hirsch pour décrire le fait que plusieurs générations d'Autochtones héritent des traumatismes causés par la colonisation, ceux-ci leur étant transmis si intensément qu'ils s'intègrent réellement à leur mémoire, quand bien même ils n'auraient pas vécu ces événements directement. Wright explore ainsi les effets à long terme des traumatismes causés par la colonisation (Hall, 2016, 5).

Plains of Promise raconte l'histoire d'Ivy, envoyée de force dans la Mission chrétienne de St Dominic, après qu'elle a été renvoyée avec sa mère de la station d'élevage où celle-ci travaillait comme domestique. Ne supportant pas la séparation d'avec sa fille qui, parce qu'elle a un père blanc, lui a été retirée, la mère d'Ivy se suicide. Violée par le missionnaire Errol Jipp, Ivy se retrouve enceinte alors qu'elle n'est qu'une adolescente. Celui-ci, pour cacher ses abus sexuels, la marie de force à Elliott. Immédiatement après son accouchement, le bébé d'Ivy lui est retiré : un épisode de violence s'ensuit entre Elliott et Ivy, à la suite duquel celle-ci est internée dans l'asile de Sycamore Heights. À la faveur d'un changement de politique, Ivy est relâchée et envoyée chez une vieille femme appelée Bessie. La cohabitation se passe mal et se termine dans une explosion violente qui souffle la maison et tue Bessie. Ivy, quant à elle, se réfugie dans une décharge. Une ellipse temporelle de grande portée couvre l'enfance de sa fille Mary Nelson, qui ne réapparaît qu'une fois devenue une jeune adulte. Après avoir appris qu'elle a été adoptée et est d'ascendance aborigène, Mary postule dans une organisation aborigène nationale, la Coalition of Aboriginal Governments (206), dans l'espoir de retrouver ses origines et l'identité de sa mère. Manipulée par son collègue Buddy Doolan qui ne lui révèle pas toutes les informations qu'il détient, elle donne naissance à une fille qu'elle a avec lui, Jessie. Après s'être éloignée de l'organisation, Mary accepte finalement une mission qui lui permettra de s'installer dans la communauté d'où vient sa mère. Elle finira par la rencontrer à l'occasion d'une nuit dans le *bush*, où elle l'aperçoit l'espace d'un éclair. Les retrouvailles ne dureront pas, car Mary et Jessie sont expulsées par le conseil aborigène local.

I | GENRE

Les deux ouvrages sont des romans racontés par un narrateur ou une narratrice hétérodiégétique, dont on ne connaît pas l'identité et qui n'est pas un personnage de l'histoire. Cette narratrice est omnisciente, elle adopte une focalisation zéro lui permettant de révéler les pensées de ses différents personnages. Dans *Carpentaria*, le récit de création, qui évoque le Serpent ancestral et a, en partie, valeur d'explication météorologique, est placé en incipit : ce sont les mouvements du serpent qui vont expliquer les divers phénomènes affectant Desperance, qu'il s'agisse du détournement de la rivière qui en fait un «waterless port» (3), des cyclones ou encore des tremblements de terre[1]. Dans *Plains of Promise*, une fable qui constitue la conclusion du roman porte sur la survie d'un oisillon aquatique qui, ayant perdu les siens, est contraint de vivre avec des corbeaux qui l'oppriment. L'oiseau femelle parviendra à transmettre à sa descendance son savoir écologique, qui consiste à faire revenir l'eau dans les Grands Lacs, mais celui-ci finit par se perdre en raison du traumatisme qui a affecté ces différentes générations. Dans un dénouement tragique est annoncé l'assèchement définitif du Grand Lac, dont la disparition à la suite de la destruction mentale des oiseaux aquatiques dénonce les conséquences environnementales dramatiques liées aux perturbations d'un écosystème. Placée en excipit des *Plains of Promise*, où plusieurs femmes, comme l'oiseau aquatique, voient leurs filles leur être arrachées, cette fable semble évoquer l'impact écologique et social de la colonisation, dans la mesure où les Premières Nations se perçoivent comme des protectrices de leurs terres ancestrales («custodians»). Le personnage masculin autochtone des *Plains of Promise*, Elliott, perçoit ainsi sa responsabilité au sein de cet écosystème : «It was his duty to do his utmost to maintain harmony in the world that owned him» (73). Dans les deux romans, la nature a donc le rôle d'un actant souvent personnifié; ce que Frances Devlin-Glass rattache, s'appuyant sur les catégories de Tamisari et Bradley, à une conception Super/Vitale où les éléments peuvent être, en fonction des contextes, uniquement ce qu'ils semblent être ou dotés de pouvoirs (Devlin-Glass, 2008, 395).

Cette épistémologie autochtone, déconnectée de l'épistémologie occidentale et de son opposition courante entre nature et culture, est évoquée dans les deux romans, mais de manière plus pathétique dans *Plains of Promise*, qui souligne les ruptures engendrées par la colonisation tout en affirmant la permanence de la souveraineté autochtone

1. Pour une explication du Serpent comme élément vital et supervital, voir Frances Devlin-Glass, p. 392–407.

et la résistance. Le champ lexical de la guerre rend compte de cette condamnation du colonialisme depuis le point de vue des colonisés :

> No one was able to look after the land any more, not all the time, the way they used to in the olden days. Life was so different now that the white man had taken the lot. It was like a war, an undeclared war. A war with no name. And the Aboriginal man was put into their prison camps, like prisoners in the two world wars. But nobody called it a war: it was simply a situation, that's all. Protection. Assimilation... different words that amounted to annihilation... (74)

Dans *Carpentaria*, les mots non traduits en langue anglaise opèrent comme des synecdoques de cette autre manière de connaître, à l'instar de Norm et de son savoir astronomique (485-6). *Plains of Promise* ne recourt pas, contrairement à *Carpentaria*, à l'« hétérolinguisme »[1] ni à la satire systématique de la langue anglaise comme synecdoque de la culture impériale dominante, bien qu'un court épisode, où Gloria se joue des stéréotypes raciaux en imitant le sociolecte de la reine d'Angleterre, signale déjà un intérêt de l'autrice pour les rapports de pouvoir tels qu'ils se jouent au niveau linguistique :

> Mission-trained in the Queen's language, Gloria mimicked the white people she imagined in that small country town. [...] In the butcher's shop they had talked to her real loud and slow, thinking she was just a black nig-nog: 'Whatta it be today, ma'am?' (*Plains*, 284)

II | PERSONNAGES

Ivy Koopundi Andrews, personnage féminin sur lequel se concentre la première moitié des *Plains of Promise*, annonce en partie celui d'Angel Day qui, dans *Carpentaria*, joue le rôle d'une reine du recyclage dans la décharge qui borde Desperance. Après l'explosion de la maison où vivait Ivy depuis sa sortie de l'hôpital psychiatrique de Sycamore Heights, elle se réfugie en effet dans la décharge où elle survit avec un troupeau grandissant de chèvres. Lorsque la ville décide de raser la décharge par mesure d'hygiène, Ivy échappe de peu à la mort, tant elle ressemble à l'une des chèvres accusées de répandre la tuberculose (*Plains*, 199-202).

---

1. J'emprunte ce terme à Jean-Marc Moura pour parler de la coexistence de différentes langues dans un même texte. Il s'agit d'une caractéristique des littératures postcoloniales qui représentent différentes communautés. Jean-Marc Moura, *Littératures francophones et théorie postcoloniale*, Paris, Presses universitaires de France, 2019, p. 84.

Quant à Elliott «the Traveller» (*Plains*, 43), envoyé par les anciens de la Mission pour enquêter sur la terre ancestrale d'Ivy et pour l'y ramener, il rappelle les figures de Norm et de Will Phantom lorsque ceux-ci doivent convoquer leur savoir cartographique ancestral pour se repérer. Comme Will initié par Joseph Midnight (*Carpentaria*, 360), Elliott dispose de chants hérités de sa parentèle pour s'orienter. Ainsi, lors de son premier voyage : «Elliott journeyed discreetly, singing the songs taught by his father and uncle-fathers, each step through the song-map unlocking the land» (*Plains*, 43). Comme Will fondant ses pas dans ceux des kangourous pour échapper aux hommes de la mine qui le recherchent (*Carpentaria*, 170-1), les mouvements d'Elliott sont comparés à ceux de son animal totem, les grues brolga : «Sometimes his mouvements were as graceful as his totem, the brolga» (*Plains*, 43). À l'instar de Norm, herméneute de la nature (*Carpentaria*, 260), Elliott interprète les éléments naturels et entre en dialogue avec les animaux. Ainsi lors de son second voyage avec les pigeons, dont il craint d'abord qu'ils ne le mettent en danger en révélant sa présence : «Over the passing of many nights he repeatedly whispered to the pigeons, urging them to take flight and seek the safety of cover» (*Plains*, 73). Elliott, de même que Will et les différents personnages aborigènes de *Carpentaria*, est l'héritier d'un savoir ancestral concernant la terre : «he was trained in religious knowledge of the land by the thoughts of the elders, through a straight line of law since time began and the land and everything in it had been created» (*Plains*, 73).

III | REGISTRE

Carpentaria repose sur une juxtaposition de registres : au satirique, lié au traitement ironique des personnages blancs d'Uptown[1], s'ajoute l'épique. Celui-ci consiste en une célébration des héros autochtones, à l'image de Will s'opposant à l'entreprise internationale qui exploite la mine de Gurfurritt. Dans *Plains of Promise*, le registre est plutôt pathétique, comme l'illustre le passage de l'accouchement, solitaire, d'Ivy à la suite des viols d'Errol Jipp alors qu'elle n'est qu'une adolescente (*Plains*, 156-157). Les dénouements des deux œuvres

1. Pour une étude de la satire de la blanchité dans *Carpentaria*, voir Anne Brewster, 2010, p. 85.

contrastent d'ailleurs, puisqu'au tragique, dans *Plains of Promise*, de la réunion finale entre Ivy, sa fille Mary et sa petite-fille Jessie, vite séparées par le conseil de la communauté de St Dominic, s'oppose la vision utopique du retour de Norm avec son petit-fils Bala sur sa terre ancestrale, après que les traces de la colonisation ont été balayées par le cyclone.

IV | THÈMES

Carpentaria et *Plains of Promise* partagent de nombreux thèmes, au premier rang desquels se trouve une critique des institutions (post)coloniales, représentées dans ces romans par l'école, la police et la religion. Dans *Carpentaria*, la critique de l'école est menée à travers le personnage de Kevin Phantom, dont la réussite scolaire, illustrée par ses essais sur l'auteur non-autochtone Tim Winton, n'a pour effet que de l'aliéner de son savoir ancestral (101-102). Dans *Plains of Promise*, les souffrances d'Ivy à l'école soulignent la violence de l'institution et l'absurdité du savoir qui y est transmis (51-52).

Bien que moins développée que dans *Carpentaria*, où l'agent Truthful apparaît à la fois inutile et dangereux[1], la satire de la police est déjà esquissée dans *Plains of Promise* avec Gloria, la cousine d'Ivy, lorsqu'elle est arrêtée par le « Protector of Aborigines » local et envoyée à la Mission car il considère avoir suffisamment de prostituées dans sa région (119-120). Le sentiment de sa propre importance et son sens moral revendiqué (« the police sergeant in a small country town presents a powerful presence in his uniform: a big man not open to persuasion », 119) contrastent de manière ironique avec l'explication pragmatique de sa décision par la narratrice (« It simply made life a lot easier... », 119). L'usage antiphrastique du terme « persuasion » – puisque le Protecteur des Aborigènes est en fait sous l'influence des colons de la ville à qui il veut plaire[2] – et son langage familier rapporté

1. Je renvoie notamment à son comportement de prédateur sexuel avec Girlie, une des filles Phantom, et à la mort des trois jeunes retenus en détention pour le meurtre de Gordie. Respectivement Wright, *Carpentaria*, p. 216-217 et p. 343.

2. La répétition du terme « comprendre » contribue à ironiser sur son incorruptibilité (« His *understanding* of the law is by the letter. He *understands* the harshness of the townspeople... »), de même que le champ lexical du « consensus ». Wright, *Plains*, p. 119. Je souligne.

au discours direct (« Ya shoulda known better to know ya shoulda kept ya nose clean and outta town », 120) participent aussi à la satire de ce personnage incarnant l'autorité.

Quant à la religion chrétienne, elle fait l'objet d'un traitement ironique dans les deux romans : dans *Carpentaria*, Mozzie Fishman l'accuse de différents maux tels que l'alcoolisme[1] et Norm souligne sa complicité avec le suprématisme blanc[2], tandis que dans *Plains of Promise*, l'hypocrisie du missionnaire Errol Jipp, les abus sexuels qu'il perpètre et sa mauvaise gestion de la communauté[3] fondent la satire du christianisme. La dénonciation des violences sexuelles est donc commune aux deux ouvrages, qui les relient à des institutions liées à la colonisation – la police dans *Carpentaria* où Truthful abuse de Girlie Phantom dans l'espoir de progresser dans son enquête, la religion dans *Plains of Promise* où Jipp se déresponsabilise de ses actes pédophiles en accusant sa femme[4].

La politique, les affaires autochtones et en particulier les dilemmes auxquels doivent faire face les communautés autochtones en Australie sont également des thèmes présents dans les deux romans : si dans *Carpentaria* les communautés autochtones sont divisées sur la ligne à tenir face aux entreprises internationales qui veulent exploiter les ressources de la région du golfe de Carpentarie, dans *Plains of Promise* la complexité de la situation dans laquelle se trouvent les Autochtones est exprimée par l'opposition entre l'organisation nationale autochtone pour laquelle Mary et Buddy travaillent et les bureaucrates autochtones du gouvernement fédéral[5], ainsi que celle entre cette même coalition nationale et les conseils locaux.

Plains of Promise annonce déjà des préoccupations qui seront développées près d'une décennie plus tard dans *Carpentaria*, notamment les effets persistants et toujours actuels de la colonisation,

---

1. Voir Wright, *Carpentaria*, p. 136 : « He said he believed Christian beliefs had indoctrinated Aboriginal communities like grog and it was true to say it was even the cause of grog ».
2. Voir Wright, *Carpentaria*, p. 491 : « He told her he believed in the Bible because the white people had prospered by believing in what the Bible had told them ».
3. Elle donne lieu, entre autres, à une épidémie de dysenterie. Voir Wright, *Plains*, p. 39.
4. Voir Wright, *Plains*, p. 29 : « 'You have made me taste the filth. Get out of my sight,' he [Errol] hissed at her [Beverly Jipp] ».
5. Voir Wright, *Plains*, p. 211 : « 'Those buggers up at Canberra can't get a thing right,' he declared on his return. He meant the Aboriginal bureaucracy in the federal capital ».

dénoncés à travers des récits se déroulant sur plusieurs générations de personnages principaux autochtones. La critique du colonialisme y est menée par le biais de ses différentes institutions – scolaire, policière et religieuse – incarnées par différents personnages non-autochtones dont le sentiment de leur propre importance contraste de manière ironique avec leurs actions, inefficaces ou violentes. Les deux romans s'inscrivent dans une épistémologie aborigène où le monde naturel est animé. Mais là où *Carpentaria* interrompt fréquemment l'anglais pour recourir à l'hétérolinguisme et souligner ainsi la permanence de cette épistémologie, *Plains of Promise* souligne plutôt, en adoptant un registre pathétique, la rupture dans la transmission de ce savoir causée par la colonisation et les politiques (post)coloniales telles que les Générations Volées. L'échec de la réunion familiale entre les trois générations de femmes des *Plains of Promise* et sa vision tragique, renforcée par la fable des oiseaux aquatiques en excipit, tranchent ainsi avec la réconciliation locale ultime et utopique de Norm avec le camp autochtone de l'Est mené par son rival Joseph Midnight, dont la petite-fille est la mère de son petit-fils Bala, avec qui il retourne sur les terres ancestrales sur lesquelles il est souverain.

CONCLUDING REMARKS

Susan Barrett

"Anyone can find hope in the stories: the big stories and the little ones in between" (Carpentaria, 12)

Carpentaria is an extraordinarily innovative novel and, as we hope *Carpentaria: The Law of the Land* has shown, there are many ways of reading it; as Arnaud Barras says its "literary power [...] resides in its ability to open up a spectrum of responses without ever confining itself to one" (2021, 169). It describes unflinchingly the terrible living conditions and daily racism that many rural Aboriginal Australians face, but it is not a bleak novel. There are many comic elements, and the novel ends on a hopeful note that Norm and his grandson will be able to build a new life with the old Dreaming stories on the site of his original house which is no longer on the edge of the white town of Desperance.

The novel draws its inspiration not only from Aboriginal culture but also from other oral and written literary traditions from all over the world. By blending them seamlessly together, and by subverting the subgenres she borrows, Wright has created a stylistically original work which challenges the dualism and binary thought processes that formed such an integral part of colonisation. The Aboriginal characters are, without a doubt, at the centre of the work but they are portrayed with all their quirks and foibles, thus portraying a complex Aboriginal world and avoiding a simple inversion of the Other of white colonial novels.

One of *Carpentaria*'s most striking features is the presence of the land as a character. Far from being a supernatural element that has nothing to do with the real world, the ancestral beings, who formed the landscape and all living-beings, are shown to permeate every moment of human life. The novel illustrates how mining, pollution and the waste created by capitalist society damage not only the land but also the humans who live in it – a timely message in the current climate change crisis.

Despite its serious messages, Wright has said that "most of all *Carpentaria* was written with the desire to create a work of art" (Writing, Kindle) and as she said in the foreword to this book, "The best way to read *Carpentaria* is just to enjoy it."

Annexes

GLOSSAIRE

I | Terminologie (Estelle Castro-Koshy & Laura Singeot)

a) Termes à employer et écueils à éviter

Il n'est pas aisé de savoir quels termes utiliser pour désigner les populations autochtones d'Australie, tant en anglais qu'en français, d'autant plus qu'il faut être sensible à leur connotation dans les deux langues et aux évolutions de perception des différents termes. Dans le glossaire de *Welcome to Country*, la géographe et anthropologue Marcia Langton liste les termes dont l'utilisation est à privilégier :

> **Aboriginal people, Torres Strait Islander people, Indigenous people, First Australians, First Nations peoples, or First People:** These terms are all generally acceptable when referring to the Aboriginal and Torres Strait Islander people of Australia. Despite much political correctness and nitpicking, none of these terms is offensive. Confusion arises among non-Indigenous people because of the long history of race hate towards Aboriginal people. Colonial and early twentieth-century laws used terms such as 'natives', 'aborigines', 'full-bloods', 'half-castes', and others. These terms are offensive because of their expression of racial supremacy and grading of people according to discredited race theories. (Langton, 2018, 104)

En français, le terme « Aborigène » est employé pour désigner les peuples autochtones du continent. Les Insulaires du détroit de Torres (Torres Strait Islanders ou Torres Strait Islander people) sont l'autre groupe autochtone australien, le détroit de Torres se situant entre la pointe nord-est de l'Australie et la Nouvelle-Guinée.

Aujourd'hui, les termes « First Nations », inspirés du contexte canadien, sont de plus en plus utilisés en Australie, notamment parmi les écrivains aborigènes et insulaires du détroit de Torres, comme le montre par exemple le nom du *First Nations Australia Writers Network*[1]. Les termes « Premières Nations », utilisés communément dans le contexte canadien, commencent à être utilisés pour le contexte australien pour traduire « First Nations ».

---

1. Leur page de présentation (https://www.fnawn.com.au/) décrit le réseau comme suit : « the peak body for Aboriginal and/or Torres Strait Islander writers, poets and storytellers, advocating and lobbying on their behalf, supporting ongoing development opportunities, in order to sustain and enhance First Nations Australian writing and storytelling. We believe in the sovereignty of First Nations writers and their communities, and work to foster writing from around the continent. »

La traduction en français par « Peuples Premiers » est sans doute moins heureuse à l'heure actuelle, car elle peut évoquer les termes connotés péjorativement de « Sociétés Primitives », expression encore trop souvent utilisée. L'expression « First Australians » a notamment été utilisée par la réalisatrice Rachel Perkins pour la série documentaire éponyme sur l'histoire autochtone de l'Australie. Pour certains, l'expression « First Australians » n'est pas judicieuse puisque cette partie de la population n'a été reconnue comme australienne que très tardivement, après le référendum de 1967, faisant d'eux les « derniers Australiens » (Pearson)[1].

« Indigenous Australians » englobe les Aborigènes et les Insulaires du détroit de Torres et se traduit par « peuples autochtones australiens/d'Australie ». Toutefois, quand ce terme est utilisé pour ne pas répéter « Aboriginal people » ou « Torres Strait Islander people », en français on peut le traduire par « Aborigènes » ou « Insulaires du détroit de Torres » (en fonction des peuples auxquels il est fait référence). Depuis le vote de la Déclaration des Nations Unies sur les droits des peuples autochtones (2007), il convient de traduire « Indigenous » par « autochtone » puisque c'est le terme qui a été retenu par les délégations autochtones pour s'auto-désigner, le terme « indigène » étant en général considéré comme péjoratif en raison de son utilisation dans les colonies françaises et du code de l'Indigénat. Utilisé très fréquemment pendant la décennie qui a suivi cette Déclaration, les termes « Indigenous Australians » sont désormais moins utilisés que « First Nations peoples » dans certains domaines en Australie[2].

Les termes ci-dessus n'attestent toutefois pas de la très grande diversité des peuples aborigènes et insulaires du détroit de Torres : il est estimé qu'il y avait environ 400 groupes linguistiques différents avant l'arrivée des colons sur le territoire australien. Les Aborigènes se présentent par leur nom de groupe, clan, nation ou de tribu. Ainsi, Alexis Wright est waanyi. Pour ne citer que quelques auteurs traduits en français, Anita Heiss et Tara June Winch sont wiradjuri, Philip McLaren est kamilaroi, Terri Janke est wuthati/meriam (à la fois aborigène et insulaire du détroit de Torres), Kim Scott est noongar. Inclure le nom de groupe quand il est connu est respectueux.

Les termes « Aboriginal people » et « Indigenous people » ont aussi pu être considérés comme un refus de reconnaître la diversité des peuples aborigènes et insulaires du détroit de Torres et être rejetés par des personnes qui préfèrent utiliser le nom précis de leur groupe (Waanyi, Noongar), des noms faisant référence aux Aborigènes d'une région (Murri pour le Queensland, Koori pour la Nouvelle-Galles du Sud), etc. D'autres dénominations telles « salt/freshwater people », peuple d'eau salée, peuple d'eau douce, ou encore « rainforest/spinifex/desert people » se réfèrent directement à l'environnement écologique de leur territoire ancestral (« country »)[3].

---

1. Voir par exemple : https://indigenousx.com.au/appropriate-terminology-for-aboriginal-and-torres-strait-islander-people-its-complicated/
2. Les termes à privilégier dans cinq ou dix ans ne seront donc peut-être pas les mêmes.
3. Voir : https://aiatsis.gov.au/explore/indigenous-australians-aboriginal-and-torres-strait-islander-people

Toutefois, les termes « Aboriginal people » et « Torres Strait Islander people » sont jugés importants dans le contexte de revendications pan-aborigènes/autochtones et pour les personnes faisant partie des Générations Volées qui ont été enlevées à leur famille et qui savent qu'elles sont aborigènes ou insulaires du détroit de Torres mais n'ont pu retrouver leur famille et leur communauté d'appartenance.

Certains termes, comme « natives », qui font référence au contexte colonial raciste, ne sont plus utilisés. D'autres sont tombés en désuétude. Le nom commun « Aborigine », que Wright utilise avec facétie dans le roman comme adjectif (118, 123) pour se moquer des bureaucrates ou des universitaires, mais qu'Angel Day utilise comme il se doit (en tant que nom) en faisant référence au « legal service for Aborigines » (38), est de moins en moins utilisé et ne fait pas partie des termes généralement recommandés. Il était jusque dans les années 2000 utilisé et considéré comme respectueux dans bien des contextes, notamment universitaires. Sa connotation méliorative se retrouve notamment dans la chanson célèbre « Nothing I Would Rather Be » de la comédie musicale *Bran Nue Dae* de Jimmy Chi[1].

b] Mots et expressions utilisés dans *Carpentaria*

Les traductions des termes en français qui suivent sont tirées de la traduction de Pierre Furlan aux éditions Actes Sud (2009).

Le terme « Mob » est fréquemment utilisé par les Aborigènes et Insulaires du détroit de Torres pour définir une communauté ou un groupe d'individus. Dans *Carpentaria*, ce terme est notamment employé lorsque ces personnes sont liées par une loyauté spécifique ou occupe un même espace géographique : « The Pricklebush mob » (6), « Uptown whitefella mob » (55), « Fishman mob » (363) ou « us mob » (413), par exemple. La traduction française affiche respectivement « les gens de Pricklebush » (16), « les Blancs des beaux quartiers » (66), « les gars de Fishman » (373) ou encore simplement « nous » (422). « Edge people » (57, 60, 316) est traduit par « les gens de la marge/la périphérie » (68, 71, 328) et « fringe people/mob » (20, 57) devient en français « les gens qui vivaient en bordure de la ville » (31) ou « ceux de la périphérie » (68).

Le terme « blackfella » est un terme qui désigne les Aborigènes dans *Carpentaria*, mais peut aussi désigner les Insulaires du détroit de Torres (et parfois, en fonction des contextes, être traduit par « les Noirs »). Il appartient au registre informel comme l'indique l'orthographe et est communément utilisé par les autochtones entre eux. Son pendant « whitefella » (« les Blancs ») apparaît tout aussi souvent dans *Carpentaria* et n'est en général pas utilisé par les Blancs. Synonyme d'Aborigène et/ou Insulaire du détroit de Torres, le terme « blackfella », tout comme les termes « Black » ou « Blak »

---

1. La chanson peut s'écouter dans sa forme théâtrale : https://aso.gov.au/titles/documentaries/bran-nue-dae/clip2/ ; et telle qu'elle a été reprise pour l'adaptation de la comédie musicale au cinéma dans le film de Rachel Perkins : https://www.youtube.com/watch?v=ZTiXSmQET2E

dans la plupart des contextes, ne renvoie pas à la couleur de la peau et peut donc désigner un Aborigène ou un Insulaire du détroit de Torres très clair de peau.

Enfin, les diverses communautés autochtones se nomment également selon leur lien à différents types d'eaux : par exemple, les ancêtres de Norm Phantom sont « the river people » (2, 6)/« les gens du fleuve » ou « les hommes du fleuve » (12, 16). Norm est aussi [a] saltwater man : « A *saltwater man* who insisted he belonged to the sea like fish » (386)/« C'était un homme de l'élément salé qui insistait qu'il appartenait à la mer comme les poissons » (396). On pourrait aussi proposer comme traduction « un homme du pays de l'eau salée » ou « de la terre de l'eau salée ». Enfin, « The Pricklebush mob » (6)/« Les gens de Pricklebush » (16), qui devient « les habitants des buissons épineux » (16) s'il s'agit de « the prickle bush mob » (6), est un autre nom lié au territoire.

c) L'épineuse question des termes injurieux et racistes

Des termes injurieux et racistes apparaissent ponctuellement dans le récit : « niggers » (341, 376), ainsi que le terme « darkies » (326) utilisé une fois. En français, si l'abréviation « Abo » peut de prime abord sembler pratique lors de prise de notes, il convient de préciser que dans le contexte australien, « Abo/s » et « Abos » est un terme méprisant voire insultant. C'est le maire raciste, Bruiser, qui l'utilise (34).

Un seul passage dans le roman renvoie, dans une phrase ironique, aux catégories racistes coloniales construites selon le « pourcentage de sang » des individus : « What Uptown liked to call tritaroon, quadroon, octaroon, full blood, or if speaking about themselves, friends and neighbours » (306)/« Ceux que dans les beaux quartiers on aimait désigner sous le nom de métis, de quarterons, de huitième de sang, ou de purs Abos – ou alors, s'ils parlaient de Blancs, sous le nom de voisins et amis » (318).

L'insulte raciste « coons » apparaît trois fois dans *Carpentaria* (32, 328, 432). Le terme témoigne toujours en anglais du racisme et du mépris des personnages qui l'utilisent. Il est notamment utilisé par le maire Bruiser dès le chapitre 2 :

> 'Ya mean coons?' Sanguine-voiced, the local mayor was speaking. A big, beefy, six-two, no-fuss man, who liked to call chalk chalk, or night night. That was his motto. He overshadowed the town with his power.
>
> 'Excuse me, Mr Bruiser, Mayor, you don't have to talk like that. We are just saying that they are an eyesore, so what are you going to do about it?' (32)

La voix de la communauté australienne blanche souligne bien le fait que parler de la sorte ne se fait pas, même si elle ne condamne ni le contenu des propos du maire raciste ni ne le critique directement. Par la suite, Kevin est surnommé « the party coon boy » (328) par les hommes aux cagoules blanches qui le torturent et le traînent derrière leur voiture au chapitre 10. Enfin, la dernière occurrence intervient lorsqu'Angel Day est envoyée par Mozzie Fishman loin de Desperance pour sa sécurité. Elle arrive dans une ville dont les graffitis témoignent de l'ambiance raciste qui peut encore régner en Australie : « Curt messages painted over public signs told the story of the town to the whole world passing on the highway. Kill All Coons, or similar, left on the hill for posterity's sake» (432). Ce passage rappelle le témoignage d'Alexis Wright sur son enfance et la ville où elle a grandi dans son essai «A dream of belonging: for Indigenous Australians, the fabled 'outback' is home» :

> I have fond memories of Cloncurry as a town of relatives and families. A town where closely connected families supported each other. Yet there was also the loneliness of being racially hemmed in and stereotyped in narratives based on racially divisive myths – the stories of the mind that defined the outback, about what it meant to belong.
>
> It probably did not help my mental wellbeing that the name of the town painted across the old water reservoir sitting on the top of a hill had been vandalised and changed from Cloncurry to Cooncurry. It remained there for several years. Years later, while visiting my mother, I found similar messages on the walls of the newly constructed dam. Hopefully, such offensive vandalism does not happen today. I remember my mother telling me at the time to not worry about it. Don't cause any fuss. (Dream)

II | Australian English in the novel (Susan Barrett)

Aussie battler : australien ordinaire, de la classe ouvrière, qui ne se laisse jamais décourager face à l'adversité

banana state : terme péjoratif pour l'État de Queensland

bickies: au sens propre, des biscuits ; en argot australien, une grosse somme d'argent

billycan : boîte de conserve vide utilisée pour faire bouillir l'eau sur un feu de camp

black stump «**this side of the black stump**» : expression qui signifie la limite de la civilisation (tout ce qui est civilisé se trouve de ce côté de la souche brûlée) – «**beyond the black stump**» : endroit très isolé, loin de tout

blackfella : Aborigène ou Insulaire du détroit de Torres (Aborigène dans *Carpentaria*)

blackfella mob : un groupe d'Aborigènes

bogan : stéréotype de l'Australien qui vivait dans les banlieues défavorisées des grandes villes et faisait partie de la classe ouvrière

boong : terme raciste et insultant qui désigne une personne aborigène

bush : terme générique pour des lieux peu peuplés et dont la végétation varie en fonction des climats (arbres, arbustes et/ou broussailles)

camel train : chameaux de trait (utilisés pour transporter les marchandises dans les endroits arides avant l'arrivée des voitures automobiles)

cattle stations : grand élevage de vaches à l'intérieur du pays

chook : un poulet

coon : terme raciste et très insultant pour désigner une personne aborigène

darkies : terme péjoratif, utilisé surtout au XIXe siècle et au début du XXe, pour désigner les Aborigènes

doona : une couette

dunny : WC extérieur

dunny cart : chariot qui circulait la nuit pour ramasser les excréments humains

eskies : glacière

flying doctor : médecin qui se déplace en avion dans les endroits reculés à l'intérieur de l'Australie
grog : terme générique pour l'alcool
googie-egg : œuf à la coque
humpy (sing)/**humpies** (pl) : petit abri temporaire, fabriqué avec des branches, des écorces, ou de la tôle par les Aborigènes
kangaroo court : tribunal populaire, sans existence légale
louvred homes : maisons aux volets faits de lattes horizontales qui permettent de garder la fraîcheur
Myall : terme péjoratif utilisé surtout au XIXe siècle pour désigner un Aborigène vivant de manière traditionnelle
outback : (terme des Australians blancs) l'intérieur du continent australien, aride ou semi-aride, loin des zones urbaines
never never : zone rurale très isolée
pastoralist : propriétaire d'un grand élevage de moutons ou de vaches
rednecks : terme péjoratif pour désigner des personnes politiquement conservatrices (« *conservative* »), généralement utilisé pour des personnes en milieu rural
stock camps : lieu où est logé le personnel qui s'occupe des vaches sur les grands élevages
stubby : (sing)/**stubbies** (pl) : petite bouteille de bière
Surfers Paradise : district du Gold Coast dans le Queensland, très populaire auprès des touristes australiens et internationaux
swag : sac de couchage et petite tente combinés
swagman : ouvrier agricole qui allait d'une ferme à une autre, en apportant ses affaires dans un « swag »
TAFE : acronyme pour « Technical And Further Education », établissement d'enseignement professionnel
thongs : des claquettes
tucker : terme générique pour la nourriture
Yellow Peril : terme raciste qui désigne le risque d'invasion du nord de l'Australie par les Chinois ou autres peuples asiatiques voisins

BIBLIOGRAPHIE

*** : lecture incontournable
** : lecture très fortement conseillée
* : lecture fortement conseillée

I | Alexis Wright

a) Carpentaria

*****Wright Alexis, *Carpentaria* (2006), London, Constable, 2009.**

*****—, *Carpentaria*, Audible Audiobook - Unabridged. Isaac Drandich (narrator), Tullamarine, Bolinda, 2008.**

—, trad. fr. P. Furlan, *Carpentarie*, Arles, Actes Sud, 2009.

L'écoute du livre lu par l'acteur aborigène Isaac Drandich est conseillée en sus de la lecture du livre. Elle permet notamment d'entendre ce que sont les langues, voix, l'humour du roman, de mieux percevoir que l'on se trouve d'emblée dans l'Australie aborigène, et de prendre du plaisir à découvrir ce roman magistral.

b) Other Works by Alexis Wright

I) Novels

—, *Plains of Promise*, St Lucia, University of Queensland Press, 1997.

—, *The Swan Book*, Artarmon, Giramondo, 2013.

II) Non-fiction

—, *Tracker: Stories of Tracker Tilmouth*, Artarmon, Giramondo, 2017.

**—, *Croire en l'incroyable*, trad. fr. S. Porte, Arles, Actes Sud, 2000. (Unpublished in English)

— (ed.), *Take Power Like This Old Man Here: An Anthology of Writings Celebrating Twenty Years of Land Rights in Central Australia 1977-1997*, Alice Springs, Jukurrpa Books, 1998.

—, *Grog War*, Broome, Magabala Books, 1997.

III) Short Stories and novella

—, "Odyssey of the Horizon", *in* King Natalie (ed.), *Tracey Moffatt: my Horizon*, Thames and Hudson Australia, 2017, https://natalieking.com.au/wp-content/uploads/2018/07/TraceyMoffatt-MyHorizon_VeniceBiennale2018.pdf

—, trad.fr. S. Kandé, M. De Gouvenain, *Le Pacte du serpent arc-en-ciel*, Arles, Actes Sud, 2002. (Unpublished in English)

—, "The Chinky Apple Tree", *in* DAVIES Kerry (ed.), *Across Country: Stories from Aboriginal Australia*, Sydney, ABC Books, 2001, p. 218-23.

—, "When Devils Call", *in* DAVIES Kerry (ed.), *Across Country: Stories from Aboriginal Australia*, Sydney, ABC Books, 2001, p. 224-28.

IV] Articles and Essays

*—, "A Dream of Belonging for Indigenous Australians, the Fabled Outback is Home", *The Guardian*, 18 May, 2021, https://www.theguardian.com/australia-news/2021/may/18/a-dream-of-belonging-for-indigenous-australians-the-fabled-outback-is-home

**—, "The Inward Migration in Apocalyptic Times", *Emergence Magazine*, 27 January 2021, https://emergencemagazine.org/essay/the-inward-migration-in-apocalyptic-times/

**—, "Broken Sense of Place", *in* JOSE Nicholas, MADDEN Benjamin, *Antipodean China: Reflections on Literary Exchange*, Artarmon, Giramondo, 2021. (Available on Kindle)

**—, "The Power of Story", *in* JOSE Nicholas, MADDEN Benjamin, *Antipodean China: Reflections on Literary Exchange*, Artarmon, Giramondo, 2021. (Available on Kindle)

**—, "In Times Like These, What would Oodgeroo do?", *The Monthly*, December 2020-January 2021, https://www.themonthly.com.au/issue/2020/december/1606741200/alexis-wright/times-these-what-would-oodgeroo-do#mtr

**—, "A Self-governing Literature", *Meanjin*, Winter 2020, https://meanjin.com.au/essays/a-self-governing-literature/

—, "The Road Ahead Is Hard: Now is not the Time to Kill off Studies in the Humanities", *The Guardian*, 22 June 2020, https://www.theguardian.com/commentisfree/2020/jun/22/the-road-ahead-is-hard-now-is-not-the-time-to-kill-off-studies-in-the-humanities

—, "Want to Stop Australia's Fires? Listen to Aboriginal People", *The New York Times*, 15 January 2020, https://www.nytimes.com/2020/01/15/opinion/australia-fires-aboriginal-people.html

**"—, "A Journey in Writing Place", *Meanjin*, Winter 2019, n° 78/2, p. 44-53, https://meanjin.com.au/essays/a-journey-in-writing-place/

**"—, "The Ancient Library and a Self-Governing Literature", *Sydney Review of Books*, June 2019, https://sydneyreviewofbooks.com/essay/the-ancient-library-and-a-self-governing-literature/

**—, "We all Smell the Smoke, we all Feel the Heat: This Environmental Catastrophe is Global", *The Guardian*, 17 May 2019, https://www.theguardian.com/environment/2019/may/18/we-all-smell-the-smoke-we-all-feel-the-heat-this-environmental-catastrophe-is-global

—, "Telling the Untold Stories: Alexis Wright on Censorship", *Overland*, 18 February 2019, https://overland.org.au/2019/02/telling-the-untold-stories-alexis-wright-on-censorship/

—, "The Power and Purpose of Literature: Boisbouvier Oration 2018", *Meanjin*, Summer 2018, https://meanjin.com.au/essays/the-power-and-purpose-of-literature/

—, "Hey Ancestor", *The Guardian*, 25 January 2018, https://www.theguardian.com/commentisfree/2018/jan/26/alexis-wright-hey-ancestor

**—, "The Big Book about Small Town Australia that Travelled the World", *The Guardian*, 7 September 2017, https://www.theguardian.com/culture/2017/sep/08/the-big-book-about-small-town-australia-that-travelled-the-world

**—, "What Happens When You Tell Somebody Else's Story?", *Meanjin*, Summer 2016, https://meanjin.com.au/essays/what-happens-when-you-tell-somebody-elses-story/

*—, "Where to Point the Spears?", *in* OBOE Annalisa, BASSI Shaul (eds.), *Experiences of Freedom in Postcolonial Literatures and Cultures*, London, Routledge, 2011, p. 35-42.

**—, "Deep Weather", *Meanjin*, Autumn 2011, https://meanjin.com.au/essays/deep-weather/

*—, "Open Letter: Talking about an Indigenous Tomorrow", *ABC News*, 29 March 2011, https://www.abc.net.au/news/2011-03-30/talking_about_an_indigenous_tomorrow/45734

—, "A Question of Fear", *in* TSIOLKAS Christos, HAIGH Gideon, WRIGHT Alexis, *Tolerance, Prejudice and Fear: Sydney PEN Voices, the Three Writers Project*, St Leonards Allen & Unwin, 2008, p. 129-169.

*****—, "On Writing *Carpentaria*", *Heat*, 2007, n° 13, p. 79-95. (Also available in NG Lynda (ed.), *Indigenous Transnationalism: Alexis Wright's* Carpentaria).** (Available on Kindle)

—, "We Have a Vision. What we Need is Authority", *The Advertiser*, 30 June 2007, p. 8-10.

—, "Embracing the Indigenous Vision", *Meanjin*, 2006, n° 65, p. 104-108.

**—, "The Politics of Writing", *Southerly*, 2003, n° 62/2, p. 10-20.

—, "One Hundred Milleniums Plus Two: Maintaining Traditional Indigenous Geographies Minus Two Centuries of Lost Life in the Geography of Australian Ignorance", *in* BALLYN Susan *et al.* (eds.), *Changing Geographies: Essays on Australia*, Barcelona, Universitat de Barcelona, 2001, p. 135-143.

—, "A Family Document", *in* HALLIGAN Marion (ed.), *Storykeepers*, Sydney, Duffy & Snellgrove, 2001, p. 223-42.

*—, "Breaking Taboos", *Australian Humanities Review*, September-November 1998, n° 11, http://australianhumanitiesreview.org/1998/09/01/breaking-taboos/

II) Interviews with Alexis Wright

a) Interviews with Alexis Wright about *Carpentaria*

**INDYK Ivor, "Alexis Wright in Conversation with Ivor Indyk", Western Sydney University, 24 October 2014, https://www.youtube.com/watch?v=W8Xvut04Bbo

O'BRIEN Kerry, "Alexis Wright Interview", 21 June 2007, Televised on the ABC's 7:30 report, *in Hecate*, 2007, n° 33/1, p. 215-219, http://www.uws.edu.au/__data/assets/pdf_file/0009/57906/Alexis_Wright_Interview.pdf

b) Interviews with Alexis Wright about her work in general

BRASCH Nic, "Alexis Wright", *The Garret Podcast: Writers on Writing*, April 20th, 2018, https://thegarretpodcast.com/alexis-wright/

*VERNAY Jean-François, "An interview with Alexis Wright", *Antipodes*, December 2004, n° 18/2, p. 119-122.

WRIGHT Alexis, "Alexis Wright at the Sydney Writers' Festival 2014", *The Monthly Video*, 12 September 2014, https://www.youtube.com/watch?v=sh_XvQecHB4

III) Articles and books on *Carpentaria*

a) Books on *Carpentaria*

*****CASTRO-KOSHY Estelle, LEHARTEL Temiti (eds.), *Alexis Wright*, Carpentaria, Paris, Ellipses, 2021.**

***Alexis Wright*, Carpentaria brings together 16 essays by 18 French and international scholars offering innovative, contextual, and microreading analyses of *Carpentaria*.**

*****NG Lynda (ed.), *Indigenous Transnationalism: Alexis Wright's* Carpentaria, Artarmon, Giramondo, 2018.** (Available on Kindle)

***Indigenous Transnationalism* brings together essays by literary scholars from seven countries who highlight the ties *Carpentaria* has to other writers/novels and literary traditions in different parts of the world and analyse the distinctiveness of Wright's writing.**

b) Journal issue on Alexis Wright

***Antipodes: A Global Journal of Australian/New Zealand Literature*, 2019, n° 33/1, https://digitalcommons.wayne.edu/antipodes/vol33/iss1/

c) Articles and book chapters on *Carpentaria*

*****ALAI, "On *Carpentaria*", *in* JOSE Nicholas, MADDEN Benjamin (eds.), *Antipodean China: Reflections on Literary Exchange*, Artarmon, Giramondo, 2021. (Available on Kindle)**

In this essay, Alai highlights Alexis Wright's talent for writing, in particular, her depiction of the sea "in a way that is even more soul-stirring than Hemingway's". The writer also foregrounds how *Carpentaria* breaks "the linear dimension of time". *Antipodean China: Reflections on Literary Exchange* includes important essays by Alexis Wright.

*ATKINSON Mira, "Australia", *in Reading Australia*, 2015, https://readingaustralia.com.au/essays/carpentaria/

**BARRAS Arnaud, "Mapping Carpentaria: Voices, Stories and Journeys of the Gulf Country", in CASTRO-KOSHY Estelle, LEHARTEL Temiti (eds.), *Alexis Wright*, Carpentaria, Paris, Ellipses, 2021, p. 169-183 (An earlier version is available at: https://arnaudbarras.ch/documents/barras_mapping%20carpentaria_unpublished.pdf)

**BARRETT Susan, "'This Land is Me': Indigenous Australian Story-telling and Ecological Knowledge", 2013, *ELOHI*, n° 3, p. 29-40, https://journals.openedition.org/elohi/592

**BIRNS Nicholas, "The Notions of Permanence: Autochthony, Indigeneneity, Locality in Alexis Wright's Carpentaria", *in* NG Lynda (ed.), *Indigenous Transnationalism: Alexis Wright's* Carpentaria, Artarmon, Giramondo, 2018. (Available on Kindle)

*****BIRRELL Kathleen, "*Carpentaria* by Alexis Wright", *Law, Culture and the Humanities*, 2009, n° 5, p. 156-170. (Also available in CASTRO-KOSHY Estelle, LEHARTEL Temiti (eds.), *Alexis Wright*, Carpentaria, Paris, Ellipses, 2021).**

*****—, "A Law of Alterity" *in* BIRRELL Kathleen, *Indigeneity: Before and Beyond the Law*, London, Routledge, 2016, ch. 15.**

Birrell's work argues that *Carpentaria* is "a remarkable rendering of Australian indigeneities" and provides "a radical rendering of the transformative capacity of Indigenous Law". She also highlights how the novel defies conventional literary forms. Birrell's review summarizes the main points she develops in her book chapter.

*****BREWSTER Anne, "Indigenous Sovereignty and the Crisis of Whiteness in Alexis Wright's *Carpentaria*", *Australian Literary Studies*, 2010, n° 25/4,** https://doi.org/10.20314/als.10d6ac2daf

In this article Anne Brewster analyses the relationship between the white settlers and the Indigenous inhabitants of Desperance through the theoretical lens of critical whiteness studies. Brewster shows how, by placing the Indigenous characters in the subject position, the novel defamiliarises whiteness and normalises an Indigenous world view. She examines in detail the concept of indigenous sovereignty, which she situates both in the larger Australian historical context and in Aboriginal literature.

**CASTRO Estelle, "Pré-occupation(s) et souffle du lieu dans *Carpentaria* d'Alexis Wright", *Loxias*, 2009, n° 25, http://revel.unice.fr/loxias/index.html?id=2917

*****CASTRO-KOSHY Estelle, "The Poetics of Relation in *Carpentaria*", *in* NG Lynda (ed.), *Indigenous Transnationalism: Alexis Wright's* Carpentaria, Artarmon, Giramondo, 2018, p. 118-137.**

This essay shows how *Carpentaria* allows the reader to apprehend a poetics of relation through an Indigenous perspective. It analyses the distinctive "imagining role of language" (Bachelard), the use of "ancestral realism" (Mateata-Allain), and humour in the novel. Connections between *Carpentaria* and Patrick Chamoiseau's *Texaco* are also drawn. This essay also shows that French and Francophone philosophy and thought have been influenced by Aboriginal thought, narratives and concepts.

DALEY Linda, "Alexis Wright's Fiction as World Making", *Contemporary Women's Writing*, 2016, n° 10/1, p. 8–23.

**DEVLIN-GLASS Frances, "A Politics of the Dreamtime: Destructive and Regenerative Rainbows in Alexis Wright's *Carpentaria*", *Australian Literary Studies*, 2008, n° 23/4, p. 392-407.

EAGLE Chester, "Singing the Country: a First Look at *Carpentaria* by Alexis Wright", *in The Well in the Shadow: A Writer's Journey through Australian Literature*, Fitzroy, Trojan Press, 2010.

*HALL Demelza, "The Isle of Refuse in Alexis Wright's *Carpentaria*: Reconstructing Heterotopic Space", *Southerly*, 2012, n° 72/3, https://www.academia.edu/3823178/The_Isle_of_Refuse_in_Alexis_Wright_s_Carpentaria_Reconstituting_Heterotopic_Space

HAYLOCK Bridget, "Enlisting Rage and Speaking Place: Alexis Wright's *Carpentaria*", *in Traumatic Imprints: Performance, Art, Literature and Theoretical Practice*, Brill 2011, p. 91-101.

KOSUGI Sei, "Indigenous Knowledge and Global Translation : Reconstruction of Australia through Aboriginal Imagination in Alexis Wright's *Carpentaria*", *in* DEVY N., DAVIS Geoffrey V., CHAKRAVARTY K. K. (eds.), *Performing Identities: Celebrating Indigeneity in the Arts*, London, Routledge, 2015, ch. 16. (Available on Kindle)

*****LEANE Jeanine, "Historyless people", *in* MCGRATH Ann, JEBB Mary Anne (eds.), *Long History, Deep Time: Deepening Histories of Places*, Canberra, ANU Press, 2015, p. 151-162,** https://press-files.anu.edu.au/downloads/press/p319821/html/ch09.xhtml#footnote-403-backlink

This article, by the Indigenous poet and academic Jeanine Leane, examines how *Carpentaria* challenges the Western concepts of time, history and science-based knowledge. It argues that Aboriginal Dreaming is not a static place or time, as Western discourse often implies, but is rather a continually evolving narrative in which past and present co-exist simultaneously.

**LOOMES Louise, "'Armageddon Begins Here': Apocalypse in Alexis Wright's *Carpentaria*", *LiNQ*, 2014, n° 41, p. 124-138, https://journals.jcu.edu.au/linq/article/view/3181

LOWRY Elizabeth, "The Fishman Lives the Lore", *London Review of Books*, April 2004, n° 30/8, p. 26-27. http://www.uws.edu.au/__data/assets/pdf_file/0011/57926/lowr01_3008.pdf

**MEAD Philip, "The Geopolitical Underground: Alexis Wright's *Carpentaria*, Mining, and the Sacred", *in* NEUMAIER Beate, SCHAFFER Kay (eds.), *Decolonizing the Landscape: Indigenous Cultures in Australia*, Amsterdam, Rodopi, 2014, p. 185-206.

**MINTER Peter, "Rubbish Palaces, Islands of Junk: On the Function of Tropes of Pollution in Alexis Wright's *Carpentaria*", *in* NG Lynda (ed.), *Indigenous Transnationalism: Alexis Wright's* Carpentaria, Artarmon, Giramondo, 2018. (Available on Kindle)

*MOLLOY Diane, "Finding Hope in the Stories: Alexis Wright's *Carpentaria* and the Carnivalesque Search for a New Order", *JASAL*, 2012, n° 12/3, https://openjournals.library.sydney.edu.au/index.php/JASAL/article/view/9836/9724

**NG Lynda, "Translocal Temporalities in Alexis Wright's *Carpentaria*", *in* MUNKELT Marga, SCHMITZ Markus, STEIN Mark, STROH Silke (eds.), *Postcolonial Translocations. Cultural Representation and Critical Spatial Thinking*, Amsterdam & New York, Rodopi, 2013, p. 109-26.

—, "An Abundance of Waste: *Carpentaria*'s Re-Valuation of Excess", *in* NG Lynda (ed.), *Indigenous Transnationalism: Alexis Wright's* Carpentaria, Artarmon, Giramondo, 2018. (Available on Kindle)

OSBORNE Roger, WHITLOCK Gillian, "*Carpentaria*: Reading with the Dirt of Blurbs and Front Pages", *JASAL*, 2016, n° 16/2, https://openjournals.library.sydney.edu.au/index.php/JASAL/article/view/11401/10793

**NOLAN Maggie, "Shifting Timescapes and the Significance of the Mine in Alexis Wright's *Carpentaria*", *Australian Literary Studies*, 2020, n° 35/2.

**RAVENSCROFT Alison, "Dreaming of Others: *Carpentaria* and its Critics", *Cultural Studies Review*, 2010, n° 16/2, p. 194-224.

RENES Martin, "Dreamtime Narrative and Postcolonisation: Alexis Wright's *Carpentaria* as an Antidote to the Discourse of Intervention", *Journal of the European Association for Studies on Australia*, 2011, n° 2/1, p. 102-122, http://www.easa-australianstudies.net/files/jeasa29renes.pdf

**—, "Sung by an Indigenous Siren: Epic and Epistemology in Alexis Wright's *Carpentaria*", *Coolabah*, 2019, n° 27, https://revistes.ub.edu/index.php/coolabah/article/view/30518

**RIGBY Kate, "The Poetics of Decolonization: Reading *Carpentaria* in a Feminist Ecocritical Frame", *in* GAARD Greta, ESTOK Simon C., OPPERMANN Serpil (eds.), *International Perspectives in Feminist Ecocriticism*, New York, Routledge, 2013, p. 120-136.

*RODOREDA Geoff, "Orality and Narrative Structure in Alexis Wright's *Carpentaria*", *JASAL*, 2016, n° 16/2, https://openjournals.library.sydney.edu.au/index.php/JASAL/article/view/11005

*ROWLAND Lucy, "Indigenous Temporality and Climate Change in Alexis Wright's *Carpentaria*", *Journal of Postcolonial Writing*, 2019, n° 55/4, p. 541-554.

ŠČIGULINSKÁ Jana, "Tears behind the Laughter in Alexis Wright's *Carpentaria*", *in* KACMAROVA Alena, SHATRO Bavjola, *Challenges of Anglophone Language(s), Literature and Culture*, Newcastle upon Tyne, Cambridge Scholars Press, 2017, p. 173-196, https://www.researchgate.net/publication/312897154_Challenges_to_Anglophone_Languages_Literatures_and_Cultures

SPICER Chrystopher J., "The Apocalypse and Epiphany of Cyclone in the Land of Alexis Wright's *Carpentaria*", *in* SPICER Chrystopher J., *Cyclone Country, the Language of Place and Disaster in Australian Literature*, North Carolina, McFarland & Company, 2020.

SYSON Ian, "Uncertain Magic", *Overland*, 2007, n° 187, p. 85–86, http://www.staff.vu.edu.au/syson/187rev.pdf

VAN RIJSWIJK Honni, "Stories of the Nation's Continuing Past: Responsibility for Historical Injuries in Australian Law and Alexis Wright's *Carpentaria*", *University of New South Wales Law Journal*, 2012, n° 35/2, http://classic.austlii.edu.au/au/journals/UTSLRS/2012/28.html

IV | Articles and books with sections on *Carpentaria*

ASHCROFT Bill, DEVLIN-GLASS Frances, "'Stories of the Old Country': Reinventing Dreamtime Tropes in *Poor Fellow My Country*, *Benang*, and *Carpentaria*", *in* ASHCROFT Bill, MCCREDDEN Lyn (eds.), *Intimate Horizons: The Post-Colonial Sacred in Australian Literature*, Adelaide, ATF Press, 2009, p. 205-241.

ATKINSON Meera Anne, *The Poetics of Transgenerational Trauma*, London, Bloomsbury Academic, 2017, https://www.academia.edu/33060692/The_Poetics_of_Transgenerational_Trauma_Introduction_pdf

*****BARRAS Arnaud, "Ecopoetic Encounters: Amnesia and Nostalgia in Alexis Wright's Environmental Fiction", *Australasian Journal of Ecocriticism and Cultural Ecology*, 2015, n° 5, p. 54-67**, https://openjournals.library.sydney.edu.au/index.php/Swamphen/article/view/10629/10507

Arnaud Barras has written several articles on Alexis Wright, all of which offer sensitive readings of *Carpentaria*. In this article, Barras looks at some of the difficulties non-Waanyi readers encounter when reading Wright's novels. He examines the link between body, story and country with a particular focus on the character of Elias Smith who he sees as an amnesic embodiment of Euro-Australian society.

*BEN-MESSAHEL Salhia, *Globaletics and Radicant Aesthetics in Australian Fiction*, Cambridge, Cambridge Scholars Publishing, 2017.

CASTRO Estelle, *Tradition, création et reconnaissance dans la littérature aborigène du vingtième et vingt-et-unième siècles*, Thèse de doctorat, La Sorbonne Nouvelle-Paris 3 et The University of Queensland, 2007.

CHARON Mylène, *Black Feminism : Rapports sociaux de sexe et de race dans la poésie et l'art contemporains des Premières Nations d'Australie*, Thèse de doctorat, Cergy Paris Université, 2020.

**FERRIER Carole, "'Disappearing Memory' and the Colonial Present in Recent Indigenous Women's Writing", *JASAL*, 2008, p. 37-55, https://openjournals.library.sydney.edu.au/index.php/JASAL/article/view/9627/9516

*HOLGATE Ben, "Unsettling Narratives: Re-Evaluating Magical Realism as Postcolonial Discourse through Alexis Wright's *Carpentaria* and *The Swan Book*", *Journal of Postcolonial Writing*, 2015, n° 51/6, p. 634-647.

GLEESON-WHITE Jane, "Capitalism versus the Agency of Place: an Ecocritical Reading of *That Deadman Dance* and *Carpentaria*", *JASAL*, 2013, n° 13/2, https://openjournals.library.sydney.edu.au/index.php/JASAL/article/view/9867/9756

GRIFFITHS Michael R., *The Distribution of Settlement: Appropriation and Refusal in Australian Literature and Culture*, Crawley, UWA Publishing, 2018.

JORDAN Deborah, *Climate Change Narratives in Australian Fiction*, Saarbrucken, Lambert Academic Publishing, 2014, https://www.researchgate.net/publication/276272827_Climate_Change_Narratives_in_Australian_Fiction

JOSE Nicholas, "Deconstructing the Dumpling: Australia, China, Lived Connections", *Journal of Australian Studies*, 2013, n° 37/1, p. 116-129.

JOSEPH Laura, "Opening the Gates of Hell: Regional Emergences in *Carpentaria* and *Dreamhunter*", *Southerly*, 2009, n° 69/2, p. 66-80.

—,"Dreaming Phantoms and Golems: Elements of The Place Beyond Nation in *Carpentaria* and *Dreamhunter*", *JASAL*, special issue 2009, http://pandora.nla.gov.au/pan/63067/20090910-1633/www.nla.gov.au/openpublish/index.php/jasal/article/view/848/1759.html

LE GUELLEC-MINEL Anne, "From *Carpentaria* to *The Swan Book*: Finding a Voice to Narrate and Resist the Threat of Extinction in Alexis Wright's Latest Work", *E-rea: Revue D'études Anglophones*, 2021, n° 18/2, https://journals.openedition.org/erea/11860

**LEANE Jeanine, "The Vastness of Voice", *in* NG Lynda (ed.), *Indigenous Transnationalism: Alexis Wright's* Carpentaria, Artarmon, Giramondo, 2018. (Available on Kindle)

MARTIN Richard, MEAD Philip, TRIGGER David, "The Politics of Indigeneity, Identity and Representation in Literature from North Australia's Gulf Country", *Social Identities*, 2014, n°20 / 4–5, p. 330–345.

*MEAD Philip, "Indigenous Literature and the Extractive Industries", *Australian Literary Studies*, 2013, n° 28/4, p. 31-46.

MOLLOY Diane, *Cultural Memory and Literature: Re-imagining Australia's Past*, Leiden, Brill, 2015.

*MULLANEY Julie, "Storying Sovereignty and 'Sustainable Self-Determination' in Alexis Wright's *Carpentaria* and Warwick Thornton's *Samson and Delilah*", *in* DEVY N., DAVIS Geoffrey V., CHAKRAVARTY K. K. (eds.), *Performing Identities: Celebrating Indigeneity in the Arts*, London, Routledge, 2015, ch. 9. (Available on Kindle)

**PALLEAU-PAPIN Françoise, "The 'Weight' of Words in Alexis Wright's Works", *EASA*, 2020, n° 11/1, http://www.australianstudies.eu/?p=1487

POLAK Iva, "Indigenous Australian Texts in European English Departments: A Fence, a Bridge and a Country as an Answer to the Debate over Multiculturalism", *Elope*, 2013, n° 10/2, p. 69-81.

*RAVENSCROFT Alison, "Strange Weather: Indigenous Materialisms, New Materialism, and Colonialism", *The Cambridge Journal of Postcolonial Literary Inquiry*, 2018, n° 5/3 p. 353-370.

SEFTON-ROWSTON Adelle, "Hope at the End of the World: Creation Stories and Apocalypse in Alexis Wright's *Carpentaria* and *The Swan Book*", *Antipodes*, 2016, n° 30/2, p. 355-368.

**SHOEMAKER Adam, "Hard Dreams and Indigenous Worlds in Australia's North", *Hecate*, 2008, n° 34/1, p. 55-61.

V | Anthologies of Indigenous Australian Literature

DAVIS Jack, et al. (eds.), *Paperbark: A Collection of Black Australian Writings*, (1990) St Lucia, University of Queensland Press, 2001.

DIXON R.M.W., DUWELL Martin (eds.), *The Honey-Ant Men's Love Song and Other Aboriginal Song Poems*, St Lucia, University of Queensland Press, 1990.

DOUGLAS Josie (ed.), *Untreated: Poems by Black Writers*, Alice Springs, Jukurrpa Books, 2001.

GILBERT Kevin (ed.), *Inside Black Australia: an Anthology of Aboriginal Poetry*, Ringwood, Penguin, 1988.

*HEISS, Anita, MINTER Peter (eds.), *Macquarie Pen Anthology of Aboriginal Literature*, Crows Nest, Allen and Unwin, 2008.

*—, *Anthology of Australian Aboriginal Literature*, Montreal and Kingston, McGill-Queen's University Press, 2008.

LEANE Jeanine (ed.), *Guwayu, for All Times: A Collection of First Nations Poems*, Broome, Magabala, 2020.

VAN NEERVEN Ellen (ed.), *Flock: First Nations Stories Then and Now*, St Lucia, University of Queensland Press, 2021.

*WHITTAKER Alison (ed.), *Fire Front: First Nations Poetry and Power Today*, St Lucia, University of Queensland Press, 2020.

VI | Books and Articles on Indigenous Australian Literature

BARRETT Susan, "The Translation and Marketing of Australian Literature in France", *in* DOLCE Maria Renata, RIEM NATALE Antonella (eds.), *Bernard Hickey, A Roving Cultural Ambassador: Essays in His Memory*, Udine, Forum, 2009, p. 51-60.

*BREWSTER Anne, *Giving this Country a Memory: Contemporary Aboriginal Voices of Australia*, New York, Cambria Press, 2015.

*BRUN Marilyne, "Oralité et résistance dans la littérature aborigène australienne", *in* MEYER Christine, PRESCOD Paul (eds.), *Langues choisies, langues sauvées : poétiques de la résistance*, Würzburg, Königshausen & Neumann, 2018, p. 279-293.

CASEY Maryrose, *Creating Frames: Contemporary Indigenous Theatre: 1967-1990*, St Lucia, University of Queensland Press, 2004.

**CASTRO-KOSHY Estelle, *Literature (H)as Power: A Collection of Essays and Interviews with Six Aboriginal and Torres Strait Islander Authors*, St Lucia, AustLit, 2018, https://www.austlit.edu.au/LiteratureHasPower

CHADWICK Allen, *Trans-Indigenous: Methodologies for Global Native Literary Studies*, Minneapolis, University of Minnesota Press, 2012.

—, "Indigenous Juxtapositions: Teaching Maori and Aboriginal Texts in Global Contexts", *in* BIRNS Nicholas, MOORE Nicole, SHIEFF Sarah (eds.), *Teaching Australian and New Zealand Literature*, New York City, MLA, 2016, p. 179-189.

DAVIS Jack, HODGE Bob, (eds.), *Aboriginal Writing Today: Papers from the First National Conference of Aboriginal Writers, Held in Perth, Western Australia, in 1983*, Canberra, Australian Institute of Aboriginal Studies, 1985.

DUTHIL Fanny, *Histoire de femmes aborigènes*, Paris, PUF/Le Monde, 2006.

GILFEDDER Deirdre, "Stories from the Stolen Generation: the Role of Autobiography in the National Enquiry into Separation of Children from their Aboriginal Families", *in* PERRY Susan, SCHENCK Celeste (eds.), *Eye-to Eye: Women Practising Development across Cultures*, London, Zed Books, 2001, p. 200-213.

GRIEVE-WILLIAMS Victoria, "Oodgeroo: Breaking the Iron Cycle of Settler Colonialism", *Overland Literary Journal*, 2020, https://overland.org.au/previous-issues/issue-240/feature-oodgeroo-breaking-the-iron-cycle-of-settler-colonialism/

GROSSMAN Michèle, "After Aboriginalism: Power, Knowledge and Indigenous Australian Critical Writing", *in* GROSSMAN Michèle (ed.), *Blacklines: Contemporary Critical Writing by Indigenous Australians*, Melbourne, Melbourne University Press, 2005, p. 12-23.

—, *Entangled Subjects: Indigenous/Australian Cross-Cultures of Talk, Text, and Modernity*, Amsterdam, Rodopi, 2013.

HALL Demelza, "Translating the Short Stories of Alexis Wright. Sylvie Kandé Talks to Demelza Hall about *Le Pacte Du Serpent Arc-En-Ciel*", *Journal of the Association for the Study of Australian Literature*, 2016, n° 16/2.

HEISS Anita, *Dhuuluu-Yala – to Talk Straight: Publishing Indigenous Literature*, Canberra, Aboriginal Studies Press, 2003.

—, "Black Poetics", *Meanjin*, 2006, n° 65, p. 180-191.

**—, "Indigenous Studies Told Collectively", *in The BlackWords Essays*, St Lucia, AustLit, 2019, https://www.austlit.edu.au/austlit/static/new/files/newsitefiles/Heiss_Indigenous-Stories-Told-Collectively.pdf

**—, *The BlackWords Essays*, St Lucia, AustLit, 2015, https://www.austlit.edu.au/blackwordsessays

HORAKOVA Martina, *Inscribing Difference and Resistance: Indigenous Women's Personal Non-Fiction and Life Writing in Australia and North America*, Brno, Masaryk University Press, 2017.

**LEANE Jeanine, "Teaching with BlackWords: Aboriginal and Torres Strait Islander Storytellers", St Lucia, AustLit, 2012, https://www.austlit.edu.au/austlit/static/new/files/newsitefiles/Leane-TeachingwithBlackWordsEssay.pdf

—, "Biography: David Unaipon", *AQ-Australian Quarterly*, 2015, n° 86, p. 28-30.

MUDROOROO Narogin, *Writing from the Fringe, A Study of Modern Aboriginal Literature*, South Yarra, Hyland House, 1990.

—, *The Indigenous Literature of Australia: Milli Milli Wangka*, South Melbourne, Hyland House, 1997.

PHILLIPS Sandra R., ARCHER-LEAN Clare, "Decolonising the Reading of Aboriginal and Torres Strait Islander Writing: Reflection as Transformative Practice", *Higher Education Research & Development*, 2019, n° 38/1, p. 24-37.

POLA Iva, *Futuristic World in Australian Aboriginal Fiction*, Oxford, Peter Lang, 2017.

SHARRAD Paul, "Indigenous Transnational: Pluses and Perils, and Tara June Winch", *Transnational Literature*, 2020, n° 12, p. 1-17.

*SHOEMAKER Adam, *Black Words White Page: Aboriginal Literature 1929-1988*, St Lucia, University of Queensland Press, 1989.

VAN TOORN Penny, "Early Aboriginal Writing: And the Discipline of Literary Studies", *Meanjin*, 1996, n° 55, p. 754–765.

—, *Writing Never Arrives Naked: Early Aboriginal Cultures of Writing in Australia*, Canberra, Aboriginal Studies Press, 2006.

VERNAY Jean-François, *Panorama du roman australien. Des origines à nos jours, 1831-2007*, Paris, Hermann, 2009.

WATEGO Cliff, "Backgrounds to Aboriginal Literature", *in* NELSON Emmanuel S. (ed.), *Connections: Essays on Black Literatures*, Canberra, Aboriginal Studies Press, 1988, p. 11-24.

*WHEELER Belinda (ed.), *A Companion to Australian Aboriginal Literature*, Rochester, Camden House, 2013.

VII) Indigenous Studies, History, Cultural Studies, Anthropology

ATKINSON Judy, *Trauma Trails. Recreating Song Lines: The Transgenerational Effects of Trauma in Indigenous Australia*, North Melbourne, Spinifex Press, 2002.

ATTWOOD Bain, *In the Age of Mabo: History, Aborigines, and Australia*, St Leonards, Allen & Unwin, 1996.

BEHRENDT Larissa, "In Your Dreams: Cultural Appropriation, Popular Culture and Colonialism", *Law Text Culture*, 1998, n° 4, p. 256-279.

—, "Consent in a (Neo)Colonial Society: Aboriginal Women as Sexual and Legal 'Other'", *Australian Feminist Studies*, 2000, n° 15, p. 353-367.

—, "Self-Determination and Indigenous Policy: The Rights Framework and Practical Outcomes", *Journal of Indigenous Policy*, 2002, p. 43-58.

BELFRAGE Hugh, "Wanyi and Garrwa comparative data: an update", *in* EVANS Nicholas (ed.), *The Non-Pama-Nyungan Languages of Northern Australia: Comparative Studies of the Continent's most linguistically Complex Region*, Canberra, Australian National University, "Pacific Linguistics 552 – Studies in Language Change", 2003, p. 463-471.

BERNARD Michel, *Histoire de l'Australie de 1770 à nos jours : naissance d'une nation du Pacifique*, Paris, L'Harmattan, 1995.

BIDDLE Jennifer, "Dot, Circle, Difference: Translating Central Desert Paintings", *in* DIPROSE Rosalyn, FERRELL Robyn (eds.), *Cartographies: Poststructuralism and the Mapping of Bodies and Spaces*, North Sydney, Allen and Unwin, 1991, p. 27-39.

BIRRELL Kathleen, *Indigeneity: Before and Beyond the Law*, London, Routledge, 2016.

BLAKE Barry, "Redefining Pama-Nyungan: towards the History of Australian Languages", *in* EVANS Nicholas, JOHNSON Steve (eds.), *Aboriginal Linguistics*, Armidale NSW, University of New England, p. 1-90.

BOURKE Colin, BOURKE Eleanore, EDWARDS William Howell (eds.), *Aboriginal Australia: An Introductory Reader in Aboriginal Studies*, St Lucia, University of Queensland Press, 1994.

BRADLEY John, *Yanyuwa Wuka: Language from Yanyuwa Country*, Ms, The University of Queensland, 640p.

BREEN Gavan, *Warluwarra Grammar and Dictionary*, unpublished electronic files, 1990.

—, "Wanyi and Garrwa Comparative Data", *in* EVANS Nicholas (ed.), *The Non-Pama-Nyungan Languages of Northern Australia: Comparative Studies of the Continent's most Linguistically Complex Region*, Canberra, Australian National University, "Pacific Linguistics 552 – Studies in Language Change", 2003, p. 425-462.

—, "Evolution of the Verb Conjugations in the Ngarna Languages", *in* BOWERN Claire, KOCH Harold (eds.), *Australian Languages: Classification and the Comparative Method*, Amsterdam/Philadelphia, John Benjamins, "Current Issues in Linguistic Theory", 2004, p. 223-240.

BRERETON David, PARMENTER Joni, "Indigenous Employment in the Australian Mining Industry", *Journal of Energy & Natural Resources Law*, 2008, n° 26/1, p. 66-90.

*BROOME Richard, *Aboriginal Australians: A History since 1788*, St Leonards, Allen & Unwin, 2010. (Available on Kindle)

CAPELL Arthur, *A New Approach to Australian Linguistics*, "Oceania Linguistic Monographs", n° 1, Sydney, University of Sydney, 1956.

—, *Some Linguistic Types in Australia*, "Oceania Linguistic Monographs", n° 7, Sydney, University of Sydney, 1962.

*CASTEJON Vanessa, *Les Aborigènes et l'apartheid politique australien*, Paris, L'Harmattan, 2005.

CLIFFORD James, "Indigenous Articulations", *The Contemporary Pacific*, 2001, n° 13/2, p. 468-90.

DAVISON Graeme, HIRST John, MACINTYRE Stuart, *The Oxford Companion to Australian History*, Oxford, Oxford University Press, 2001.

DE LARGY HEALY Jessica, "La déclaration de l'imagination ou l'appel au rêve de la jeunesse australienne", *Cahiers de littérature orale*, Hors-Série, 2020, p. 67-74.

DIXON Robert Malcom Ward, *Australian Languages*, Cambridge, CUP, "Cambridge Language Surveys", 2002.

DODSON Patrick, “Until the Chains are Broken: Aboriginal Unfinished Business”, *Arena Magazine*, 2000, n° 45, p. 29-31.

DYMOCK John, *Something Deep and Rich: Indigenous and Post Contact Environment and Heritage Materials Relevant to the Lawn Hill/Riversleigh District of Queensland: Report Prepared for Department of Environment and Heritage*, Queensland, 1993, Ms. 3 v.; ill., maps.

FOLEY Gary, “Black Power, Land Rights and Academic History”, *Griffith Law Review*, 2011, n° 20, p. 608-618.

GAMMAGE Bill, *The Biggest Estate on Earth : How Aborigines made Australia*, Crows Nest, Allen & Unwin, 2011.

GAY'WU Group of Women, *Songspirals: Sharing Women's Wisdom of Country Through Songlines*, Sydney, Allen & Unwin, 2019.

*GLOWCZEWSKI Barbara, *Rêves en colère: alliances aborigènes dans le Nord-Ouest australien*, Paris, Plon / Terre humaine, 2004.

—, *Réveiller les esprits de la terre*, Bellevaux, Éditions Dehors, 2021.

GRIFFITHS Billy, *Deep Time Dreaming: Uncovering Ancient Australia*, Carlton, Black Inc., 2018.

*GROSSMAN Michèle (ed.), *Blacklines: Contemporary Critical Writing by Indigenous Australians*, Carlton, Melbourne University Press, 2003.

*GRIEVES Victoria, *Aboriginal Spirituality: Aboriginal Philosophy, the Basis of Aboriginal Social and Emotional Wellbeing*, Cooperative Research Centre for Aboriginal Health, Discussion Papers Series, n° 9, 2009, https://www.lowitja.org.au/content/Document/Lowitja-Publishing/DP9-Aboriginal-Spirituality.pdf

GROVE Richard, *Green Imperialism: Colonial Expansion, Tropical Island Edens and the Origins of Environmentalism, 1600-1860*, Cambridge, Cambridge University Press, 1995.

HAEBICH Anna, *Broken Circles: Fragmenting Indigenous Families 1800-2000*, Fremantle, Fremantle Arts Centre Press, 2000.

—, *Spinning the Dream: Assimilation in Australia 1950-1970*, North Fremantle, Fremantle Press, 2008.

HARVEY Mark, “The Genetic Status of Garrwan”, *Australian Journal of Linguistics*, 2009, n° 2, p. 195-244.

HEALY J. J., *Literature and the Aborigine in Australia* (1978), St Lucia, University of Queensland Press, 1989.

HUTCHISON Abigail, “The Whanganui River as a Legal Person”, *AltLJ*, 2014, n° 39/3, p. 179-182.

KAPITONOV Ivan, *A Grammar of Kunbarlang*, PhD dissertation, The University of Melbourne, 2019.

KEEN Sandra, “Yukulta”, *in* DIXON Robert Malcolm Ward, BLAKE Barry (eds.), *Handbook of Australian Languages*, vol.3, Canberra, Australian National University Press, 1983, p. 190-304.

KELLY Lynne, “Songlines in Sea and Sky”, *in* NEALE Margo, KELLY Lynne (eds.), *Songlines: the Power and Promise*, Thames & Hudson Australia Pty Ltd, 2020.

KIRTON Jean, CHARLIE Bella, *Further Aspects of the Grammar of Yanyuwa, Northern Australia*, Canberra, Australian National University, “Pacific Linguistics, Series C-131”, 1996.

LANGTON Marcia, *Burning Questions : Emerging Environmental Issues for Indigenous Peoples in Northern Australia*, Darwin, Northern Territory University, 1998.

—,“The Fire that is at the Centre of Each Family: Landscapes of the Ancients”, *in Visions of Future Landscapes*, Proceedings of the 1999 Australian Academy of Science, Fenner Conference on the Environment, 2-5 May 1999, Canberra. Canberra, ACT, Bureau of Rural Sciences, 2000, p.169–178.

—, “The Resource Curse”, *Griffith Review*, 28, June 2010, https://www.griffithreview.com/articles/the-resource-curse/

**—, *Welcome to Country: A Travel Guide to Indigenous Australia*, Melbourne, Hardie Grant Travel, 2018.

LAUGHREN Mary, “Serial Verbs in Waanyi and its Neighbours”, *in* AUSTIN Peter, KOCH Harold, SIMPSON Jane (eds.), *Language, Land and Song: Studies in Honour of Luise Hercus*. Batchelor, N.T., Australia, Batchelor Institute Press, 2018a, p. 139-157.

—, “Asymmetrical Distinctions in Waanyi Kinship Terminology”, *in* MCCONVELL Patrick, KELLY Piers, LACRAMPE Sebastien (eds.), *Skin, Kin and Clan: the Dynamics of Social Categories in Indigenous Australia*, Acton ACT, Australia, ANU Press, 2018b, p. 391-429.

LE ROUX Géraldine, «*Solwata*, un contre-courant anthropocénique. Réflexion sur la circulation des filet-fantômes dans le détroit de Torres (Australie)», *in* BOUVET, Yvanne, PAGES-JONES Kimberley (dir.), *Discours sur la mer, Résistance des pratiques*, Rennes, PUR, 2020.

—, «Vingt milles filets autour de la mer – Twenty thousand nets under the sea», *in* JACOB Stéphane, *L'art des ghostnets*, catalogue d'exposition bilingue, Paris, Arts d'Australie-Édition, 2016.

—, “Transforming Representations of Marine Pollution. For a New Understanding of the Artistic Qualities and Social Values of Ghost Nets”, Castro-Koshy Estelle, Le Roux Géraldine (eds.), *Visual Creativity and Narrative Research in and on Oceania, AnthroVision,n° 4/1*, 2016: https://journals.openedition.org/anthrovision/2221

MACINTYRE Stuart, *A Concise History of Australia*, Cambridge, Cambridge University Press, 2009.

MADDISON Sarah, *Black Politics: Inside the Complexity of Aboriginal Political Culture*, Crows Nest, Allen & Unwin, 2009.

MCGRATH Ann, JEBB Mary Anne Jebb (eds.), *Long History, Deep Time: Deepening Histories of Place*, Canberra, ANU press, 2015.

MCKINNON Crystal, *Expressing Indigenous Sovereignty: the Production of Embodied Texts in Social Protest and the Arts*, La Trobe University, 2018.

MCNIVEN Ian, RUSSEL Lynette, *Appropriated Pasts: Indigenous Peoples and the Colonial Culture of Archaeology*, Lanham, Altamira Press, 2005.

MERLE Isabelle, «Le Mabo Case. L'Australie face à son passé colonial», *Annales. Histoire, Sciences Sociales*, 1998, n° 53/2, p. 209-229.

MORETON-ROBINSON Aileen, *Talkin' up to the White Woman: Indigenous Women and Feminism*, St Lucia, University of Queensland Press, 2000.
— (ed.), *Whitening Race: Essays in Social and Cultural Criticism*, Canberra, Aboriginal Studies Press, 2004.
— (ed.), *Sovereign Subjects*, Crows Nest, Allen and Unwin, 2007.
—, *The White Possessive: Property, Power, and Indigenous Sovereignty*, University of Minnesota Press, 2015.
*MORETON Romaine, *The Right to Dream*, PhD diss., University of Sydney, 2006, https://www.academia.edu/38677397/The_Right_to_Dream
MORRISSEY Philip, "Stalking Aboriginal Culture: the Wanda Koolmatrie Affair", *Australian Feminist Studies*, 2003, n° 18, p. 299-307.
MOWALJARLAI David, "The Law Report: Aboriginal Law" transcript, ABC Radio, 1995.
MUECKE Stephen, BENTERRAK Krim, ROE Paddy, *Reading the Country*, Fremantle, Western Australia, Fremantle Arts Centre Press, 1984.
—, *Ancient and Modern: Time, Culture and Indigenous Philosophy*, Sydney: University of New South Wales Press, 2004.
*—, SHOEMAKER Adam, *Aboriginal Australians: First Nations of an Ancient Continent*, London, Thames & Hudson, 2009.
MULVANEY John, KAMMINGA Johan, *Prehistory of Australia*, St Leonards NSW, Allen & Unwin, 1999.
MUSHIN Ilana, *A Grammar of (Western) Garrwa*, Boston/Berlin, De Gruyter Mouton, "Pacific Linguistics 637", 2012.
NATIONAL OCEANS OFFICE, *Sea Country: an Indigenous Perspective: The South-east Regional Marine Plan Assessment Reports*, Hobart, National Oceans Office, 2002.
NEIDJIE, Bill, *Story about Feeling* Magabala Books, Broome, 1989.
NEUMAIER Beate, SCHAFFER Kay (eds.), *Decolonizing the Landscape: Indigenous Cultures in Australia*, Amsterdam, Rodopi, 2014.
OFFICE OF TREATY SETTLEMENTS, *Ruruku Whakatupua Te Mana O Te Awa Tupua*, Office of Treaty Settlements, 2002, n 1, http://nz01.terabyte.co.nz/ots/DocumentLibrary%5C140805RurukuWhakatupua-TeManaOTeAwaTupua.pdf
OSBORNE Charles, *A Tentative Description of the Wanji Language*, [dated] February 1966. Ms.
PARSONS Meg, FISHER Karen, CREASE Roa Petra, "Legal and Ontological Pluralism: Recognising Rivers as More-Than-Human Entities", *in* PARSONS Meg, FISHER Karen, CREASE Roa Petra, *Decolonising Blue Spaces in the Anthropocene*, Cham, Switzerland, Palgrave Macmillan, 2021.
PASCOE Bruce, *Dark Emu*, Broome, Magabala Books, 2014.
—, trad. fr. A. Baquier, *L'Émeu dans la nuit. L'Australie aborigène et la naissance de l'agriculture*, Paris, Pétra Éditions, à paraitre 2021.
PATRICK Wanta, Steve Jampijinpa, *Cultural Studies Review*, 2015, n° 21/1, https://epress.lib.uts.edu.au/journals/index.php/csrj/article/view/4420/4754
PEARSON Noel, *Up from the Mission: Selected Writings*, Collingwood, Black Inc, 2011.
PIQUET Martine, *Australie plurielle: gestion de la diversité ethnique en Australie de 1788 à nos jours*, Paris, L'Harmattan, 2004.

PONS Xavier, *L'Australie et ses populations*, Bruxelles, Complexe, 1983.
RADIN Margaret, "Property and Personhood", *Stanford Law Review*, 1982, n° 34, p. 957-1015.
REECE Bob, "Inventing Aborigines", *Aboriginal History Journal*, 1987, n° 11/1, p. 14-23.
REYNOLDS Henry, *The Other Side of the Frontier: Aboriginal Resistance to the European Invasion of Australia* (1981), Revised Edition, Sydney: University of New South Wales Press, 2006.
—, *The Law of the Land* (1987), Third Edition, Camberwell, Penguin, 2003.
—, *Frontier: Aborigines, Settlers and Land*, Sydney, Allen & Unwin, 1987.
—, *Dispossession, Black Australians and White Invaders*, Sydney, Allen & Unwin, 1989.
—, *Aboriginal Sovereignty: Reflections on Race, State and Nation*, St Leonards, Allen & Unwin, 1996.
—, *Why weren't we Told? A Personal Search for the Truth about our History*, Ringwood, Viking, 1999.
—, *An Indelible Stain? The Question of Genocide in Australia's History*, Ringwood, Viking, 2001.
—, *Unnecessary Wars*, Sydney, New South, 2016.
RICKARD John, *Australia: A Cultural History*, New York, Longman, 1996.
ROBERTS Tony, *Frontier Justice: A History of the Gulf Country to 1900*, St Lucia Qld Australia, UQP, 2005.
*ROSE Deborah Bird, *Dingo Makes Us Human* (1992), Cambridge, Cambridge University Press, 2000.
— *Nourishing Terrains: Australian Aboriginal Views of Landscape and Wilderness*, Canberra, Australian Heritage Commission, 1996, https://www.academia.edu/4539641/Nourishing_Terrains_Australian_Aboriginal_views_of_Landscape_and_Wilderness_Australian_Heritage_Commission_Canberra_1996
—, D'AMICO Sharon, DAIYI Nancy, DEVERAUX Kathy, DAIYI Margaret, FORD Linda, BRIGHT April, *Country of the Heart: An Indigenous Australian Homeland*, Canberra, Aboriginal Studies Press, 2002.
SCOTT Kim, BROWN Hazel, *Kayang and Me*, Fremantle, W.A, Freemantle Arts Centre Press, 2005.
STOCKTON Eugene, *The Aboriginal Gift: Spirituality for a Nation* Newtown, NSW, Millenium Books, 1995, p. 77-78.
STEFFENSEN Victor, *Fire Country: How Indigenous Fire Management Could Help Save Australia*, Richmond, Hardie Grant Travel, 2020.
STRELEIN Lisa, *Compromised Jurisprudence: Native Title Cases Since Mabo*, Canberra, Aboriginal Studies Press, 2009.
SUTTON Peter, *Native Title in Australia*, Cambridge, Cambridge University Press, 2003.
TAÇON Paul, S. C., WILSON Meredith, CHIPPINDALE Christopher, "Birth of the Rainbow Serpent in Arnhem Land Rock Art and Oral History", *Archaeology in Oceania*, 1996, n° 31, p. 103-124.
*TAÇON, Paul S. C, "Connecting to the Ancestors: Why Rock Art is Important for Indigenous Australians and their Well-being", *Rock Art Research*, 2019, n° 36/1,

p. 5-14, https://search.informit.com.au/documentSummary;dn=392956435680766;res=IELIND

TRIGGER David, *Nicholson River (Waanyi/Garawa) Land Claim*, Darwin, Northern Land Council, 1982, Ts. 134p.

—, "Language, Linguistic Groups and Status Relations at Doomadgee, an Aboriginal Settlement in Northwest Queensland, Australia", *Oceania*, 1987, n° 57/3, p. 217-238.

—, "Mining, Landscape and the Culture of the Development Ideology in Australia", *Ecumene*, 1997a, n° 4/2, p. 161-180.

VAN NEERVEN Ellen, "The Country Is Like a Body", *Right Now: Human Rights in Australia*, 26 October, 2015, https://rightnow.org.au/essay/the-country-is-like-a-body/

WHITE Richard, *Inventing Australia: Images and Identity 1688-1980*, St Leonards, Allen & Unwin, 1981.

WILSON Ronald Darling and WILKIE Meredith, *Bringing Them Home: Report of the National Inquiry into the Separation of Aboriginal and Torres Strait Islander Children from their Families*, Sydney, Australia, Human Rights and Equal Opportunity Commission, 1997.

**WOLFE Patrick, "Settler Colonialism and the Elimination of the Native", *Journal of Genocide Research*, 2006, n° 8/4, p. 387-409.

—, *Traces of History: Elementary Structures of Race*, London, Verso, 2016.

YUNUPINGU Galarrwuy, "Indigenous Art in the Olympic Age", *Art and Australia*, 1998, n° 35/1, p. 64-67.

VIII] Books and Articles on the Gulf of Carpentaria

BRADLEY John, YANYUWA families, *Singing Saltwater Country: Journey to the Songlines of Carpentaria*, St Leonards, Allen & Unwin, 2010.

MARTIN Richard, *The Gulf Country: The Story of People and Place in Outback Queensland*, St Leonards, Allen and Unwin, 2019. (Available on Kindle)

ROBERTS Tony, *Frontier Justice: A History of the Gulf Country to 1900*, Brisbane, University of Queensland Press, 2005.

TAÇON Paul, S.C., "Rainbow Colour and Power among the Waanyi of Northwest Queensland", *Cambridge Archaeological Journal*, 2008, n° 18/2, p. 163–76.

**TRIGGER David, "Change and succession in Australian Aboriginal Claims to Land", *in* TONER, P. (ed.), *Strings of Connection: Essays in Honour of Ian Keen*, Canberra, ANU Press, 2001, p. 53-73, http://press-files.anu.edu.au/downloads/press/p325141/pdf/ch032.pdf

**—, "Reflections on Century Mine", *in* SMITH Diane Evelyn, FINLAYSON Julie (eds.), *Fighting over Country: Anthropological Perspectives*, Canberra, Instant Colour Press, 1997b, p. 110-128, https://openresearch-repository.anu.edu.au/bitstream/1885/145209/1/CAEPR_Mono12.pdf

TRIGGER David, MARTIN Richard, "Place, Indigeneity, and Identity in Australia's Gulf Country", *American Anthropologist*, n° 118/4, p. 824-837.

TRIGGER David, ROBINSON Michael, “Mining, Land Claims and the Negotiation of Indigenous Interests: Research from the Queensland Gulf Country and the Pilbara Region of Western Australia”, *Senri Ethnological Studies*, 2001, n° 59, p. 101-116.

IX) Postcolonial Theory and Decolonial Theory

ASHCROFT, Bill, GRIFFITHS Gareth, TIFFIN Helen (eds.), *The Post-Colonial Studies Reader*, Second Edition, London, Routledge, 2006.

*ASHCROFT, Bill, GRIFFITHS Gareth, TIFFIN Helen, *The Empire Writes Back: Theory and Practice in Post-Colonial Literatures*, London & New York, Routledge, 1989.

BREWSTER Anne, *Literary Formations: Post-Colonialism, Nationalism, Globalism*, Melbourne, Melbourne University Publishing, 1995.

*CÉSAIRE Aimé, *Discours sur le colonialisme* (1950), Paris, Présence Africaine, 2000.

CLIFFORD James, “Indigenous Articulations”, *The Contemporary Pacific*, 2001, n° 13/ 2, p. 468-90.

CROWLEY Patrick, HIDDLESTON Jane (eds), *Postcolonial Poetics: Genre and Form*, Liverpool, Liverpool University Press, 2011.

FANON Frantz, *Peau noire, masques blancs*, Paris, Seuil, 1952.

—, *Les damnés de la terre*, (1961), Paris, Gallimard, 1991.

GROVE Richard, *Green Imperialism: Colonial Expansion, Tropical Island Edens and the Origins of Environmentalism, 1600-1860*, Cambridge, Cambridge University Press, 1995.

HAVEMANN Paul (ed.), *Indigenous Peoples' Rights in Australia, Canada, and New Zealand*, Oxford, Oxford University Press, 1999.

HOY Helen, *How Should I Read These? Native Women Writers in Canada*, Toronto, University of Toronto Press, 2001.

HUGGAN Graham, *The Post-Colonial Exotic: Marketing the Margins*, London, Routledge, 2001.

JUSTICE Daniel Heath, *Why Indigenous Literatures Matter*, Waterloo, Wilfrid Laurier University Press, 2018. (Available on Kindle)

MATEATA-ALLAIN Kareva, “Ma'ohi Women Writers of Colonial French Polynesia: Passive Resistance toward a Post(-)colonial Literature”, *Jouvert*, 2003, n° 7/2, https://legacy.chass.ncsu.edu/jouvert/v7i2/mateat.htm

MEMMI Albert, *Portrait du colonisé, précédé de : Portrait du colonisateur* (1957), Paris, Gallimard, 2002.

MOURA Jean-Marc, *Littératures francophones et théorie postcoloniale*, Paris, Presses Universitaires de France, 2019.

SAID Edward, *Culture and Imperialism*, London, Vintage, 1993.

SCOTT David, “The Tragic Vision in Postcolonial Time”, *PMLA*, 2014, n° 129/ 4, p. 799-808.

*SMITH Linda Tuhiwai, *Decolonizing Methodologies: Research and Indigenous Peoples*, London/Dunedin, Zed Books/University of Otago Press, 1999. (Available on Kindle)

X) Complementary references

ALLEN Graham, "Intertextuality", *The Literary Encyclopedia*, https://www.litencyc.com/

ARIZTI Barbara, "Personal Trauma/Historical Trauma in Tim Winton's *Dirt Music*" *in Cross / Cultures*, suppl. *The Splintered Glass*, Leiden, 2011, n° 136, p. 175-189.

BAKHTIN Mikhail, *The Dialogic Imagination* (1981), ed. and trans. EMERSON Caryl and HOLQUIST Michael, Austin, University of Texas Press, 2008.

—, "The Epic and the Novel: Towards a Methodology for the Study in the Novel", *in The Dialogic Imagination* (1981), ed. and trans. EMERSON Caryl and HOLQUIST Michael, Austin, University of Texas Press, 2008.

—, *Problems of Dostoevsky's Poetics*, ed. and trans. EMERSON Caryl, Manchester, Manchester University Press, 1984.

BALDICK Chris (ed.), *Oxford Dictionary of Literary Terms*, Oxford, Oxford University Press, 2015. (Available on Kindle)

BARTHES Roland, *Le bruissement de la langue*, Paris, Seuil, 1984.

BARRETT Susan, "'What I say will not be understood': Intertextuality as a subversive force in Nadine Gordimer's *Burger's Daughter*", *E-Rea*, 2004, n° 2/1, https://journals.openedition.org/erea/491

BEN-MESSAHEL Salhia, WINTON Tim, "An Interview with Tim Winton", *Antipodes*, 2012, n° 26/1, p. 9-12.

BIDDLE Jennifer, LEA Tess, "Hyperrealism and Other Indigenous Forms of 'Faking It with the Truth'", *Visual Anthropology Review*, 2018, n° 34/1, p. 5–14.

CHANDLER David, "An Introduction to Genre Theory", 1997, http://www.aber.ac.uk/media/Documents/intgenre/chandler_genre_theory.pdf

DEVATINE Flora Aurima, CASTRO-KOSHY Estelle, «Poétiques, éthique et transmission sur la toile : l'univers littéraire et le patrimoine culturel de Flora Aurima Devatine, Nathalie Heirani Salmon-Hudry et Chantal Spitz», *Anthrovision*, 2016, n° 4/1, https://journals.openedition.org/anthrovision/2307

DIMOCK Wai Chee, "Genre as World System: Epic and Novel on Four Continents", *Narrative*, n° 14/1, 2006, p. 85-101.

DIXON Robert, "Tim Winton, *Cloudstreet* and the Field of Australian Literature", *Westerly*, 2005, n° 50/Nov., p. 240-260.

GARRARD Greg, *Ecocriticism*, New York, Routledge, 2004.

GENETTE Gérard, «Discours du récit : essai de méthode», *Figures III*, Paris, Seuil, «Poétique», 1972.

GIBBS Leah Maree, ATCHISON Jennifer M., MACFARLANE Ingereth, "Camel Country: Assemblage, Belonging and Scale in Invasive Species Geographies", *Geoforum*, 2015, n° 58, p. 1-37, https://ro.uow.edu.au/cgi/viewcontent.cgi?article=2711&context=sspapers

GLOTFELTY Cheryll, "Introduction", *in* GLOTFELTY Cheryll et FROMM Harold (eds.), *The Ecocriticism Reader: Landmarks in Literary Ecology*, London, University of Georgia Press, 1996.

GORDIMER Nadine, "The Essential Gesture", *in The Essential Gesture: Writing, Politics and Places* (1988), Middlesex, Penguin, 1989, p. 285-300.

GRAULUND Rune, “Grotesque”, *Oxford Research Encyclopaedias, Literature*, https://doi.org/10.1093/acrefore/9780190201098.013.1067

HAGGARD, Henry Rider, *Allan Quatermain* (1887), London, Puffin, 1990.

HEISE Ursula, *A Sense of Place and Sense of Planet, the Environmental Imagination of the Global*, New York, Oxford University Press, 2008.

KLARER Mario, *An Introduction to Literary Studies*, London, Routledge, 2013.

KRISTEVA Julia, “Word, Dialogue and Novel”, *in* ROUDIEZ Leon (ed.), *Desire in Language: A Semiotic Approach to Literature and Art*, New York, Colombia University Press, 1980, p. 64-91.

LACHMANN Renate, ESHELMAN Raoul, DAVIS Marc, “Bakhtin and Carnival: Culture as Counter-Culture”, *Cultural Critique*, 1988-1989, n° 11 (Winter), p. 115-152.

MUECKE Stephen, “Devastation”, *in* HAWKINS Gay, MUECKE Stephen (eds.), *Culture and Waste: the Destruction and Creation of Value*, Lanham, Maryland, Rowman & Littlefield Publishers, 2003.

NEELAWALA Prasad, WILSON Clevo, ATHUKORALA Wasantha, “The Impact of Mining and Smelting Activities on Property Values: a Study of Mount Isa City, Queensland, Australia”, *The Australian Journal of Agricultural and Resource Economics*, 2012, n° 57, p. 60–78.

SLEMON Stephen, “Magic Realism as Postcolonial Discourse”, *in* ZAMORA Lois Parkinson, FARIS Wendy B., *Magical Realism: Theory, History, Community*, Durham & London, Duke University Press, 1995, p. 407–426.

SMITH Ellen, “Remapping *Capricornia*: Xavier Herbert's Cosmopolitan Imagination”, *Cultural Studies Review*, n° 23/2, p. 126-140, http://dx.doi.org/10.5130/csr.v23i2.5822

TYNAN Aidan, *The Desert in Modern Literature and Philosophy: Wasteland Aesthetics*, Edinburgh, Edinburgh University Press, 2020.

WATTS Ian, *The Rise of the Novel: Studies in Defoe, Richardson, and Fielding*, Berkeley, University of California Press, 1957.

YAEGER Patricia, “Trash as Archive, Trash as Enlightenment”, *in* HAWKINS Gay, MUECKE Stephen (eds.), *Culture and Waste: the Destruction and Creation of Value*, Lanham, Maryland, Rowman & Littlefield Publishers, 2003.

XI) Websites

a) On terminology

Australian Institute of Aboriginal and Torres Strait Islander Studies, https://aiatsis.gov.au/explore/indigenous-australians-aboriginal-and-torres-strait-islander-people

IndigenousX, *https*://indigenousx.com.au/appropriate-terminology-for-aboriginal-and-torres-strait-islander-people-its-complicated/

b) On Treaties, statements and history

Agreements, Treaties and Negotiated Settlements, https://www.atns.net.au/

Anti-Discrimination Commission Queensland, Aboriginal people in Queensland: a brief human rights history https://www.qhrc.qld.gov.au/__data/assets/pdf_file/0013/10606/Aboriginal-timeline-FINAL-updated-25-July-2018.pdf

Australian Mining History Association, https://www.mininghistory.asn.au/mining-history/

Colonial Frontier Massacres in Australia 1788-1930, https://c21ch.newcastle.edu.au/colonialmassacres/

Mabo and Others v Queensland (N°2), https://www.foundingdocs.gov.au/item-did-33.html

Uluru Statement from the Heart, https://ulurustatement.org

c) On Queensland, and more particularly the Gulf of Carpentaria

Australian Bureau of Statistics (about Carpentaria), https://quickstats.censusdata.abs.gov.au/census_services/getproduct/census/2016/quickstat/LGA32250

Burke Shire Council, Local History, https://www.burke.qld.gov.au/our-region/history/a-brief-history-of-the-gulf-of-carpentaria

Carpentaria Land Council Aboriginal Corporation, "The Century Mine Dispute", http://www.clcac.com.au/native-title/our-story/02

History of Mount Isa, https://www.qld.gov.au/firstnations/cultural-awareness-heritage-arts/community-histories/community-histories-m/community-histories-mount-isa

New Century Mine, https://newcenturyresources.com/century-mine-project/

***World101x, Full Interview with UQ Anthropologist David Trigger*, https://www.youtube.com/watch?v=CnAzFkIj8fI&t=558s

d) Other

The Aboriginal and Torres Strait Islander Curricula, The University of Melbourne, Melbourne Graduate School of Education, https://education.unimelb.edu.au/aboriginal-and-torres-strait-islander-curricula

Libraries Tasmania Animated Version of William Gould's Sketchbook of Fishes, https://www.youtube.com/watch?v=vRle_ym5llQ

Patrick White's Nobel Prize, https://www.nma.gov.au/defining-moments/resources/patrick-white-wins-nobel-prize

Tracks (n.d.): The Story Behind Milpirri, https://tracksdance.com.au/story-behind-milpirri

Notes on Contributors

Susan Barrett is of Anglo-Australian origin and has been a senior lecturer at Bordeaux-Montaigne University for twenty years. She wrote her doctoral thesis on white South African women's novels from 1883 to 1994. She later extended her research interests to cover Australian literature. She is particularly interested in questions of marginality, and how both personal and national history are inscribed in works of literature. She has published numerous articles in France and abroad on both Australian and South African fiction, including several articles on Alexis Wright. More recently she has worked on mental health policies in Great Britain and has had several articles on this topic published in French journals.

Estelle Castro-Koshy is a French scholar with over sixty publications who has worked with Australian First Nations writers, performers and filmmakers, since 2003 and with Indigenous French Polynesian writers and artists since 2006. An Adjunct Senior Research Fellow at James Cook University, she is also a translator and an editor. Her articles on *Carpentaria* have been published in the journal *Loxias* and in Lynda Ng's edited book *Indigenous Transnationalism*, and her essay on Alexis Wright's *Croire en l'incroyable* and *Le Pacte du serpent arc-en-ciel* co-written with Philippe Guerre has been published in the journal *Antipodes*. She is currently completing a book on Australian First Nations literature (Actes Sud, 2022) and an edited volume on Indigenous Tahitian poet Flora Aurima Devatine.

Mylène Charon est chercheuse associée au laboratoire Héritages : Culture/s, Patrimoine/s, Création/s (CY Cergy Paris Université, CNRS et ministère de la Culture). Elle est enseignante en licence de lettres à CY Cergy Paris Université. Elle a soutenu sa thèse, *Blak Feminism : rapports sociaux de sexe et de race dans la poésie et l'art* *contemporains des Premières Nations d'Australie* sous la direction de Rémi Astruc en 2020 à CY Cergy Paris Université.

Jessica De Largy Healy is an anthropologist at the Laboratoire d'ethnologie et de sociologie comparative, Centre National de la Recherche Scientifique – Université Paris Nanterre, and an Honorary Fellow at the Indigenous Studies Unit, School of Population and Global Health, The University of Melbourne. She has worked with Indigenous communities in Victoria's Western District and for the past two decades in the East Arnhem region. Her research concerns Indigenous repatriation processes and practices and she has published extensively on the many creative ways in which museum and archival collections are reinvested locally through art, ritual, new media and collaborative exhibitions.

Eugenia Flynn is a writer and researcher. Her doctoral thesis aims to advance the writing of Australian Indigenous women and non-binary people, through Indigenous-centred approaches to reading Indigenous literature. Eugenia is a Tiwi, Larrakia, Chinese Malaysian and Muslim woman who works within her multiple communities to create change through literature, art and community engaged practice. Her work can be found in *IndigenousX*, *Peril* magazine, and the anthology *#MeToo: Stories From the Australian Movement*.

Victoria Grieve-Williams is Warraimaay and a historian who incorporates interdisciplinary approaches to developing Indigenous knowledges in Australia.

Mary Laughren is an honorary senior research fellow at The University of Queensland where she taught linguistics between 1993 and 2009. She was awarded her Doctorat de 3ème cycle in linguistics from the University of Nice in 1973 for a thesis on a Senoufo language of Côte d'Ivoire. Since 1975 she has documented and researched Australian languages, particularly the Warlpiri and Waanyi languages. Her publications are listed in The University of Queensland's eSpace https://espace.library.uq.edu.au/

Laura Singeot, PhD, teaches English at Paris Saclay University, France. Her interest as a researcher lies first in the representations of Indigeneity in contemporary Indigenous literatures in Australia and

New Zealand-Aotearoa. She examines the rewritings of colonial history and epistemologies in contemporary Pacific fiction, and the renewal of artistic forms. She has also published on museology and the visual arts of the Pacific, especially new digital art. Her next research projects explore poetry, eco-criticism and the inclusion of contemporary Indigenous art pieces in urban environments.

David Trigger is Professor Emeritus of Anthropology at The University of Queensland and Adjunct Professor at The University of Western Australia. He is the Principal Partner in David S Trigger & Associates consulting anthropologists. His most recent works address senses of historical place that both overlap and diverge for people of diverse ancestries. In Australian Aboriginal Studies, Professor Trigger has carried out more than 40 years of research on Indigenous systems of land tenure, including applied research on resource development negotiations, land claims, native title and cultural heritage.

See: http://www.socialscience.uq.edu.au/david-trigger

Remerciements

The authors would like to warmly thank Alexis Wright for her time and generosity in answering our questions and providing us with information that was not yet available in the public domain.

They thank Alexis Wright and Toly Sawenko for the permission to reproduce the magnificent photographs of the Gulf Country and Alexis Wright taken by Toly Sawenko.

They thank Lily Sawenko for the permission to reproduce her beautiful portrait of Alexis Wright.

They would also like to thank David Trigger for his advice about mining in the Gulf Country, and all the contributors, Mylène Charon, Jessica De Largy Healy, Eugenia Flynn, Victoria Grieve-Williams, Mary Laughren and David Trigger for having agreed to work with them at such short notice and with a very tight deadline.

They thank Giovanni Picci, directeur éditorial des Langues, Belin Éducation, for his clear and calm vision for this book.

Cet ouvrage a été mis en pages par

<pixellence>

Imprimé en France
par JOUVE-PRINT
733, rue Saint-Léonard, 53100 Mayenne
septembre 2021 - N° 2967230D

JOUVE-PRINT est titulaire du label imprim'vert®